AF693127

Chinese Policy and Presence in the Arctic

Edited by

Timo Koivurova and Sanna Kopra

BRILL
NIJHOFF

LEIDEN | BOSTON

Library of Congress Cataloging-in-Publication Data

Names: Koivurova, Timo, editor. | Kopra, Sanna, editor. | Finland. Valtioneuvosto. Kanslia, sponsoring body.
Title: Chinese policy and presence in the Arctic / edited by Timo Koivurova and Sanna Kopra.
Description: Leiden ; Boston : Brill | Nijhoff, 2020. | Series: Studies in polar law, 2589-6822 ; volume 3 | Includes index.
Identifiers: LCCN 2020002045 (print) | LCCN 2020002046 (ebook) | ISBN 9789004408418 (hardback) | ISBN 9789004408425 (ebook)
Subjects: LCSH: Arctic Regions--International status. | China--Foreign relations--Arctic Regions. | Arctic Regions--Politics and government. | China--Foreign relations--Finland. | Finland--Foreign relations--China.
Classification: LCC KZ4110.P65 C476 2020 (print) | LCC KZ4110.P65 (ebook) | DDC 341.4/209113--dc23
LC record available at https://lccn.loc.gov/2020002045
LC ebook record available at https://lccn.loc.gov/2020002046

Typeface for the Latin, Greek, and Cyrillic scripts: "Brill". See and download: brill.com/brill-typeface.

ISSN 2589-6822
ISBN 978-90-04-40841-8 (hardback)
ISBN 978-90-04-40842-5 (e-book)

Copyright 2020 by Koninklijke Brill NV, Leiden, The Netherlands.
Koninklijke Brill NV incorporates the imprints Brill, Brill Hes & De Graaf, Brill Nijhoff, Brill Rodopi, Brill Sense, Hotei Publishing, mentis Verlag, Verlag Ferdinand Schöningh and Wilhelm Fink Verlag.
All rights reserved. No part of this publication may be reproduced, translated, stored in a retrieval system, or transmitted in any form or by any means, electronic, mechanical, photocopying, recording or otherwise, without prior written permission from the publisher.
Authorization to photocopy items for internal or personal use is granted by Koninklijke Brill NV provided that the appropriate fees are paid directly to The Copyright Clearance Center, 222 Rosewood Drive, Suite 910, Danvers, MA 01923, USA. Fees are subject to change.

This book is printed on acid-free paper and produced in a sustainable manner.

Contents

Preface and Acknowledgements

The Arctic region has globalized rapidly during the past decade. Many non-Arctic states, including the People's Republic of China, have become increasingly interested in partaking in regional affairs and governance in the High North. Amongst Arctic states and stakeholders, this development has not only opened up new (economic) opportunities but has also raised concerns about China's aims and motives in the Arctic.

In order to offer a balanced and multi-faceted picture of China's Arctic activities, we, the editors, and Liisa Kauppila, Marc Lanteigne, Mingming Shi, Malgorzata (Gosia) Smieszek, Adam Stepien, Juha Käpylä, Harri Mikkola, Egill Þór Níelsson and Matti Nojonen compiled a report entitled "China in the Arctic; and the Opportunities and Challenges for Chinese-Finnish Arctic Co-operation" as a part of a broader advisory project called "Finland's Arctic Council chairmanship in the times of increasing uncertainty",[1] funded by Finnish Government's Analysis, Assessment and Research Activities unit (part of the government's call for expertise in 2016). The report, published in February 2019, captured the attention of the media and the general public, not only in Finland but also at a global level, which indicates the public desire for knowledge of China's policy and presence in the Arctic. This prompted us to develop our report into an edited volume – a choice that enables us to offer a more comprehensive account of China's role in the Arctic. Most of the authors of the report stayed onboard and some new experts joined us during the writing process of this book. We wish to thank all these talented researchers, as this book would never have seen the light of the day without their valuable contributions. Our thanks also extend to Anna Riipinen, who assisted us in the editorial process. All remaining errors and/or omissions are naturally the sole responsibility of the chapter authors and/or us, the editors.

As this book grew out of a project funded by the Finnish Government's Analysis, Assessment and Research Activities unit, we would like to express our sincere gratitude to the Finnish Prime Minister's Office, not only for funding our work but also for permitting us to republish some parts of the above-mentioned report. In addition, Sanna Kopra wishes to thank the Academy of Finland (project no. 315402) for funding her research on China's role in the Arctic.

Timo Koivurova and Sanna Kopra
Rovaniemi, Finland
February, 2020

1 See Finnish Government's Analysis, Assessment and Research Activities website at https://tietokayttoon.fi/hankkeet/hanke-esittely/-/asset_publisher/suomen-puheenjohtajuus-arktisessa-neuvostossa-kasvaneen-epavarmuuden-aikakaudella, retrieved September 24, 2019.

Abbreviations

A2/AD	Anti-access/Anti-denial
AC	Arctic Council
ADIZ	Air defence identification zone (China)
AEC	Arctic Economic Council
AIIB	Asian Infrastructure Investment Bank
AMSA	Arctic Marine Shipping Assessment
APEC	Asia-Pacific Economic Cooperation
ASO	Atmosphere-Sea-Ice-Ocean
ASSW	Arctic Science Summit Week
BASIC	Brazil, South Africa, India and China grouping
BAT	Baidu, Alibaba, Tencent firms
BFRS	Brominated flame retardants
BRI	Belt and Road Initiative
BRICS	Brazil-Russia-India-China-South Africa group
CAA	China Arctic and Antarctic Administration
CAMCE	CAMC Engineering Ltd.
CAS	Chinese Academy of Sciences
CAO	Central Arctic Ocean
CCAC	Climate and Clean Air Coalition
CCAMLR	Convention for the Conservation of Antarctic Marine Living Resources
CCCC	China Communications Construction Company
CDEM	Construction, design, equipment and manning standards (law of the sea)
CIAO	China - Iceland Arctic Science Observatory (earlier China-Iceland Joint Aurora Observatory)
CNARC	China-Nordic Arctic Research Centre
CNOOC	China National Offshore Oil Corporation
CNPC	China National Petroleum Corporation
CO_2	Carbon Dioxide
COP	Conference of Parties
COSCO	China Ocean Shipping Company
CPEC	China-Pakistan Economic Corridor
CSSC	China State Shipbuilding Corporation
CWEC	CSSC Wärtsilä Engine Co Ltd
EFTA	European Free Trade Area
EU	European Union
FinChi	Finland-China Innovation Centre
FDI	Foreign Direct Investment

FONOPS	Freedom of Navigation Operations (US)
FTA	Free Trade Agreement
GDP	Gross Domestic Product
GPS	Global Positioning System
IASC	International Arctic Science Committee
IGY	International Geophysical Year
ICSU	International Council of Scientific Unions
ICT	Information and communication technology
IMO	International Maritime Organization
IPCC	Intergovernmental Panel on Climate Change
IPRS	Intellectual property rights
IPY	International Polar Year
KMI	Korea Maritime Institute
KOPRI	Korea Polar Research Institute
LNG	Liquefied natural gas
MARPOL	International Convention for the Prevention of Pollution from Ships
MCC	Microcrystalline cellulose
MNR	Ministry of Natural Resources (China)
MOSAIC	The International Multidisciplinary drifting Observatory for the study of the Arctic Climate
MOST	Ministry of Science and Technology (China)
MOU	Memorandum of Understanding
NATO	North Atlantic Treaty Organization
NDB	New Development Bank
NDC	Nationally determined contribution (Paris Agreement)
NDRC	National Development and Reform Commission (China)
NEP	Northeast Passage
NPC	National People's Congress (China)
NSR	Northern Sea Route
NWP	Northwest Passage
ODI	Outward Direct Investment
OECD	Organization for Economic Cooperation and Development
PCA	Permanent Court of Arbitration
PLA	People's Liberation Army (China)
POPS	Persistent organic pollutants
PPP	Public-private partnership
PRC	People's Republic of China
PRIC	Polar Research Institute of China
R&D	Research and development
RANNIS	Icelandic Centre for Research

REES	Rare earth elements
RFE	Russian Far East
ROC	Republic of China
SAOS	Senior Arctic Officials (Arctic Council)
SCAR	Scientific Committee on Antarctic Research
SCS	South China Sea
SLCPS	Short-Lived Climate Pollutants/Forcers
SOA	State Oceanic Administration (China)
SOE	State owned enterprise
SOLAS	International Convention for the Safety of Life at Sea
SYKE	Finnish Environment Institute
UN	United Nations
UNFCCC	United Nations Framework Convention on Climate Change
UNIFI	Universities Finland
UNPFII	United Nations Permanent Forum on Indigenous Issues
UNCLOS	UN Convention on the Law of the Sea
UNSC	United Nations Security Council
US	United States
USGS	United States Geological Survey
USSR	Union of Soviet Socialist Republics
VMI	National Forest Inventory (Finland)
VTT	Technical Research Centre of Finland
WTO	World Trade Organization

Notes on Contributors

Karoliina Hurri
(MSc in Development Geography) is a Ph.D. Candidate in World Politics in the Aleksanteri Institute at the University of Helsinki. Her dissertation "The Construction of China's Leadership Role in International Climate Politics" is funded by The Tiina and Antti Herlin Foundation.

Liisa Kauppila
(M.Soc.Sci., MA in Futures Studies) is a Ph.D. Candidate at the Centre for East Asian Studies, University of Turku, Finland. Her current research focuses on China's Arctic engagement, regionalisation, relational theory and China's role in alternative Arctic futures.

Timo Koivurova
is a research professor and director of the Arctic Centre, University of Lapland. He was a lead editor in Arctic Law and Governance; the Role of China and Finland (Hart, 2017) and his research focuses on governance issues in the Arctic.

Sanna Kopra
is an Academy of Finland postdoctoral researcher in the Arctic Centre at University of Lapland and a visiting scholar in the Aleksanteri Institute at University of Helsinki, Finland. She is the author of *China and Great Power Responsibility for Climate Change* (Routledge, 2019). Kopra's current research focuses on China's Arctic engagement and great powers' leadership in international climate politics.

Juha Käpylä
works as a Senior Research Fellow at the Finnish Institute of International Affairs (FIIA). He earned his Ph.D. in International Relations from the University of Tampere, Finland, where he has also worked as a researcher prior to joining FIIA. Käpylä's research interests include Arctic geopolitics and geo-economics, and International Relations metatheory.

Marc Lanteigne
is an Associate Professor at UiT: The Arctic University of Norway, specialising in Chinese and East Asian politics and foreign policy, including Chinese relations with Europe and the Arctic region. He is the author of *Chinese Foreign Policy: An Introduction* (Fourth Edition, 2019), as well as numerous articles and

chapters on Chinese politics. Lanteigne is the editor of the Arctic online news blog *Over the Circle*.

Harri Mikkola
(Ph.D. in Political Science) works as a Senior Research Fellow at the Finnish Institute of International Affairs (FIIA). Mikkola has published several expert analyses on the Arctic region's transformation. His other fields of expertise include defence and security policy, hybrid war and influencing, societal resilience, security of supply as well as defence market issues.

Egill Thor Nielsson
is a Ph.D. Candidate at the University of Iceland and University of Lapland, and Senior Adviser at the Icelandic Centre for Research (Rannís). Previously, he was Executive Secretary of the China-Nordic Arctic Research Center (CNARC) and a Visiting Scholar at the Polar Research Institute of China (PRIC) and the Shanghai Institutes for International Studies (SIIS). His research focus is on China-Nordic Arctic Relations in the context of policy, science and economy.

Matti Nojonen
(M.A. Sinology and Ph.D. in Economics and Business) is a Professor of Chinese Culture and Society at University of Lapland. He specializes both on traditional Chinese strategic culture and contemporary Chinese political economy and strategic behavior of China. Nojonen has translated into Finnish Chinese strategy classics (Gaudeamus Helsinki University Press) and is currently working on book manuscript "The Philosophy and Concepts of Traditional Chinese Strategic Thinking".

Malgorzata (Gosia) Smieszek
is a political scientist and a researcher at the Arctic Centre, University of Lapland in Finland. She studies questions of Arctic governance, in particular the Arctic Council, and science-policy interface. Smieszek has been the Chair of International Arctic Science Committee (IASC) Action Group on Communicating Arctic Science to Policy-Makers (CASP) and a representative of IASC to the meetings of the Arctic Council. She is a co-founder of a non-profit association "Women of the Arctic" (www.genderisnotplanb.com).

Adam Stepien
is political scientist working at the Arctic Centre of the University of Lapland. He focuses in his work on Arctic governance, and in particular on the role of the European Union in the Arctic. Recently, he has been working on northern

regional development policies, indigenous politics and cross-sectoral policy-making. He has participated in a number of policy support and advisory projects.

Yulia Yamineva
is a Senior Researcher (docent) at the Centre for Climate, Energy and Environmental Law, University of Eastern Finland. Her research focuses on legal and governance issues pertaining to climate change, air pollution and science-policy interface. This work has been published in leading legal and interdisciplinary journals including Transnational Environmental Law, Environmental Science & Policy, and Nature Climate Change. Yamineva holds a Ph.D. in International Studies from the University of Cambridge.

CHAPTER 1

Introduction to China's Arctic Engagement

Sanna Kopra and Timo Koivurova

Although the People's Republic of China (hereafter China) lacks territory and waters above the Arctic Circle (ca. 66°33′ N), it has become an increasingly influential actor in Arctic affairs during the past decade. In 2007, China started to take part in the work of the Arctic Council, the key intergovernmental forum in the region, and in 2013, its observer application was accepted. In June 2017, the Polar Silk Road (a series of planned Arctic shipping routes) was officially added to President Xi Jinping's flagship project, the Belt and Road Initiative (BRI). In January 2018, the Chinese government published its long-awaited first Arctic strategy. According to the strategy, China is a "near-Arctic state" that respects the sovereign rights of the eight Arctic states (Canada, Denmark, Finland, Iceland, Norway, Russia, Sweden, and the United States) but has legitimate rights in the region as well. Furthermore, Chinese scholars conduct polar research onboard icebreaker research vessels MV *Xuelong* and MV *Xuelong* 2 – the latter, delivered in 2019, being the first domestically-built icebreaker in China – and Chinese corporations have become partners in various economic projects in the Arctic, especially in Russia's Siberia, where massive projects of liquefied natural gas take place. The development of infrastructure along the Polar Silk Road is also of interest to Chinese investors. Lastly, China's policies indirectly influence the future of the Arctic, given the state's status as an emerging great power and the biggest carbon dioxide emitter in the world. Without a doubt, both factors are important: first, the Arctic is not untouched by international economic and geopolitical fluctuations, and second, climate change proceeds faster in polar regions than elsewhere on the globe.

Due to China's autocratic governance system and the poor track record of Chinese companies in other parts of the world, among other issues, China's growing footprint in the Arctic region has caused concerns and speculations amongst the regional actors. Although Beijing has stressed that it has no military intentions in the Arctic, the country's growing maritime power and its rising presence in other oceans, including the Indian and Pacific, has led some scholars to question the motives of Chinese engagement in the region. Accordingly, they view China's increasing involvement in the Arctic in unfavorable and hostile terms, and they interpret Chinese actions in the region predominantly in security and military terms. Critics have pointed to the potential for

© KONINKLIJKE BRILL NV, LEIDEN, 2020 | DOI:10.1163/9789004408425_002

the 'dual-use' of Chinese facilities in the Arctic and warned against China silently expanding its influence and dominance through scientific and economic engagement. Other scholars, however, have found this approach to be highly reductionist and limited in the necessarily nuanced analysis of Chinese Arctic policy. This latter group notes that such concerns have much to do with the fact that China is an emerging great power and therefore seen as having a strategic agenda in much of its activities in the High North. In any event, these disagreements over China's underlying Arctic interests demonstrate the necessity of academic research on China's policy and presence in the Arctic.

Despite a rapidly growing number of academic papers elaborating China's Arctic interests (e.g. Chen, 2012; Jakobsen, 2010; Jakobsen & Peng, 2012; Koivurova et al., 2017; Kopra, 2013; Lanteigne, 2014; Lanteigne & Ping, 2015; Sørensen & Klimenko, 2017; Tonami, 2014; Yang, 2014), extensive reviews of China's policy and presence in the Arctic remain close to zero (but see Brady, 2017). This book seeks to fill this gap in literature by elaborating on China's evolving Arctic interests, policies and strategies. The book builds on and expands the findings of our report "China in the Arctic", prepared for the Finnish Prime Minister's Office in 2019 (Koivurova et al., 2019). The publication of the report drew a lot of attention from both national and international media, which also demonstrates the public's thirst for knowledge of China's plans and visions in the High North. In response to these calls, this book offers a comprehensive account of China's diplomatic, economic, environmental, scientific and strategic contribution to the Arctic region. In this way, the book aims to increase understanding of Beijing's polar interests and potential influence on the future of the region – intellectual capital that not only helps regional decision-makers and stakeholders plan their future activities but also possibly makes the cooperation between China and the Arctic states easier.

1.1 Organization of the Book

As China's Arctic policy is not separated from the other national interests of the country, Chapter 2 by Marc Lanteigne and colleagues gives an introduction to China's overall foreign policy interests. It also reviews the ongoing global economic, political and legal transformations that undoubtedly shape China's overall interests in the region. Chapter 3 by Timo Koivurova and colleagues moves to study China's evolving Arctic policy. It demonstrates that the release of Beijing's first official Arctic strategy in 2018 was the culmination of a long process that Beijing undertook over the previous decade to demonstrate its growing knowledge of, and commitment to, the Arctic region in order to be accepted as a legitimate Arctic actor. It also briefly reviews the Arctic states' responses to Beijing's Arctic strategies.

Chapter 4 by Malgorzata (Gosia) Smieszek and colleagues elaborates on the development of Chinese scientific activities in the Arctic since the 1980s as well as the contribution of the Chinese experts to the Arctic Council's activities since 2007. Clearly, climate change is a key interest of Chinese scientists – a pressing political problem that is also addressed in Chapter 5 by Sanna Kopra and colleagues. Clearly, climate change cannot be solved simply by regional cooperation in the Arctic; truly global efforts are necessary. Therefore, Chapter 5 focuses on China's contribution to international climate negotiations under the UN climate regime and also reviews China's potential to reduce black carbon emissions. The chapter also briefly examines China's broader ecological footprint in the Arctic.

Chapter 6 by Adam Stępień and colleagues scrutinizes China's economic presence in the Arctic. It offers an extensive outline of the on-going and planned economic activities in which Chinese stakeholders are involved. In addition to economic benefits, the chapter suggests that such activities may consist of various concerns and risks, especially for the small Arctic states. Chapter 7 by Stępień and colleagues offers a case study of China's economic cooperation with one of the eight Arctic states, namely Finland, where Chinese investors are involved in plans to build a new Arctic railway, to name just one project. In this way, the chapter sheds light on the opportunities and concerns that China's growing Arctic interest may bring in Finland and beyond. Finally, Chapter 8 summarizes the findings of the book and discusses the risks and future prospects of China's role in the Arctic.

Literature

Brady, A.M. (2017). *China as a polar great power.* Washington, D.C. and Cambridge, England: Woodrow Wilson Center Press.

Chen, G. (2012). China's emerging Arctic strategy. *The Polar Journal,* 2(2), 358–371.

Jakobson, L. (2010). China Prepares for an Ice-Free Arctic. *SIPRI Insights on Peace and Security,* No. 2010/2. Solna, Sweden: SIPRI.

Jakobson, L., & Peng, J. (2012). China's Arctic Aspirations. *SIPRI Policy Paper, 34.* Solna, Sweden: SIPRI.

Koivurova, T., Qin, T., Duyck, S., & Nykänen, T. (Eds.) (2017). *Arctic Law and Governance: The Role of China and Finland.* Oxford, England: Hart Publishing Ltd.

Koivurova, T., Kauppila, L., Kopra, S., Lanteigne, M., Shi, M., Smieszek, M., ... Nojonen, M. (2019). *China in the Arctic: and the Opportunities and Challenges for Chinese-Finnish Arctic Co-operation.* Helsinki, Finland: Prime Minister's Office. Retrieved August 16, 2019 from: http://julkaisut.valtioneuvosto.fi/handle/10024/161371.

Kopra, S. (2013). China's Arctic Interests. In L. Heininen, H. Exner-Pirot & J. Plouffe (Eds.) *Arctic Yearbook 2013* (pp. 107–122). Akureyri, Iceland: Northern Research Forum.

Lanteigne, M. (2014). *China's Emerging Arctic Strategies: Economics and Institutions.* [Occasional Papers]. Institute of International Affairs, the Centre for Arctic Policy Studies. Reykjavík, Iceland: University of Iceland.

Lanteigne, M., & Ping, S. (2015). China's Developing Arctic Policies: Myths and Misconceptions. *Journal of China and International Relations,* 3(1), 1–25.

Sørensen, C.T.N., & Klimenko, E. (2017). Emerging Chinese-Russian Cooperation in the Arctic. Possibilities and Constraints. *SIPRI Policy Paper, 46.* Stockholm, Sweden: SIPRI.

Tonami, A. (2014). The Arctic Policy of China and Japan: Multi-Layered Economic and Strategic Motivations. *The Polar Journal,* 4(1), 105–126.

Yang, J. (2014). China's Arctic Policy. In O.K. Young, D.K. Jong & K. Yoon (Eds.), *The Arctic in World Affairs. North Pacific Dialogue on International Cooperation in a Changing Arctic* (pp. 172–187). Soul, South Korea and Honolulu, Hawaii: Korea Maritime Institute and East West Center.

CHAPTER 2

China's Rise in a Changing World

Marc Lanteigne, Timo Koivurova and Matti Nojonen

2.1 Introduction

Chinese foreign policy is dictated by changing global and regional events, but also by internal dynamics in China, including the fact that there is a greater understanding of foreign policy issues in the country well beyond that of the government and its major agencies. During the past decades, China has sought to modernize both its government and its economy to reflect the current international sphere. Beijing is also seeking to expand its security interests in order to better protect its citizens and assets abroad and to increase the country's general influence in world politics. Undoubtedly, these dynamics also shape China's policy in the Arctic; the state's cross-regional diplomacy is not separated from the party-state's overall foreign policy goals and doctrines. Therefore, this chapter offers a review of China's foreign policy and economic interests – China's Arctic engagement cannot be fully understood without understanding the broader picture of China's foreign affairs.

2.2 Internal Developments in China

Internally, many recent developments have had a clear impact on Chinese foreign policy. These have included ongoing domestic economic reform, the combating of corruption, the drive to reduce environmental damage, and the promotion of liberalized trade to improve Chinese businesses. Moreover, there is now a greater concentration of domestic and foreign policy decision-making power by President Xi Jinping (习近平). This consolidation was most prominently illustrated by the decision at the country's National People's Congress (NPC *Quanguo Renmin Daibiao Dahui* 全国人民代表大会) meeting in March 2018 to remove term limits for the position of president, thus giving Mr Xi the power to shape both China's domestic policy and its international relations for an indefinite period (Buckley & Bradsher, 2018; Tepperman, 2018). The question now is what Beijing's foreign policy and strategic priorities will be in the near future, and whether China's ongoing rise as a great power will lead to

© KONINKLIJKE BRILL NV, LEIDEN, 2020 | DOI:10.1163/9789004408425_003

greater cooperation or competition on a regional and potentially even global scale.

There is also an expansion of various ministries and departments that are involved in foreign affairs as Chinese influence in world affairs grows. Recent additions have included a dedicated aid agency as well as a greater concentration on environmental affairs. The ongoing importance of the People's Liberation Army (*Zhongguo Renmin Jiefangjun* 中国人民解放军), or PLA, in foreign policy concerns is still of much relevance, given that the PLA retains strong decision-making powers within the Chinese government, a legacy of the country's revolutionary era under Mao Zedong (毛泽东) between 1949 and 1976. Chinese foreign policy interests have been greatly expanded over the past three decades, with an emphasis on developing Chinese interests on the global stage as opposed to primarily within the Asia-Pacific region. Under the administrations of Hu Jintao (胡锦涛) in 2002–12 and now Xi Jinping, Beijing's foreign policy interests have expanded well beyond the Pacific Rim to include Africa, Eurasia, Europe, and the Middle East. The Arctic is one of the most recent examples of Beijing's commitment to cross-regional diplomacy as the country grows more confident of its great power status. The development of the Belt and Road Initiative (*Yidaiyilu Changyi* 一带一路倡议), or BRI, first announced by President Xi in 2013, has been the most recent manifestation of China's economic diplomacy and strategic thinking on the international level (PRC Foreign Ministry, 2013).

At the same time, Chinese bilateral diplomacy efforts are ongoing. Since the 1990s, under the presidency of Jiang Zemin (江泽民) between 1992–2002, Beijing often developed bilateral diplomacy in the form of strategic partnership arrangements, and under President Hu, China became more comfortable with developing bilateral free trade agreements (FTAs) once China was admitted to the World Trade Organisation (WTO) after fifteen long years of negotiations (Lanteigne, 2013). FTAs have been a little-noticed opening for China to develop its Arctic policies, as China penned an FTA with Iceland in 2013 and has been in similar negotiations with Norway since 2017 after diplomatic relations were fully restored the previous year following a six-year freeze due to tensions related to awarding the Nobel Peace Prize to Liu Xiaobo in 2010 (Watts & Weaver, 2010). In the case of Russia's Vladimir Putin government, there has been much enthusiastic talk about the emergence of an 'Ice Silk Road' (although specifics are still not determined), which would link both states as well as the Nordic region through the Arctic. Current projects such as the Yamal project, as well as potential infrastructure such as the cross-Siberian railways and fibre optic links that may link Finland with China, would form part of this 'road'.

2.3 Challenging American Hegemony

The growing trade frictions between China and the United States (U.S.), especially since the start of 2018, can be seen as one manifestation of power rivalry between the two great powers and a possible power transition. The two sides have engaged in retaliatory tariffs on each other's goods since the middle of 2018, partially spurred by Washington's concerns about a leap in China's high technology capabilities as part of its 'Made in China 2025' (*Zhongguo Zhizao 2025* 中国制造2025), including artificial intelligence, robotics, quantum computing, driverless vehicles, and blockchain (*qukuailian* 区块链) applications (Tse & Wu, 2018). The American government under Trump is concerned that the Chinese government's push towards more advanced manufacturing by Chinese industries is a direct challenge to U.S. technological superiority. From a wider viewpoint, the U.S. is concerned about eventually being overtaken in terms of overall gross domestic product (GDP) by China in the coming years. Additionally, China has been building its political and military power on a global scale and has become more involved in diplomatic endeavours as well as peacekeeping and peace-building in parts of the world that are well-beyond the Pacific Rim. Although China's military spending, reported at about US$175 billion for 2018, remains far behind that of the United States, especially given the possibility for the U.S. military budget for next year to rise to levels of US$700 billion or more (Rajagopalan, 2018; Stein, 2018), China's power projection capabilities have developed considerably in the past decade, as has been seen in the Indian Ocean and deeper into the Pacific region.

Thus, it can be argued that China under President Xi has now developed to the point of becoming a confident great power,[1] after many years of settling carefully into that role. One of the Chinese leader's first domestic initiatives after taking power, for example, was the concept of the 'China Dream' (*Zhongguomeng* 中国梦) (Xi, 2014). In contrast to the American dream that is based on an idea of individualism and his/her free possibilities to pursue personal interests, the Chinese dream is a collective dream monopolized by the Party. It also refers to China's growing economic power, rejuvenation and widening opportunities for people in the country (Wang, 2014). There is much debate about whether China is abandoning a long-held foreign policy philosophy, in existence in some form since the leadership of Deng Xiaoping (邓小平) in the 1980s, of "keeping a low profile" (*taoguang yanghui* 韬光养晦). There has also been the argument that this Dengist philosophy has been superseded by the

1 This means that the country no longer fears subjugation by other great powers, as was the case during much of the Cold War.

idea of 'trying to accomplish something' (*yousuo zuowei* 有所作为) under Xi, and that more recently Chinese foreign policy has been marked by a greater 'assertiveness', although that term is also widely open to interpretation (Wang, 2014; Johnston, 2013).

It is notable that Beijing is rapidly changing its Dengist traditional approach to international issues. Namely, soon after Xi Jinping came to power, Beijing changed its overall strategic narrative, pointing in the direction that China is rapidly altering its traditional 'passive', 'never seek leadership' and 'non-intervention' principles in its foreign policy conduct. In 2014, the Politburo announced that China needs to strengthen its institutional power in multilateral institutions and to move from 'side-by observer' and 'follower' to 'active participant' and 'guiding actor' (Xinhua Agency, 2014). In other words, Beijing aims at becoming a rule-maker and an active shaper of the architecture, rules and norms of international institutions. At the 2016 Group of Twenty (G20) meeting in Hangzhou, Xi Jinping proudly announced a new political slogan that China should become a 'guiding power' of the world (*Zhongguo yinling shijie* 中国引领世界), marking a clear demarcation from the traditional Dengist 'keep a low profile and never seek leadership' principles (G20 meeting, n.d.).

Furthermore, in a concerted fashion, the Xi government has stipulated new laws that provide Beijing the right to send troops overseas to prevent or counter terrorist activities that threaten Chinese people or assets, thus paving the way for abandoning the treasured foreign policy principle of 'non-intervention' (The U.S.-China Business Council, 2015). For example, China is increasing its security forces' presence in Tajikistan and Afghanistan, and based on international media reports, China has already participated in joint counter-terrorist operations in Afghanistan during the past year (Clover, 2017, February 26). China is also reportedly building a military base in Afghanistan, but Beijing denies that it has troops or will send combat troops to Afghanistan (Putz, 2018, August 29). China has also established hundreds of private or semi-private armed security companies that provide security services to Chinese State-Owned Enterprises (SOEs) in politically unstable environments, including a number of Belt and Road partner countries such as African states (Legarda & Nouwens, 2018, August 16). Few outspoken Chinese scholars and politicians have pointed out that abandoning Dengist foreign policy principles is not only wrong, but China is too weak to seek the position that Xi's regime aims to reach. Scholars warn that the imminent economic risks instigated by the post-2018 Sino-American trade war combined with the radical shift in foreign policy conduct could turn out to be a damaging imperial overstretch for the current regime (Sheng, 2018, October 25; Barmé, 2018, August 1). What can be said, however, is that the Arctic is the latest example of the growing comprehensive approach that Beijing has taken in its foreign policy development.

As noted above, relations between China and the United States have become more problematic, partly as a result of expanded Chinese economic and military power, but also due to the current turn towards greater isolationism, unilateralism and transactionalism by the Donald Trump government since 2017 (Sinkkonen, 2018). These events have led to intensified debates over whether a 'power transition' (Organski, 1968; Tammen et al., 2001) will take place between China and the U.S. in the coming decades. History has demonstrated, with some exceptions, that such transitions often result in war if dissatisfied challenger power aligns against a satisfied status quo power. This has also been referred to in recent media as the 'Thucydides Trap' (Allison, 2017), drawing parallels to the ancient rivalry between the city states of Athens and Sparta. As the centenary of the First World War was observed starting 2014, there was also some debate as to whether similar conditions that caused a regional Balkan conflict to escalate into a global conflict were being replicated in the Pacific Rim.

However, as both states are nuclear powers, the possibility of a great power war along the lines of conflicts on the nineteenth and twentieth centuries are seen as far less likely. In addition, solving today's global problems such as climate change and pandemic diseases provides a strong impetus for cooperation amongst great powers. Moreover, in contrast to previous centuries, the growing number of institutions, regimes and other forms of communication, not to mention global markets, may act as a restraint against a plunge into an overt Sino-American conflict (see, however, Henry M. Paulson Jr., 2018). Nonetheless, the world might be entering into, or is perhaps already in, a period of more overt great power rivalry as Chinese power reaches American levels.

Even during his election campaign, Donald Trump was openly hostile to China and its alleged detrimental policies for the United States. This strategic competition is being felt most acutely in the Pacific Ocean (but also in the Indian Ocean, a major conduit for the Belt and Road), including disputes regarding maritime security, disputed islands, and border demarcation such as the ongoing disputed status of the South and East China Seas. In China, this has led to concerns about containment by the United States and its allies.

Over the past half-decade, the situation in the South China Sea (SCS *Nanhai* 南海) has worsened as China has increased its military presence, including via the so-called 'Third Force' of a Chinese maritime militia, supplementing Chinese naval and coast guard vessels, on some of the islands within the area Beijing claims as its 'historical waters' (Strategic Comments, 2016). This has been viewed as a type of 'hybrid warfare' in the SCS via developing a layered maritime presence. These acts have caused concern for the region's states and the United States. Over the past three years, China has begun to augment disputed reefs, first by adding sand to transform them into de facto islands and then placing various types of infrastructure on them, including runways, monitoring equipment, port facilities and weaponry, including missiles. Despite periodic U.S.-led 'freedom of navigation operations' (FONOPs) in the SCS by American military planes and vessels since the previous U.S. administration of President Barack Obama, Beijing continues to fortify its positions in the SCS, suggesting an 'anti-access/area denial' (A2/AD) strategy in the region, which may hamper the entrance of American or other foreign military vessels into the waterway in the coming years (Erickson, 2016).

2.4 Evolving Economic Interests Abroad

There is also a growing importance of 'economic security' as China develops its great power status, with related concerns about more overt trade competition. After many years of GDP development levels often in the double digits, economic growth has slowed down in China to below seven percent. However, fears of a 'hard landing', meaning a sharp downturn in the Chinese economy leading to a recession and potentially a cascade effect involving the greater global financial system, have been so far proven unfounded. Thus far, Beijing has managed to work with its slower economic growth successfully, remaining an island of stability in the global markets as other regions, including Europe, are still struggling to continue on the path towards recovery. The emerging trade war with the United States since the middle of 2018 is also a wild card in China's short-term economic policies. Concerns about the long term fallout from the trade conflict with Washington has prompted the Xi government to further develop ties with alternative markets, including Europe, Russia, the Middle East and Latin America, with varying degrees of success. There have also been emerging negative effects on China's domestic environmental policies, including cases in which polluting factories that had previously been shut down have since been reopened due to economic strains exacerbated by the Sino-U.S. trade war starting in 2018 (Cai, 2018).

There is also a quiet transition in place between the secondary and tertiary economies, but manufacturing remains the cornerstone of the Chinese economy and so the country is still sensitive to the state of the global trading system. While manufacturing continues to be the mainstay of China's economic growth, there has been much greater attention paid to the tertiary/services sector, including various forms of e-commerce. China is also an innovator in the areas of financial technology, including mobile payments, microloans, and online retail. Witness the massive online sales in China during 'Singles Day' (*Guanggun jie* 光棍节) in the country every 11 November – the online store Alibaba recorded a record profit of US$30.8 billion in sales on that day in 2018 (Rapoza, 2018). Much attention has been paid in this area to the so-called 'BAT' firms, meaning the technology giants Baidu (百度), Alibaba (阿里巴巴) and Tencent (腾讯) as well as their subsidiary companies. From a wider viewpoint, there is also no shortage of 'unicorns', (privately held startup firms valued at over US$1 billion) and even 'decacorns' (firms with a net worth of ten billion dollars US) within the Chinese economy (Yu & Zhang, 2018; Fannin, 2017).

Nonetheless, challenges to the Chinese economy remain. The rapid growth not only of regional level governmental debt, but also rapidly growing domestic debt ratio has created serious structural challenges for the sustainability of the Chinese economic growth model. The current trade war and the possibility of greater economic protectionism in the United States and other Western economies are also potential hazards for Beijing. The Belt and Road processes have also been challenged by concerns about Chinese 'debt traps' among some BRI partners, including Djibouti, Pakistan and Sri Lanka (Hurley, Morris & Portelance, 2018). This has led to the question of whether Beijing will be able to reconcile its economic challenges at home with the large amount of startup capital that will be needed in building the Belt and Road networks.

In addition, there are ongoing concerns about energy security as China's economy modernises, including access to fossil fuels but also the technology to improve Chinese energy efficiency. China's indigenous energy supplies remain dominated by coal, which is polluting, expensive and difficult to transport, as well as being inefficient. Thus, there has been a great deal of enthusiasm for alternative resources, including oil, natural gas, nuclear power, and greener alternatives such as hydro-electricity, wind power, and thermal energy. There is a clear need for more varied sources of energy from different parts of the world in order to move the country away from its high dependency on coal. Many regions, including the Arctic, are seen as sources of oil, gas, liquefied natural gas (LNG) and potentially other types of energy as the Chinese economy matures. Connected to this is China's growing need for other raw materials such as metals and minerals, including those required for high-technology and 'green' technologies such as cobalt, columbite-tantalites (coltan) and rare earth elements (REEs) (Kalantzakos, 2017). One of the reasons why the Arctic has recently assumed a stronger profile in China's resource diplomacy is that not only is more of the region becoming accessible to resource extraction due to climate change, but the Arctic States are viewed as politically stable and generally predictable, which is not the case with other resource-rich regions.

2.5 China as a Maker of Norms and Institutions

As part of Beijing's widening diplomatic interests, China has begun to practice greater 'structural power' in the areas of establishing new rules and norms in the international system. These have included the development of alternative organizations that operate outside of the existing framework established by the West. These include the Asian Infrastructure Investment Bank (AIIB), a financial institution that began operations in January 2016, with a membership that includes all of the Arctic States, save the United States (Dollar, 2015). However, the function of the AIIB remains questionable, as it has remained rather passive in its lending activities. The AIIB, that was supposedly seen as a new regional financial institution established and initiated by Beijing, has approved loans only of less than 10USD billion since the bank began its operations four years ago. Instead, it is evident that China continues to rely heavily on bilateral agreements in providing loans to recipient countries. For instance, two Chinese policy-banks, China Export and Import Bank and China Development Bank, have provided roughly three times more loans to Kazakhstan alone than the AIIB's total to some dozen countries. There is also the New Development Bank (NDB), which began in 2015 as an offshoot of the BRICS (*Jinzhuan Guojia* 金砖国家) grouping. The BRICS has linked China with other large emerging markets, namely Brazil, India, Russia and South Africa.

Although China has no interest in creating exclusionary organizations to directly balance the West, along the lines of a Cold War Soviet-led Comecon or a Warsaw Pact, China is nonetheless beginning to develop as a 'norm-maker' in addition to being a 'norm-taker' in the area of international regime-building (Hirono & Lanteigne, 2012). This means that after many years of China's accepting rules and regimes that were largely created and developed by the United States and other parts of the West, especially when China first opened up to the international community in the late 1970s-80s and when the country engaged in the 'deep reform' processes in the 1990s under Jiang Zemin (Dittmer & Liu, 2006), Beijing is now interested in developing norms of its own, including organizations that do not follow Western guidelines.

The most prominent of these new regimes has been the Belt and Road Initiative (BRI), introduced by President Xi in 2013. It can be argued that the BRI is a prominent example of China's interests in norm-making, given that the initiative represents a Chinese commitment to building an alternative economic pole not only for the Asia-Pacific but also for other regions, including the Arctic. It is notable that the Belt and Road Initiative does not have any official strategy or any national approving institution governing the policies, approvals or accumulating economic activities that Chinese companies are doing in the name of BRI. Instead, Beijing has provided fast and cheap capital for companies and regional governments that claim to make an investment under the banner of BRI. Consequently, countless companies and local governments utilize this financial stimulus to internationalize by proclaiming to be part of the Belt and Road Initiative. As a result, the plethora of Belt and Road investments in various investment sectors are astonishing, ranging from traditional logistical infrastructure and power plants to 'softer' investments, such as sports facilities and arranging of cultural and scientific events that are all financed by various actors through the loose BRI finance.

However, the Belt and Road initiative is also witnessing the build up of trade corridors that are being created in order to expand Chinese trade with key partners in Africa, Europe, Eurasia, Russia and South Asia. The 'Belt' encompasses overland routes that connect China with Europe via Russia and Central Asia, with the centerpiece being the China-Pakistan Economic Corridor (*Zhongguo-Bajisitan Jingji Zoulang* 中国-巴基斯坦经济走廊) or CPEC, and associated transportation and communication routes planned across the Central Asia/Caucasus region. It is very likely that Siberia will play an expanded part in the 'Belt' via new transportation and communication links, given the potential of expanding Chinese trade with Northern Europe and the greater Arctic.

The 'Road' is, more specifically, a set of sea routes connecting the Chinese coastal regions with economies in the Indian Ocean, the Mediterranean and the Pacific Ocean, all the way to Latin America. Connected to the development of these routes has been Chinese investment in ports throughout the Indian Ocean region, including in Pakistan, Sri Lanka and Myanmar as well as in Greece (Piraeus) (Kynge et al., 2017). At present, there are over sixty countries, including Finland, that are involved in some fashion with the building of the Belt and Road via regional and bilateral agreements.

In 2017, the Arctic was formally added to the Belt and Road as a result of a Chinese governmental report that designated the Arctic Ocean as a 'blue economic passage' (*lanse jingji tongdao* 蓝色经济通道) that could be used for enhanced Chinese trade between Asia and Northern Europe. Although it is unlikely that the Arctic will be a primary conduit for the BRI, especially compared to Eurasia and the Indian Ocean, the addition of the Arctic does underscore Chinese interests in utilizing the region for future economic projects in addition to scientific ones (see Chapters 4, 6, and 7 in this volume).

2.6 Aspects of Continuity in Chinese Foreign Policy

Even if many changes have occurred, there are also stable aspects in current-day Chinese foreign policy. Many internal elements are still very much the same, such as the state-guided capitalism, nationalism and the ongoing economic growth that collectively serve as the drivers behind the wide acceptance of the country's political system, and, indeed, the acceptance of a communist one-party system. All of these internal dynamics still manifest in many areas of foreign policy as stable elements. At the same time, it is evident that China is hardening its stance on a number of security issues that are related to its "core interests" and there is increasing evidence that China is utilizing its economic leverage, or debt-trap practices, to interfere with other countries' internal affairs, thus challenging the much cherished non-interference principle of Beijing (Mattlin and Nojonen 2015; Patey, 2017).

China has been consistent in its reliance on the fundamental principles of public international law ever since the start of the reform era in the 1980s, and this view was exemplified in its first ever Arctic policy. Territorial sovereignty, the equality of states, non-interference in the internal affairs of other states and non-use of force against other states have been constant features of China's foreign policy since as far back as the Mao era, notable in the ongoing status of the 'Five Principles of Peaceful Co-existence' (*Heping Gongchu Wuxiang Yuanze* 和平共处五项原则) left over from that period. However, in practice the approach to these features has been open to interpretation. For example, Beijing has become more accepting of humanitarian intervention in the case of civil conflicts, such as in the case of the East Timor conflict and more recently in the civil wars in Mali and South Sudan. Beijing has also been sensitive to any international policies that affect areas viewed by the Chinese government as strictly domestic affairs, including the status of Taiwan, the territories of Tibet and Xinjiang, as well as security in the East and South China Seas.

As one of the permanent members of the United Nations Security Council (UNSC), China has been generally against military interventions into sovereign states, especially if there is no clear Security Council authorization, or if these interventions are conducted by military alliances. Two major examples are the American and North Atlantic Treaty Organization (NATO) actions against Yugoslavia in 1999, and the Washington-led 'coalition of the willing' against Iraq in 2003. In the case of the Arctic, Beijing has also affirmed that it respects the sovereignty and sovereign rights of Arctic States, a requirement that all Observers needed to fulfill as part of the Council's 'Nuuk Criteria' (Graczyk & Koivurova, 2014).

Beijing has also been a fairly strong supporter of regulatory action in many other fields of international policy such as the law of the sea, international environmental law or indigenous people's rights (internationally) – all areas that are of importance from the viewpoint of the Arctic.

China is a party to the United Nations Convention on the Law of the Sea (UNCLOS), unlike the United States. The U.S. does accept most of UNCLOS to be legally binding as customary international law. Even if many accuse China of violating UNCLOS in the South China Sea, the country itself perceives that it is behaving on the basis of the law of the sea. China questioned the jurisdiction of the Permanent Court of Arbitration (PCA) that was established on the initiative of the Philippines (on the basis of UNCLOS) and dismissed the ruling of the PCA in 2016 that decided, to a large extent, against Chinese interests in the SCS (Panda, 2016). The Philippines challenged the historic rights of China in the South China Sea, as many other countries have done, given that Beijing's alleged historic rights, as exemplified by the 'nine dashed line', overlapped with those sovereign rights of the Philippines. Chinese claims to the SCS have also overlapped claims made by Vietnam as well as Malaysia and Brunei (Hayton, 2014).

China did not participate in the proceedings of the PCA. The arbitral tribunal did not accept the historic rights claim of China. China sees that its historic rights over the South China Sea are firmly grounded in the customary law of the sea, and that the arbitral tribunal did not have jurisdiction to even examine the dispute. From a general point of view, China has placed a lot of emphasis on observing UNCLOS. Beijing has also been strident in its claims to the Diaoyu (also known as the Senkaku in Japanese) Islands in the East China Sea despite overlapping Japanese claims. In 2013, China implemented an 'air defence identification zone' (ADIZ) over the East China Sea, which further underscored the seriousness of its claim (Burke & Cevallos, 2017).

Beijing has also actively participated in international environmental policy and law-making (see Chapter 5 in this volume). For example, after the Trump government decided in 2017 to unilaterally withdraw the U.S. from the Paris Climate Agreement, China found itself as one of the largest remaining supporters of the deal, and the Xi government has since reached out to the EU and specific European leaders in the hopes of perpetuating the agreement. China is also party to a large number of international environmental treaties, including many that are relevant in the Arctic (such as the 2001 Persistent Organic Pollutants Convention) and also the most recent fisheries agreement related to the Central Arctic Ocean (CAO).

2.7 China as an Actor in Regions Outside of its Immediate Neighborhood

During the early reformist period in China under Deng Xiaoping and during the 1990s under President Jiang Zemin, Beijing's foreign policy concerns were primarily limited to the surrounding Asia-Pacific region as well as great power relations with the United States and the Soviet Union and later the Russian Federation. Under Jiang, China was especially concerned about resolving, or at least calming, numerous border disputes remaining from the Cold War. During this period, Beijing opened diplomatic relations with former regional adversaries, including Singapore, South Korea and Vietnam, and sought to resolve border disputes including with Russia and Central Asia. China also sought to improve relations with many Southeast Asian governments that had previously been concerned about Beijing's previous support for communist movements. Jiang was primarily interested in *zhoubian* (peripheral) diplomacy in order to allow China to concentrate on delicate internal reforms, including economic reforms but also the restructuring of the Communist Party itself. After decades of poor regional relations and Cold War border conflicts with the Union of Soviet Socialist Republics (USSR), India and Vietnam, China needed a period of calm with its neighbors.

Under Hu Jintao, China began the first steps of adaptation as a great power, although there was still some sensitivity towards being seen as potentially revisionist. The Hu government initially put forward a foreign policy based on the concept of 'peaceful rise' (*heping jueqi* 和平崛起). However, after some internal debates, the concept was changed to the more politically palatable 'peaceful development' (*heping fazhan* 和平发展). Nonetheless, the Hu government began to engage in extensive summit diplomacy in many parts of the world, including in Africa and the Middle East, to demonstrate China's emerging role as a developmental and economic partner, especially given China's own history of being a developing state and a former victim of colonialism. These policies were greatly assisted by the growing unpopularity of U.S. policy under then-President George W. Bush, which was seen as increasingly unilateralist and focused to an excessive degree on anti-terrorism policies and the conflict in Iraq after 2003.

At first, China's cross-regional diplomacy was focused on bilateral agreements, including with large and medium powers such as India, Pakistan and Russia. One exception, however, was the European Union (EU), which Beijing recognized as a key economic partner and a potential alternative pole to the United States. However, China-Europe economic relations have been hampered by strong differences between European governments regarding how to engage with Beijing, as well as the EU's unwillingness to recognize China as a market economy, which is a prerequisite for FTA talks. Nonetheless, the development of the Belt and Road Initiative has added another layer to Chinese diplomacy in the EU, in particular in Central and Eastern Europe (CEE) via the '16+1' talks, which have brought together China and sixteen CEE governments since 2012 to discuss BRI-based economic cooperation (Bachulska, 2018).

China's interests in being viewed as a developmental partner has been especially prevalent in Africa, where Beijing has invested in several economies on the continent, including in resource-rich states such as Angola, the Republic of Congo (Congo-Brazzaville), the Democratic Republic of the Congo (DRC), Equatorial Guinea, Sudan, South Sudan and Zambia. Developmental diplomacy has also been active in Latin America, especially in countries that have run afoul of U.S. policy, such as Venezuela, as well as countries experiencing economic trauma since the financial downturn of a decade ago, including Brazil and Argentina. More recently, the Pacific Islands region has also been a major beneficiary of Chinese aid, to the point where Beijing is widely seen as an alternative donor to the traditional powers in the region, namely Australia and New Zealand (Lanteigne, 2012).

Unlike Africa and other developing regions, China's cross-regional diplomacy in the Arctic is less overtly based on resource-based interests. Although the potential resources of the Arctic, including raw materials and fossil fuels, are of concern to Chinese Arctic diplomacy, Beijing is also seeking greater usage of the Arctic as a transit corridor. Notably, China has also put forward the idea of the Arctic as a *de facto* 'international space', whereby non-Arctic States can have a voice in regional governance while also avoiding being seen as a 'spoiler' in the region, going against the status quo. Therefore, understanding that the Arctic is a distinct region and that Beijing is at a disadvantage compared to the Arctic Eight, China seeks to take on the persona of a 'norm entrepreneur' (Lanteigne, 2017).

At present, the Arctic is not as high a priority for Beijing in comparison with other regions, and much of its Arctic policy is still in development (see Chapter 3 in this volume). Additionally, of the two polar regions, Antarctica has been given more attention in terms of scientific projects and funding. In 1983, China signed on to the primary Antarctic Treaty, and shortly afterwards it began to construct its own research stations on the continent, the first being the Great Wall Station (*Changcheng zhan* 长城站), on the Fildes Peninsula, completed in 1985. Also in 1985, China became a consultative party to the Antarctic Treaty and it was made a full member of the Scientific Committee on Antarctic Research (SCAR) in 1986. Four Chinese bases are currently in operation, with the latest, Taishan Station (*Taishan zhan* 泰山站) on Queen Elizabeth Land in Eastern Antarctica, opening in February 2014. A fifth base is to be situated on Inexpressible Island near the shore of the Ross Sea. Unlike Taishan, it will be built to stay operational through the entire winter season, and is expected to be fully operational by 2022 (Liu, 2018). In October 2018,

Beijing announced that it was also seeking to build an airstrip on the continent to assist with Chinese scientific missions as well as accommodating the *Snow Eagle 601* aircraft used for research purposes (Feng, 2018).

Since 2006, Beijing has been a member of the Convention for the Conservation of Antarctic Marine Living Resources (CCAMLR), which oversees the waters surrounding the Antarctic continent. China's first Antarctic expedition took place in 1984, and since then the country has conducted subsequent missions on the continent via the Chinese Arctic and Antarctic Administration (CAA *Guojia Haiyangju Jidi Kaocha Bangongshi* 国家海洋局极地考察办公室), which operates under the aegis of the government's State Oceanic Administration (SOA *Guojia Haiyangju* 国家海洋局), an agency which, in turn, was incorporated into the newly-created Ministry of Natural Resources (Reuters, 2018, March 19).

In May 2017, Beijing hosted an Antarctic Treaty Consultative Meeting for the first time (Straits Times, 2017, May 24), and the Chinese government used that opportunity to outline its growing interests on the continent but also to demonstrate its status as an important contributor to multilateral Antarctica policy. Beijing also took that opportunity to publish its first Antarctic White Paper, which outlined China's growing scientific capabilities in the region. As with its dealings with the Arctic, over the past decade China has been seeking to develop a distinct identity in the Circumpolar South, noting the possibility that both polar regions may encourage greater scientific, and potentially economic, activities in the coming decades.

Nomenclature is also important in the understanding of Chinese diplomacy at both poles. *Polar* is translated in Chinese as the compound word *jidi* (极地); the two characters in the word being *ji* ('extreme') and *di* ('earth'), or in other words, 'the extremes of the earth'. Thus, in Chinese, the Arctic is the "Northern Extreme" (*Beiji* 北极); the Antarctic is the "Southern Extreme" (*Nanji* 南极); while the Tibetan Plateau, which contains the world's highest mountains, is the "Third Extreme" (*Disanji* 第三极) or 'Third Pole', referring to the Himalaya region. According to Chinese international law specialist Zou Keyuan (邹克渊), China and Antarctica's close links were forged millions of years ago as a part of the history of the ancient supercontinent of Gondwana. These claims are not made lightly; the implication is that although the two continents are now far apart, China has as much right to make a claim on the territory as other nations that currently are physically closer. From the Chinese government's perspective, the geographical connection between China and "the poles" gives added cogency and legitimacy to its claim for rights and interests in the polar regions and China's "right to speak" on polar affairs (Brady, 2017).

However, China is also aware that it is a relative neophyte to Antarctic affairs as compared with veterans including the United States, Russia, Western

Europe, Latin America, and of course Australia and New Zealand. Therefore, the Xi government has taken steps to present its Antarctic agenda as one that stresses partnerships and respect for regional laws and norms. At the same time, China is also underscoring its determination to be recognized as an Antarctic player, keeping in mind that the political situation on the continent may change considerably if the various treaty networks in the region either change or fall into abeyance.

While there are some similarities in China's policies at both poles, there are also significant differences, not least because the Arctic, unlike the Antarctic, has a permanent population and is a predominantly maritime region. Yet, there are also commonalities, as are reflected in the interest that China expresses in all three polar regions (including the 'Himalayan Pole') and its increasing presence and scientific expertise in all those regions. In addition, according to some scholars, research activities provide China with more legitimacy and give cogency to its claim for rights and interests in the polar regions (Bertelsen, Li & Gregerson, 2017).

While scientific diplomacy will probably continue to be the vanguard of Chinese Arctic interests, economic concerns are starting to attain importance as well, given China's ongoing need for energy and raw materials as well as new shipping lanes. This has led to questions about whether China may develop stronger security interests in the Arctic as its investment in the region grows, along similar lines as in the Indian Ocean, where increased Chinese trade interests were a factor in the opening of a logistics center in Djibouti in 2017.

Although there have been no open discussions as to whether China would seek to open military bases in the Arctic Ocean, some scholars view the increasing involvement of China in the Arctic in unfavourable and hostile terms, and they interpret Chinese actions in the region predominantly in security and military terms. They point to the potential of the 'dual-use' of Chinese facilities in the Arctic – a concern that was also expressed by Denmark regarding the establishment of Chinese research stations in Greenland – and warn against China's silently expanding its influence and dominance throughout the means of scientific and economic engagement. Other scholars, however, find this approach highly reductionist and limited in its nuanced analysis of Chinese Arctic policy. They note that such concerns have much to do with the fact that China is a great power and therefore is seen as having a strategic agenda in much of its activities in the Far North. Most of all, in light of very high international scrutiny that any actions of China in the Arctic receive in the media, among experts and state officials, it appears highly improbable that China could significantly extend its reach silently and thereby increase its power in the region.

2.8 Conclusion

China has now become a great power, via a process that has been moulded both by the country's internal politics and also through the actions of other states, including other great powers. At the same time, as China has risen in power, its foreign policy has not only affected the Asia-Pacific but also numerous other regions. The Arctic is but the latest part of the world to be affected by Beijing's increasingly confident cross-regional diplomacy, as this book makes clear. Overall, it can be concluded that Beijing is no longer content to be a norm-*taker* in international politics but it is more comfortable with becoming a norm-*maker*. However, there are noteworthy differences between China's Arctic engagement and its diplomacy in other parts of the world.

Literature

Allison, Graham (2017). *Destined for War: Can America and China Escape Thucydides's Trap?* Boston and New York: Mariner Books.

Bachulska, A. (2018, July 3). What's next for China's 16+1 platform in Central and Eastern Europe? *The Diplomat.* Retrieved August 25, 2018, from https://thediplomat.com/2018/07/whats-next-for-chinas-161-platform-in-central-and-eastern-europe/.

Barmé, G.R. (2018, August 1). Imminent fears, immediate hopes – A Beijing jeremiad. *China heritage, The Wairarapa Academy for New Sinology.* Retrieved August 10, 2018, from http://chinaheritage.net/journal/imminent-fears-immediate-hopes-a-beijing-jeremiad/.

Bertelsen, R.G., Li, X., & Gregersen, M.H. (2017). Chinese Arctic science diplomacy: An instrument for achieving the Chinese dream? In E. Conde & S.I. Sánchez (Eds.), *Global Challenges in the Arctic Region: Sovereignty, Environment and Ecological Balance* (pp. 442–460). London, United Kingdom & New York, NY: Routledge.

Brady, A-M. (2017). China as a polar great power. Cambridge, England: Cambridge University Press.

Buckley, C., & Bradsher, K. (2018, February 25). China moves to let Xi stay in power by abolishing term limit. *The New York Times.*

Burke, E.J., & Cevallos, A.S. (2017). In line or out of order? China's approach to ADIZ in theory and practice. *Rand.* Retrieved June 10, 2018, from https://www.rand.org/pubs/research_reports/RR2055.html.

Cai, J. (2018, November 15). Northern China's clean air targets get lost in the smog of the trade war. *South China Morning Post.* Retrieved December 10, 2018, from https://

beta.scmp.com/news/china/politics/article/2172956/northern-chinas-clean-air-targets-get-lost-smog-united-states.

Clover, C. (2017, February 26). Mystery deepens over Chinese forces in Afghanistan. *Financial Times.* Retrieved June 15, 2018, from https://www.ft.com/content/0c8a5a2a-f9b7-11e6-9516-2d969e0d3b65.

Dittmer, L., & Liu, G. (Eds.). (2006). China's deep reform: Domestic politics in transition. Oxford, England: Rowman and Littlefield.

Dollar, D. (2015, Summer). The AIIB and the "One Belt, One Road". *Brookings.* Retrieved June 15, 2018, from https://www.brookings.edu/opinions/the-aiib-and-the-one-belt-one-road/.

Erickson, A. (2016). America's security role in the South China Sea. *Naval War College Review, 69*(1): 1-14. Retrieved June 10, 2018, from https://digital-commons.usnwc.edu/cgi/viewcontent.cgi?referer=https://scholar.google.co.nz/scholar?as_ylo=2014&q=A2/AD+China+South+China+Sea&hl=en&as_sdt=0,5&httpsredir=1&article=1117&context=nwc-review.

Fannin, R. (2017, October 9). Counting decacorns? Look to Beijing. *Forbes.* Retrieved April 20, 2018, from https://www.forbes.com/sites/rebeccafannin/2017/10/09/counting-decacorns-look-to-beijing/#43bb2d0567be.

Feng, E. (2018, October 28). China to build first Antarctic airport. *Financial Times.* Retrieved October 30, 2018, from https://www.ft.com/content/6409b48a-db33-11e8-9f04-38d397e6661c.

Foreign Ministry of the People's Republic of China (2013), President Xi Jinping Delivers Important Speech and Proposes to Build a Silk Road Economic Belt with Central Asian Countries. Retrieved 31 August 2019, from https://www.fmprc.gov.cn/mfa_eng/topics_665678/xjpfwzysiesgjtfhshzzfh_665686/t1076334.shtml.

G20 meeting. (n.d.). [Website]. Retrieved June 10, 2018, from http://www.ipanda.com/special/lundaoG20/index.shtml.

Graczyk, P., & Koivurova, T. (2014). A new era in the Arctic Council's external relations? Broader consequences of the Nuuk Observer rules for Arctic governance. *Polar Record, 50*(3), 225.

Hayton, B. (2014). *The South China Sea: The struggle for power in Asia.* New Haven and London: Yale University Press.

Hirono, M., & Lanteigne, M. (2012). *China's evolving approach to peacekeeping.* London, England & New York, NY: Routledge.

Hurley, J., Morris, S., & Portelance, G. (2018, March). Examining the debt implications of the Belt and Road Initiative from a policy perspective. Centre for Global Development. CGD Policy Paper 121. Retrieved June 10, 2018, from https://www.cgdev.org/sites/default/files/examining-debt-implications-belt-and-road-initiative-policy-perspective.pdf.

Johnston, A.I. (2013). How new and assertive is China's new assertiveness? *International Security, 37*(4): 7–48.

Kalantzakos, S. (2017). China and the geopolitics of rare earths. Oxford, England: Oxford University Press.

Kynge, J., Campbell, C., Kazmin, A., & Bokhari, F. (2017, January 13). How China rules the waves. *Financial Times.* Retrieved June 10, 2018, from https://ig.ft.com/sites/china-ports/.

Lanteigne, M. (2012, June). Water dragon? China, power shifts and soft balancing in the South Pacific. *Political Science, 64*(1): 21–38.

Lanteigne, M. (2013). Commercial diplomacy and China's free trade policies. In X. Huang and R. Patman (Eds.), *Becoming a World Power: China and The International System* (pp. 71–88). Boulder, CO: Lynne Reinner.

Lanteigne, M. (2017). Have you entered the storehouses of the snow? China as a norm entrepreneur in the Arctic. *Polar Record, 53*(2): 117–130.

Legarda, H., & Nouwens, M. (2018, August 16). Guardians of the Belt and Road: The internationalization of China's private security companies. *Merics: Mercator Institute for China Studies.* Retrieved August 20, 2018, from https://www.merics.org/en/china-monitor/guardians-of-belt-and-road.

Liu, N. (2018, June 28). What does China's fifth research station mean for Antarctic governance?. *The Diplomat.* Retrieved October 21, 2018, from https://thediplomat.com/2018/06/what-does-chinas-fifth-research-station-mean-for-antarctic-governance/.

Mattlin, M. & Nojonen, M. (2015). Conditionality and Path Dependence in Chinese Lending. *Journal of Contemporary China* 24:94.

Organski, A.F.K. (1968). World politics. (Alfred A. Knopf).

Panda, A. (2016, July 12). International court issues unanimous award in Philippines v. China case on South China Sea. *The Diplomat.* Retrieved November 10, 2018, from https://thediplomat.com/2016/07/international-court-issues-unanimous-award-in-philippines-v-china-case-on-south-china-sea/.

Patey, L. (2017, Jan 24). China Made Mauricio Macri a Deal He Couldn't Refuse. *Foreign Policy.* Retrieved September 2, 2019, from https://foreignpolicy.com/2017/01/24/china-made-mauricio-macri-a-deal-he-couldnt-refuse/.

Paulson, H.M. Jr. (2018). Remarks by Henry M. Paulson, Jr., on the United States and China at a Crossroads. *Paulson Institute.* Retrieved November 10, 2018, from http://www.paulsoninstitute.org/news/2018/11/06/statement-by-henry-m-paulson-jr-on-the-united-states-and-china-at-a-crossroads/.

Putz, C. (2018, August 29). With rumored 'Training camp', China's Afghanistan presence set to grow. *The Diplomat.* Retrieved September 14, 2018, from https://thediplomat.com/2018/08/with-rumored-training-camp-chinas-afghanistan-presence-set-to-grow/.

Rajagopalan, R.P. (2018, March 7). China's 2018 military budget: New numbers, old worries. *The Diplomat.* Retrieved October 21, 2018, from https://thediplomat.com/2018/03/chinas-2018-military-budget-new-numbers-old-worries/.

Rapoza, K. (2018, November 13). Alibaba's 'Singles day' sales record – A symbol of an unstoppable China. *Forbes.* Retrieved November 20, 2018, from https://www.forbes.com/sites/kenrapoza/2018/11/13/alibabas-singles-day-sales-record-a-symbol-of-an-unstoppable-china/#12458973cd16.

Reuters. (2018, March 19). China picks rising star to run new natural resources ministry. *Reuters.* Retrieved August 20, 2018, from https://www.reuters.com/article/us-china-parliament-resources/china-picks-rising-star-to-run-new-natural-resources-ministry-idUSKBN1GV04F.

Sheng, H. (2018, October 25). Sino-US relation is critical for China's reform and opening-up. *Unirule Institute of Economics.* Retrieved November 20, 2018, from http://english.unirule.cloud/highlights/2018-10-25/1124.html.

Sinkkonen, V. (2018, November). Contextualizing the "Trump Doctrine": Realism, transactionalism and the civilizational agenda. FIIA Analysis. *Finnish Institute of International Affairs.* Retrieved December 10, 2018, from https://www.fiia.fi/julkaisu/contextualizing-the-trump-doctrine.

Stein, J. (2018, June 19). US military budget inches closer to $1 trillion mark, as concerns over federal deficit grow. *Washington Post.*

Straits Times. (2017, May 24). China to expand its presence in Antarctica. Retrieved October 20, 2018, from https://www.straitstimes.com/asia/east-asia/china-to-expand-its-presence-in-antarctica.

Strategic Comments. (2016). China's assertiveness in the South China Sea. *Strategic Comments,* 22(9): iii–iv. DOI: 10.1080/13567888.2016.1260390.

Tammen, R.L., Kugler, J., Lemke, D., Stam, A.C. III, Abdollahian, M., Alsharabati, C., Efird, B., & Organski, A.F.K. (2001). *Power Transitions: Strategies for the 21st Century.* Washington, DC: CQ Press.

Tepperman, J. (2018) China's Great Leap Backward, *Foreign Policy* October 15, Retrieved 31 August 2019, from https://foreignpolicy.com/2018/10/15/chinas-great-leap-backward-xi-jinping/.

The US-China Business Council. (2015). Unofficial translation of the counter-terrorism law of the People's Republic of China. *The US-China Business Council.* Retrieved July 15, 2018, from https://www.uschina.org/china-hub/unofficial-translation-counter-terrorism-law-peoples-republic-china.

Tse, A., & Wu, J. (2018, September 11). Why "Made in China 2025" Triggered the wrath of President Trump. *South China Morning Post.* Retrieved December 10, 2018, from https://multimedia.scmp.com/news/china/article/made-in-China-2025/index.html.

Wang, Z. (2014, March). The Chinese dream: Concept and context. *Journal of Chinese Political Science,* 19(1): 1–13.

Watts, J., & Weaver, M. (2010, October 11). China cancels meeting with Norwegian Minister after Nobel Peace Prize row. *The Guardian.* Retrieved November 25, 2018, from https://www.theguardian.com/world/2010/oct/11/china-cancels-norway-meeting.

Xi, J. (2014). *The Chinese dream of the Great Rejuvenation of the Chinese Nation*. Beijing: Foreign Languages Press.

Xinhua Agency. (2014). Website. Retrieved June 10, 2018, from http://www.xinhuanet.com/politics/2014-12/06/c_1113546075.htm.

Yu, X., & Zhang, M. (2018, March 31). At the heart of China's techno-nationalism is a hit list of 200 unicorns. *South China Morning Post.* Retrieved July 10, 2018, from https://www.scmp.com/business/companies/article/2139684/heart-chinas-techno-nationalism-hit-list-200-unicornsn.

CHAPTER 3

China's Arctic Policy

Timo Koivurova, Sanna Kopra, Marc Lanteigne, Matti Nojonen, Malgorzata (Gosia) Smieszek and Adam Stepien

3.1 Introduction

This chapter elaborates on China's evolving strategy in the Arctic. In January 2018, the Chinese government published its first-ever Arctic policy. For many, the overarching and ambitious nature of the country's Arctic policy was a surprise. China emphasized its role in global and regional governance that pertains to the Arctic but also the way it will function in the region through bilateral relations. For China, the Arctic is no longer about simply being an observer in the Arctic Council, but much more. It is therefore important to study the main parameters of this policy. This chapter will analyze mainly the specifics of China's Arctic white paper and examine a pair of specific cases, namely China's role in negotiating the Polar Code and the Arctic fisheries agreement. Special attention will be paid to the ways in which China's national policy towards the Arctic has emerged and how it has been viewed by other actors and commentators following China's role in the Arctic. As a sub-section, China's policy towards the Arctic's indigenous peoples will also be studied. It is additionally useful to explore how China's Arctic national policy compares with other Asian states that were accepted as observers into the Arctic Council. Finally, conclusions are drawn on the impact and future prospects of China's Arctic policy.

3.2 The Development of China's Arctic Policy

China's participation in Arctic international cooperation is fairly recent, even if the country became a party to the Spitsbergen Treaty in 1925. The country became a member of the International Arctic Science Committee (IASC) in 1996 but only in 2007 did it start to send delegations to the meetings of the Arctic Council, the predominant inter-governmental forum for the discussion on Arctic issues (Koivurova *et al.*, 2017). China has no territory north of the Arctic Circle, a prerequisite for membership, so the country's only option was to become a formal Observer. For this, the country needed to demonstrate an understanding of Arctic affairs, including economics, history, and peoples, to a

© KONINKLIJKE BRILL NV, LEIDEN, 2020 | DOI:10.1163/9789004408425_004

degree that would be acceptable to the eight members of the Arctic Council, some of which, including Canada, Russia and the United States, were suspicious of Beijing's motives. China was also at a disadvantage, as the country did not have a long history of engagement and exploration compared with other Observer governments. Beijing also had to address its still-tentative approaches to regional institutions, especially those that were outside of the Asia-Pacific. In short, Beijing had to quickly and effectively build an Arctic identity in the face of internal and external constraints.

There was also a perceived timing issue in Beijing's engagement of the Arctic Council. Until energy and commodity prices fell after 2014, there was much discussion about an 'Arctic scramble' for resources that would place the eight Council members at a distinct advantage (Borgerson, 2008). On one hand, China wanted to avoid the impression that it was seeking to 'gate-crash' the region and challenge Arctic governance, including the Arctic Council. However, Chinese policymakers were also wary of what could be called the 'blueberry pie' scenario, whereby the Arctic is cut up amongst the Arctic Eight, with all other countries being sidelined (Rainwater, 2013; Lanteigne, 2018). Thus, China had to find a middle ground, and a great deal of that process involved presenting itself as an Arctic partner, a process that resulted in a great deal of Arctic diplomacy on a bilateral level. In some cases, the process was extremely successful (Iceland, Russia), producing good returns (Finland, Sweden), but less so in others (Canada, Denmark, United States). Norway was the odd one out in this process until late 2016, when diplomatic relations were more fully restored. Also, Norway did not veto China's 2013 bid to become an Arctic Council observer, despite worsened bilateral relations and speculation that Oslo would seek to curtail China's bid (Watts, 2012).

The country was accepted as an Observer to the Arctic Council at the Kiruna ministerial meeting in 2013, together with other Asian applicants (Japan, South Korea, India and Singapore) and Italy. China's interest in becoming a Council Observer, along with a potential growing 'line by the front door', as is the current status of many Asian states, forced greater attention to be paid to how future Observers should be chosen. Previous applications that so far have not been successful include Greece, Mongolia, Turkey and the European Union. However, the EU, while it lacks formal Observer status, remains an Observer-in-principle, and is a common participant in Council proceedings.

During the years immediately preceding Beijing's acceptance as a formal Observer in the Arctic Council, there was a noticeable uptick of media reports and academic studies regarding the country's emerging policies in the Arctic, including references to China as both a 'near-Arctic State' (*jin beiji guojia* 近北极国家) and an 'Arctic stakeholder' (*beiji lihai guanxiguo* 北极利害关系国),

despite the fact that China does not have an Arctic border (Jakobson & Peng, 2012). The shortest distance between the Arctic Circle and China's northernmost point, in Mohe County (漠河县), Heilongjiang province at 53°33′ N, is more than 1400 kilometers.

Nonetheless, some Chinese actors argued that China's proximity to the Arctic region, as well as the effects of regional climate change on Chinese weather patterns, justify greater Chinese engagement in Arctic governance. It was also suggested in studies published in March 2017 that changing weather patterns in the Arctic, specifically ice erosion in the Arctic Ocean, coupled with increased snowfall in regions of Siberia, were contributing to reduced wind frequency, which in turn allowed for air pollution to linger over parts of coastal China in winter months (Hernández, 2017). Since then, air pollution levels well above safety levels have been recorded in coastal Chinese cities during the winter, a phenomenon commonly known as the 'airpocalypse' or *morikongqi* (末日空气) in Chinese (Yang, 2016).

However, the concept of 'near-Arctic State' was greeted with suspicion by some Western Observers and at times interpreted as an attempt by China to directly challenge political norms in the region and to act as a 'gate-crasher' in the Arctic. There were also attempts by some Western commentators to draw comparisons between China's claims to the South China Sea and the country's supposed 'assertiveness' in the Arctic Ocean, despite the fact that Beijing is not claiming any sovereignty in the latter region (Houck, 2017, August 1; Martin, 2018, May 5). A quotation by then-PLA (People's Liberation Army) Rear Admiral Yin Zhuo (尹卓), stating that "the Arctic belongs to all the people around the world, as no nation has sovereignty over it [...] China must play an indispensable role in Arctic exploration as we have one-fifth of the world's population", was used as further evidence of an emerging revisionist policy in the Arctic on China's part, despite the fact that other reports suggested that the quotation was either mistranslated or taken out of context. The complete statement was also cited as "according to the United Nations Convention on the Law of the Sea (UNCLOS), the North Pole and its surrounding areas do not belong to any single country, and the common riches in the area belong to all the people in the world". Both of these alarmist interpretations of China's behavior in the region were clearly expressed by the Secretary of State of the United States (U.S.), Mike Pompeo, in his speech just before the Arctic Council's foreign ministers meeting in Rovaniemi on May 6, 2019 (Pompeo, 2019).

Despite the fact that Beijing had taken great care to stress both scientific diplomacy and its ongoing interest to act as a partner to the Arctic States, since 2013 Chinese officials have also tacitly put forward the idea that despite not being an Arctic State, non-Arctic States such as China should nonetheless play a role, to a certain degree, in Arctic affairs, given the effects of the region in parts of the world further south.

One vivid sign of this was a speech given by then-Chinese Vice-Foreign Minister Zhang Ming (张明) at the annual Arctic Circle conference in Reykjavík in October 2015. His speech included a brief, six-point plan for China's emerging Arctic policies, namely the need for future exploration and knowledge about the region, the protection and "rational use" of the Arctic, respect for the inherent rights of Arctic States and indigenous peoples, respect for the rights of non-Arctic States and the international community, creation of a "multi-tiered co-operation framework for win-win results" in the region, and the need for continued observance of relevant international law and institutions, including UNCLOS and the Spitsbergen Treaty (Zhang, 2015). The first three points were hardly groundbreaking and were assumed to be a normal stance by an Arctic Council Observer seeking to build an Arctic identity. However, the fourth, fifth and sixth points were a tacit statement that China wished to play a more central role in future Arctic affairs. China was seeking to walk a fine line between being seen as revisionist in the Arctic but also avoiding what has been called a scenario whereby the Arctic is split up, politically and economically, between the 'Arctic Eight', with all other governments being shut out (Lanteigne, 2018).

3.3 China's Arctic White Paper in a Nutshell

By the time of adoption of China's first Arctic policy document in 2018, its stance towards the Arctic Council and Arctic governance has become clearer. Beijing evidently perceives that it will continue as an Observer in the Arctic Council, but the white paper defines its general role in Arctic governance in more expansive and ambitious terms, as is briefly explained below. This stance is clear from the beginning of the white paper, in which the country details what is taking place in the region and who should bear responsibility for the region. In particular, the White paper stipulates:

> The Arctic situation now goes beyond its original inter-Arctic States or regional nature, having a vital bearing on the interests of States outside the region and the interests of the international community as a whole, as well as on the survival, the development, and the shared future for mankind.
>
> PRC State Council, 2018

With this viewpoint, the basis for China's policy is to be among those who shoulder their share of responsibility for the development of a sustainable Arctic. Before moving to these themes, the document provides some basic information about the Arctic and recent changes in the region.

Chapter 2 of the white paper starts out by defining why China perceives itself as a "near-Arctic state". It is, according to the white paper, "one of the continental States that are closest to the Arctic Circle" but also that "[t]he natural conditions of the Arctic and their changes have a direct impact on China's climate system and ecological environment, and, in turn, on its economic interests in agriculture, forestry, fishery, marine industry and other sectors". Then the document identifies how China is already active in the Arctic and has been so for quite some time.

Chapter 3 of the paper outlines China's policy goals on the Arctic: to understand, protect, develop and participate in the governance of the Arctic "so as to safeguard the common interests of all countries and the international community in the Arctic, and [to] promote sustainable development of the Arctic" (PRC State Council, 2018). In order to realize these policy goals, the white paper elaborates basic principles for their attainment: "respect, cooperation, [a] win-win result and sustainability". "Respect" is defined as the key basis for China's participation in Arctic affairs, and "cooperation" aims to establish a relationship "of multi-level, omni-dimensional and wide-ranging cooperation in this area". Furthermore, a "win-win result" is defined to mean that all stakeholders in this area should pursue and experience mutual benefits and common progress in all fields of activities. Finally, "sustainability" as the fourth principle is defined as meaning "realizing harmonious coexistence between man and nature, better coordination between ecological protection, economic growth and social progress, better balance between utilization, management and protection, and intergenerational equity" (ibid.).

Furthermore, China's Arctic white paper categorizes Chinese policies and positions on participating in Arctic affairs, in Chapter 4, in four goals: deepening the exploration and understanding of the Arctic; protecting the eco-environment of the Arctic and addressing climate change; utilising Arctic resources in a lawful and rational manner; and, finally, participating actively in Arctic governance and international cooperation. As all the other policies are studied in other chapters of this volume, it is useful to examine here the final one – participating actively in Arctic governance and international cooperation.

In the white paper, China states that it "has worked to regulate and supervise the activities of Chinese citizens, legal persons or other organizations in the Arctic in accordance with the law to ensure that their activities accord with international law and respect the relevant national laws on environmental protection, resource conservation, and sustainable development" (PRC State Council, 2018). It also expresses that it has endeavored to consolidate its overall coordination of its Arctic policy but, importantly, that "China takes an active part in the international governance of the Arctic". For the country, it is important to uphold the current Arctic governance system with the UN Charter and the UNCLOS as its core. However, China not only foresees that the existing international frameworks are to be upheld in the Arctic, it also expresses its desire to advance international cooperation on the Arctic, for instance, under the Belt and Road Initiative, which may, in China's view, provide many joint benefits such as linking China and Europe via the Arctic Ocean by building the blue economic passage or enhancing Arctic digital connectivity, including via a potential fibre-optic link from China to the Nordic Arctic via Siberia (Nilsen 2019), both of which very much hinge on the development of the Northern Sea Route.

For the remainder of this part of the white paper, China affirms that it has a strong role in those global frameworks that influence the future of the Arctic, such as the climate regime or the International Maritime Organization, but also regionally, as an Observer in the Arctic Council. Bilateral cooperation is also seen as an extremely important part of China's collaboration with the Arctic states.

3.4 China and Arctic International Governance

As a non-Arctic state, China invokes international frameworks of rules that strongly emphasize its role in Arctic governance. China's Arctic strategy pays little attention to the role of the predominant intergovernmental regional forum, the Arctic Council, in regional governance. Yet this may not be a big surprise, given China's limited role in the Council (see Chapter 4 in this volume) – China is only an Observer, a status lower than the small Nordic states, or Indigenous Peoples' organizations that would normally be dubbed as non-governmental organizations in other intergovernmental bodies or treaty negotiations. Conversely, China emphasizes international frameworks in which it itself plays a more significant role. In particular, China's Arctic white paper reiterates that the Arctic is governed not only by the Arctic Council but international norms, rules and institutions apply to the region as well. In particular, the paper stresses the role of the United Nations and its Security Council (where China is one of the permanent members), the UNCLOS (to which China is a party), UN-specialized agencies such as the International Maritime Organization (IMO) and the treaties it produces (China is a party to many of these regimes), and the UN-based regime fighting against climate change and various other international environmental treaties (to many of which China is a party). In this way, China seeks to legitimate its role as one of the main players in Arctic governance. Clearly, China's growing presence in the Arctic countries via scientific engagement (see Chapter 4 in this volume) and economic policy (see Chapter 6 in this volume), amongst other ways, shapes regional affairs.

Furthermore, it is also useful to examine more deeply two processes that both commenced around 2010 and that have provided needed regulations for enhancing safe and environmentally sound shipping and responsible fisheries in the Arctic Ocean, as these have not been studied in other chapters of this book. The 2009 Arctic Marine Shipping Assessment (AMSA, 2009) of the Arctic Council recommended that the Arctic States take action towards a mandatory Polar Code, which would establish legally binding obligations for states and their vessels when they enter the Arctic Ocean or Southern Ocean surrounding Antarctica. As early as 2002, an Arctic shipping Code was adopted by the IMO as a recommendatory instrument for navigating in the Arctic Ocean, which was then expanded to cover the Southern Ocean via the IMO-adopted non-legally binding 2009 Polar Code (see Jensen, 2007; Polar Code, 2009).

The Polar Code was negotiated to contain both recommendatory and legally binding sections (as amendments to the existing IMO treaties such as the International Convention for the Safety of Life at Sea – SOLAS and the International Convention for the Prevention of Pollution from Ships – MARPOL) and it came into force in 2017. One of the key objectives of the states in adopting law of the sea measures is to facilitate smooth traffic and navigation. Therefore, the coastal states are generally discouraged from setting construction, design, equipment and manning (CDEM) standards beyond those accepted internationally. As a result, in order to be effective, CDEM standards specific for Arctic shipping needed to be regulated in the legally binding part of the Polar Code. As a Member State to the IMO, China states in its Arctic policy that it will abide by these standards and also that it is willing to further develop these rules, as it "supports the International Maritime Organization in playing an active role in formulating navigational rules for the Arctic" (PRC State Council, 2018).

The Arctic Council's Arctic Climate Impact Assessment of 2004/2005 (ACIA, 2005) projected that with warming waters, the fish stocks are likely to move northwards. The United States took the initiative in 2007 by presenting the proposal to the Senior Arctic Officials (SAO) of the Arctic Council that precautionary regulatory action might be needed, but the SAOs did not see that the Council would have competence in fisheries management. For this reason, in 2010 the Arctic Ocean coastal states commenced diplomatic and scientific negotiations to explore whether regulatory action was needed for the possible emergence of high seas fish stocks in the Central Arctic Ocean, an area of about

2.8 million square kilometers. The coastal states issued a declaration in 2015 not to allow their own fishing vessels to enter this area, and then invited four other states (China, Japan, South-Korea and Iceland) and the European Union for further negotiations on a legally binding agreement. The text of the agreement was approved by the parties in November 2017, and the agreement itself was signed in October 2018. With the agreement, these nine states and the EU agree to abstain from commercial fishing, which can be lifted if specified procedural and substantive criteria are met. Given that there is no commercial fishing in this high seas area, the agreement is a good example of a precautionary approach to fisheries, as nowadays about forty percent of the high seas area is already open during the summer months (Arctic Fisheries Agreement, 2018). China also played an important role in these negotiations (Liu, 2018).

3.5 China and Arctic Indigenous Peoples

Indigenous Peoples are important actors in the avenues of Arctic governance. There is a broad consensus among Arctic States and other actors in the region – at least at a declaratory level – that indigenous concerns and rights need to be seriously taken into account and that Indigenous Peoples should participate in decision-making and in any Arctic-relevant discussion. Hence, any non-Arctic state wanting to develop its Arctic policy needs to take a stance on indigenous peoples, the original residents of the region. All the non-Arctic states that aim to become observers to the Arctic Council need to justify their observer application also by demonstrating their commitment to the region's indigenous peoples. To this end, the Chinese government also commits to "respect [the Arctic region's] diverse social culture and historical traditions of the indigenous peoples" (as well as "interests and concerns of indigenous peoples") (PRC State Council, 2018), reiterating several times the phrasing found in the Arctic Council's Nuuk Observer rules (see Graczyk & Koivurova, 2014).

Between 2011 and 2013, when China obtained formal Observer status in the Arctic Council, Chinese officials approached indigenous representatives, but China did not reach out to Permanent Participant organizations the way that Singapore did, for instance, by inviting Arctic indigenous activists to visit the city-state (Stepien, 2017). Conversely, China's 2018 White Paper states that business cooperation "should accommodate the interests of local residents including the indigenous peoples" in line with the "win-win result" principle. In the same vein, Chinese operators should respect "the efforts made by the Arctic States to empower the local citizens, foster their social and economic progress, and improve education and medical services, so that the Arctic residents, including the indigenous peoples, will truly benefit from the development of Arctic resources" (PRC State Council, 2018).

There is no indication that any particular attention was given to indigenous interests in the decisions on investments in Arctic Russia. Chinese mining operators in Canada expressed views that the processes of negotiating agreements with local communities is too long and burdensome, contributing to their limited interest in the investments in Canada (e.g., Beeby, 2016, June 7).

Markedly, the statements by China in regards to Arctic Indigenous Peoples primarily reflect the approach of the respect for local/national rules and regulations. In that light, the Chinese government encourages economic actors over which it has some control to take appropriate account of indigenous rights and interests because they operate within the framework established by the Arctic States, which observe these rights. China does not state at any point that it would promote in its activities indigenous rights beyond what is required by the legal systems of the Arctic States, nor in other geographical contexts such as Africa or Latin America. This is in some contrast to the way many western states' approach to indigenous rights within, for instance, development aid, which is the main policy area in which these states encounter indigeneity.

As no actual instances of Chinese activities in the Arctic allow for the proper testing the declarations made in the 2018 White Paper, it is useful to look at China's stances towards indigenous rights globally. China perceives that there are no indigenous peoples in China, as for Beijing indigeneity arises exclusively from the context of colonisation and conquest.[1] Thus, in the view of the

1 In international law, there is no official definition specifying which groups constitute "Indigenous Peoples". However, elements characterizing Indigenous Peoples can be found in the International Labour Organization Convention no. 169 on the Rights of Indigenous and Tribal Peoples. These elements include traditional lifestyles, distinctiveness compared with majority societies, continuity of institutions and cultures from the times before colonization, invasion or settlement. Representatives of Indigenous Peoples are often critical to any attempts to define which groups are indigenous, and they underline the importance of self-definition as indigenous. While indigenous status is generally accepted in states in which colonization led to the establishment of majority white settlers societies (Americas, Australia, New Zealand, the Arctic), it is often rejected by states in Africa and Asia, where indigenous status under international law is considered to be not applicable to societies in which the majority population originates from within the region. In these parts of the world, certain groups nonetheless claim indigeneity based on their current situation (so-called 'functional indigenousness') – partly arising from the process of European colonization – or the fact of settlement and conquest of their territories by non-European groups. This leads to cases such as at the Chinese-Russian borderlands, where reindeer-herding Evenki people on the Russian side enjoy indigenous status, while Evenki inhabiting the Chinese province of Inner Mongolia are listed among officially recognized ethnic groups, without any special indigenous status.

Chinese government, the issue of indigenous rights does not apply to China itself, which means that any of China's international statements on indigenous issues are seen in Beijing as having no implications for China's internal affairs, including in relation to international criticism of the Chinese government regarding its policies towards minority ethnic groups, in particular Uighurs and Tibetans. In the UN system, China has therefore proven to be a fairly strong proponent of indigenous rights. China not only voted in favor of the 2007 UN Declaration on the Rights of Indigenous Peoples but attempted in the past to be an active and supportive actor in the area of indigenous rights, for instance by organizing a pre-sessional meeting of the UN Permanent Forum on Indigenous Issues (UNPFII) in Beijing in 2007 (Stepien, 2017). This notwithstanding, the 2018 White Paper does not mention 'indigenous rights', preferring phrases such as indigenous interests, concerns, culture and traditions.

China declares that it takes into account that "[c]ommercial activities in the region [...] exert important influence on the way of work and life of Arctic residents including the indigenous peoples" (PRC State Council, 2018). Admitting that Chinese activities may also have impacts on Arctic livelihoods is of high importance, as, in principle, it should translate to the notion of Chinese operators' responsibility. Chinese investors and financial institutions have been accused in the past of neglecting indigenous interests in places such as Africa or South America, in particular in cases of hydropower, mining and agricultural projects. Partly in response to this criticism, the Chinese government adopted a variety of guidelines with strong emphasis on the proper management of local social and environmental impacts. These guidelines are directed mainly at the state owned enterprises (SOEs) and public financial institutions. It is difficult to evaluate whether such documents have a tangible influence on the actions of these actors in particular projects (Stepien, 2017).

At the Arctic Circle China Forum held in Shanghai in May 2019, the Chinese representatives often emphasized their respect for indigenous peoples' cultures and traditions – a change in tone that surprised many in the audience (e.g. Bennett, 2019). This may indicate a learning curve in which the Chinese government has understood the importance of indigenous people's role in Arctic governance and their status as central stakeholders in many Arctic economic plans such as the planned Arctic railway through the homelands of the Sami in Finnish Lapland (see Chapter 7 in this volume). Despite Beijing's efforts to emphasize its positive and responsible interest to protect indigenous populations traditions in the Arctic region, however, Beijing's actual conduct suppressing Uighurs, Kazakhs and Tibetans do not increase foreign powers' trust in Beijing's wording.

3.6 Chinese Interests in the Arctic as Compared to Other Asian States

As noted above, five Asian states have developed their distinct Arctic policies in the past decade: China, India, Japan, Singapore and South Korea. The Republic of Korea was an early starter in developing its Arctic policies, publishing a White Paper in 2013 and stressing the need for greater education and scientific cooperation in the region. However, being a major player in shipbuilding, Seoul is also watching the emergence of shipping in the Arctic Ocean. The 2013 paper, referred to as the 'Master Plan', was written via consultation with several governmental ministries including Foreign Affairs, Trade, Fisheries and and Future Planning, as well as affiliated research institutes including the Korea Maritime Institute (KMI) and the Korea Polar Research Institute (KOPRI). The paper described three major policy goals: the building of a "co-operative Arctic partnership", the enhancement of scientific research in the region, and the exploration of new business opportunities. For example, a Korean shipping firm agreed to sign on to the Tromsø-based Arctic Economic Council (AEC) in 2017.

Korea also hosts a number of Track II initiatives, that is, informal dialogues, including the annual Korean Arctic Academy conference in Busan for students in the region, a Korea Corner at the University of Greenland in Nuuk, and an Arctic Circle Forum conference in Seoul in December 2018. At present, North Korea's Arctic interests have been limited to some shipping ventures with Russia, and also the Kim Jong-un government did announce its interest in signing the Svalbard Treaty in 2016.

Japan issued its Arctic White Paper at the Arctic Circle Assembly conference in October 2016, and although Japan has also sought to push for scientific partnerships, there was an additional stress on Arctic shipping as a strategic priority, given the high dependency Japan has for imports of resources and energy. Tokyo wishes to expand its use of the Northern Sea Route for European trade, and it is concerned both about the potential militarization of the Arctic as well as the possibility of China's seeking a dominant role in the Arctic Ocean. Nonetheless, Japanese representatives have met with their counterparts in China and South Korea for trilateral Arctic summits. While there have been agreements between the three governments to pursue joint Arctic research programs, specifics have so far been limited.

India and Singapore have thus far been more outliers in the Arctic, given their geography. India is active in polar research in a variety of areas, but it does not benefit from the opening of Arctic shipping due to its location, and to date has not published a specific Arctic policy. Singapore's situation is also distinct, since although the country has pledged support for research initiatives in the Arctic, its primary concern is the possibility of expanded Arctic shipping that may compete in the future with the Malacca Straits. As a shipping power, Singapore wishes to be front and center for the opening of the Arctic Ocean to expanded maritime traffic. However, the country is also active in Track II organizations including the Arctic Circle Assembly (including a breakout forum), and has also held Arctic conferences dedicated to information-sharing.

3.7 Perceptions of China's Arctic Policy

Thus far, the responses to Beijing's Arctic strategy have been mixed and have been viewed differently in various parts of the Arctic region. The Nordic states have been largely positive about greater Chinese engagement, especially with the prospect of an 'Ice Silk Road' (*Bingshang Sichouzhilu* 冰上丝绸之路) emerging in the region (Global Times, 2019, April 7). This development would mean increased numbers of Chinese cargo vessels making use of the Northern Sea Route (NSR) in the Arctic Ocean between Siberia and Northern Europe, but also other communication and transportation projects that would link China with Arctic States and organizations. Canada and Russia, states that have traditionally been more wary about their Arctic sovereignty, have been cautious of Beijing's longer-term goals in the region. However, the Sino-Russian relationship in the region has arguably been one of convenience; Chinese support has been crucial for Russian economic initiatives in Siberia and the Russian Far East (RFE), such as the Yamal liquified natural gas (LNG) initiative (Reuters, 2018, July 19). The United States is becoming more concerned about the growing Russian and Chinese strategic interests in the Arctic, including an emerging 'icebreaker gap' and the possibility of shared Sino-Russian technology exchanges, such as in the area of nuclear powered icebreakers and submarines.

In particular, some alarmist studies suggest that Beijing is seeking to overturn the political and legal status quo in the region, both in the hopes of gaining access to emerging regional resources and establishing a strategic presence in a region that may grow in global importance in the coming decades. These studies also suggest a 'stealth' or 'sneaking' approach on China's part to the region, masking a longer-term hard security strategy in the region (Brady, 2017; Robinson, 2013). This alarmism was further consolidated by Mike Pompeo's (2019) speech, which was actually not a planned event but announced by the U.S. just before the foreign ministers meeting in Rovaniemi.

Secretary of State Pompeo posed questions about the Arctic policies of Russia and China, the latter being the major opponent for the current Trump administration. In particular, Pompeo criticized China's description of itself as a near-Arctic state. According to him, such a category does not exist in Arctic governance, and thus it "entitles China to exactly nothing" (Pompeo, 2019). Yet it should be noted that China has *not* claimed that its status as a near-Arctic state would entitle it to any additional rights or privileges. Pompeo also mentioned the "positive" investments by China to the region, which he views as beneficial from the U.S. point of view. Yet, when it comes to China's role in the Northern Sea Route, the tone of Pompeo's speech changed clearly: He warned about a "very familiar pattern" in which "Beijing attempts to develop critical infrastructure using Chinese money, Chinese companies, and Chinese workers – in some cases, to establish a permanent Chinese security presence" (Pompeo, 2019). In particular, Pompeo (2019) reminded the audience of the potential security impacts of Chinese Arctic activities:

> Our Pentagon warned just last week that China could use its civilian research presence in the Arctic to strengthen its military presence, including our deployment of submarines – including deployment of submarines to the region as a deterrent against nuclear attack. We need to examine these activities closely, and we need – and we keep the experience we have learned of other nations in mind.

Finally, Pompeo (2019) posed provocative questions about the future of the Arctic region, demonstrating very clearly that in his opinion, China's growing presence in the region would result in "militarization and competing territorial claims" as well as "ecological devastation". This amount of alarmism from the U.S. Secretary of State against Chinese policy and presence in the Arctic surely made many question what China is indeed doing in the Arctic.

While a certain amount of criticism towards China's cross-regional diplomacy may be justified, we should remember that critics of China's Arctic policy tend to ignore several factors. First, China has no Arctic geography, and therefore, before building its Arctic policy, it must gain the acceptance of the Arctic States, including some, such as Russia, that have traditionally been very protective of safeguarding their sovereignty in the Arctic. An overt revisionist approach to the Arctic on China's part would invite a serious backlash that may result in higher costs for Chinese regional interests. Second, unlike other states, including in Europe but also some of China's neighbors such as Japan, Singapore and South Korea, China is a rising great power and is therefore under much more overt international scrutiny in the Arctic. While Beijing does not want to be left out of emerging trends in the Arctic region, it cannot afford to be seen as a gatecrasher or a spoiler, and so it must find a middle ground that both includes scientific diplomacy and also seeks Arctic partnerships on a bilateral and regional level. Third, as China settles into its great power status, it is finding itself under greater challenge by the United States, as can be seen in security areas such as the South China Sea, but also in the economic realm as Washington begins to push back via an emerging trade war against what it sees as unfair Chinese trade practices as well as concerns about being leapfrogged by Chinese firms in areas of high technology. Thus, Beijing can ill-afford to see the Arctic become another potential area of great power competition. In short, while China may indeed become a "polar great power" as one study argued (Brady, 2017), it does not necessarily follow that China is seeking to upset the status quo in the Arctic, especially since the economic, political and strategic atmosphere in the Arctic greatly favors cooperation over confrontation.

3.8 Conclusion

China has by now established itself very clearly as an Arctic actor, the final touch being the adoption of the country's first ever Arctic policy in 2018. As a great power entering the Arctic, it is clear that most attention of all non-Arctic states has been targeted in China, even if its neighbours Japan and South Korea have also advanced fairly ambitious Arctic policies. To legitimate its regional role, the Chinese government has sought to define the Arctic as a global commons and China as a 'near-Arctic state'. It can be concluded that China's presence in international cooperation in the Arctic has grown significantly from 2007 onwards, when it started to send delegations to the Arctic Council Senior Arctic Official (SAO) meetings. China's view is that the Arctic is being governed on both global and regional levels. This view became evident at the latest in its 2018 Arctic strategy. China perceives the Arctic Council as only one segment of a broader network of Arctic governance, and that its own expanded role in international affairs successfully demonstrates that it is already one of the relevant parties in Arctic governance. In this way, China also shifts the attention from the region to larger policy frameworks in which the Arctic's future will, to an extent, be determined. From this vantage point, it is China, together with other permanent members of the UN Security Council, that have responsibility for maintaining peace and security in the Arctic. It is China and the rest of the international community who are committed to managing the oceans via UNCLOS, mitigating climate change via the Paris Agreement and combating other environmental problems through various international environmental treaties, and so on. China's approach to indigenous peoples' rights remains complex.

Literature

ACIA. (2005). *Arctic climate impact assessment.* Arctic Monitoring and Assessment Programme.

AMSA. (2009). *Arctic marine shipping assessment.* Arctic Council: Protection of Arctic Marine Environment.

Arctic Fisheries Agreement. (2018). Agreement to prevent unregulated high seas fisheries in the Central Arctic ocean. Retrieved December 15, 2018, from https://eur-lex.europa.eu/legal-content/EN/TXT/?uri=COM:2018:0454:FIN.

Beeby, D. (2016, June 7). Chinese mining companies feel misled by Canada, report says. *CBC News.* Retrieved October 8, 2018, from https://www.cbc.ca/news/politics/china-mining-ambassador-investors-infrastructure-1.3619228.

Bennett, M. (2019, May 10) China reveals Arctic geopolitics to be above Pompeo's pay grade. *Cryopolitics.* Retrieved September 2, 2019, from http://www.cryopolitics.com/2019/05/10/china-reveals-arctic-geopolitics-above-pompeos-pay-grade/.

Borgerson, S.G. (2008). Arctic meltdown: The economic and security implications of global warming. *Foreign Affairs, 87*(2), 63–77.

Brady, A-M. (2017). China as a polar great power. Cambridge, England: Cambridge University Press.

Graczyk, P., & Koivurova, T. (2014). A new era in the Arctic Council's external relations? Broader consequences of the Nuuk observer rules for Arctic Governance. *Polar Record, 50*(3), 225–236.

Hernández, J.C. (2017, March 24). Climate change may be intensifying China's smog crisis. *The New York Times.* Retrieved October 10, 2018, from https://www.nytimes.com/2017/03/24/world/asia/china-air-pollution-smog-climate-change.html.

Houck, C. (2017, August 1). The Arctic could be the next South China Sea, says coast guard commandant. *Defense One.* Retrieved October 21, 2018, from https://www.defenseone.com/threats/2017/08/arctic-could-be-next-south-china-sea-top-coast-guard-admiral/139917/.

Jakobson, L., & Peng, J. (2012, November). China's Arctic aspirations. SIPRI Policy Paper 34. *Stockholm International Peace Research Institute.* Retrieved June 10, 2018, from https://www.sipri.org/publications/2012/sipri-policy-papers/chinas-arctic-aspirations.

Jensen, Ø. (2007). The IMO guidelines for ships operating in Arctic ice-covered waters from voluntary to mandatory tool for navigation safety and environmental protection? *Fridtjof Nansen Institute.* Retrieved June 10, 2018, from https://www.fni.no/getfile.php/131675-1469868943/Filer/Publikasjoner/FNI-R0207.pdf.

Koivurova, T., Hasanat, W., Graczyk, P., & Kuusama, T. (2017). China as an Observer in the Arctic Council. In T. Koivurova, T. Qin, T. Nykänen and S. Duyck (Eds.), *Arctic*

Law and Governance: The Role of China and Finland (pp. 153–180). Oxford, England: Hart Publishing, Studies in International Law.

Lanteigne, M. (2018, September 12). Kiina kurottaa pohjoiseen. [China Reaches the North]. *Ulkopolitiikka*. Retrieved September 15, 2018, from https://www.ulkopolitiikka.fi/lehti/3-2018/kiina-kurottaa-pohjoiseen/.

Liu, N. (2018, June 20). How has China shaped Arctic fisheries governance?. *The Diplomat*. Retrieved October 21, 2018, from https://thediplomat.com/2018/06/how-has-china-shaped-arctic-fisheries-governance/.

Martin, J. (2018, May 5). Polar politics: How the South China Sea illuminates China's role in the Arctic. *The Observer*. Retrieved October 21, 2018, from https://www.theObserver-qiaa.org/polar-politics-how-the-south-china-sea-illuminates-chinas-role-in-the-arctic/.

Nilsen, T. (2019). Major step towards a Europe-Asia Arctic cable link. The Independent Barents Observer. June 6, 2019, from https://thebarentsobserver.com/en/industry-and-energy/2019/06/mou-signed-set-arctic-telecom-cable-company.

Polar Code. (2009). IMO guidelines for ships operating in Polar waters. *Arctic Portal Library*. Retrieved October 21, 2018, from http://library.arcticportal.org/1475/.

Pompeo, M. (2019) Looking North: Sharpening America's Arctic Focus. United States Department of State, May 6. From https://www.state.gov/looking-north-sharpening-americas-arctic-focus/.

PRC State Council. (2018, January 26). Full text: China's Arctic policy. Retrieved March 12, 2018, from http://english.gov.cn/archive/white_paper/2018/01/26/content_281476026660336.htm.

Reuters (2018). Russia's Novatek ships first LNG cargo to China via Arctic. July 19, from https://www.reuters.com/article/us-novatek-cnpc-lng/russias-novatek-ships-first-lng-cargo-to-china-via-arctic-idUSKBN1K90YN.

Rainwater, S. (2013, Spring). Race to the North: China's Arctic strategy and its implications. *Naval War College Review*, *66*(2), Article 7. Retrieved June 10, 2018, from https://digital-commons.usnwc.edu/cgi/viewcontent.cgi?referer=https://www.google.com/&httpsredir=1&article=1371&context=nwc-review.

Robinson, R.W. Jr. (2013, September). China's "Long con" in the Arctic. *MacDonald-Laurier Institute Commentary*. Retrieved October 20, 2018, from https://www.macdonaldlaurier.ca/files/pdf/MLIChina%27sLongConInTheArctic09-13Draft4-1.pdf.

Stepien, A. (2017). Incentives, practices and opportunities for Arctic external actors' engagement with indigenous peoples: China and the European Union. In T. Koivurova, T. Qin, S. Duyck and T. Nykänen (Eds.), *Arctic Law and Governance: The Role of China and Finland*. Ireland, United Kingdom: Hart Publishing.

Watts, J. (2012, January 25). Norway could shut China out of Arctic Council after diplomatic snubs. *The Guardian*. Retrieved November 25, 2018, from https://www.theguardian.com/world/2012/jan/25/norway-china-arctic-council.

Yang, Y. (2016, December 20). China's 'airpocalypse' hits half a billion people. *Financial Times.* Retrieved July 15, 2018, from https://www.ft.com/content/46cbaeea-c669-11e6-8f29-9445cac8966f.

Zhang, M. (2015, October 17) China in the Arctic – Practices and Policies. The 3rd Arctic Circle Assembly, Reykjavik, Iceland.

Zhang Y. (2019). Ice Silk Road framework welcomed by countries, sets new direction for Arctic cooperation. *Global Times*. April 7, from http://www.globaltimes.cn/content/1144928.shtml.

CHAPTER 4

China and Arctic Science

Malgorzata (Gosia) Smieszek, Timo Koivurova and Egill Thor Nielsson

4.1 Introduction

As for a non-Arctic state, scientific activities have been the foundation for China's polar engagement and, according to China's White Paper on the Arctic, exploring and understanding the Arctic "serves as the priority and focus for China in its Arctic activities" (PRC State Council, 2018). Among its policy goals and basic principles on the Arctic, Chinese authorities declare that:

> To understand the Arctic, China will improve the capacity and capability in scientific research on the Arctic, pursue a deeper understanding and knowledge of the Arctic science, and explore the natural laws behind its changes and development, so as to create favorable conditions for mankind to better protect, develop, and govern the Arctic. (*ibid.*)

With the above statement and China's rise in terms of its global and polar science position in mind, the aim of this chapter is to cast light on the history, development and current state of China's research engagement in the Arctic.

4.2 Science in the Arctic

Scientific knowledge is critical to the understanding of the Earth's poles and of the drivers and consequences of the rapidly advancing climate change in the Arctic. Science is also, next to other forms of organized knowledge, a source of key insights to sustainable development of the Arctic as well as of the rest of the planet. We know today that the Arctic plays a critical role in the Earth's climate system and serves as an indicator of global changes. However, our comprehension of the complex processes that unfold in the region and how they are interconnected with global weather patterns, ocean circulation and carbon cycle remains limited. Filling those gaps in our knowledge is essential and even more urgent, considering the pace of change that the Arctic is undergoing.

© KONINKLIJKE BRILL NV, LEIDEN, 2020 | DOI:10.1163/9789004408425_005

Yet, gaining scientific knowledge about the polar regions presents great challenges and the scale of operations in the demanding, remote conditions oftentimes exceeds the capacity of any single nation, making international collaboration of paramount importance. In the much distant past, both the Arctic and the Antarctic were first explored by individuals and small groups organized under national flags, and the conduct of research in the two poles was largely dominated by patriotic rivalries and separate competitive national explorations. The major breakthrough to that form of conducting research in the regions came with the first International Polar Year (IPY, 1882–1883), which not only collected an enormous amount of material and information but also represented the first successful attempt at collaboration by different countries in the field of scientific research (Barr & Luedecke, 2010; Smieszek, 2017). The second IPY took place fifty years later in 1932–33 and the third, under the banner of International Geophysical Year (IGY), in 1957–1958.[1] Initiatives such as the International Polar Years (IPYs) have served the purpose of facilitating research cooperation among countries, and the fourth IPY (2007–2009) was the largest, most comprehensive coordinated campaign ever mounted to explore the Earth's polar regions. In general, it could be said that science has been one of the major platforms for collaboration in the Arctic – both during the Cold War and increasingly after its end. Moreover, scientific presence and research have traditionally been the main forms of engagement in the polar regions – both for Arctic and non-Arctic countries alike. As in the case of the Antarctic, where participation in the decision-making under the Antarctic Treaty is limited to only those countries (aside from the original signatories) that demonstrate their interest in Antarctica "by conducting substantial scientific research activity there" (Article IX.2), so the Observer status with the Arctic Council (AC) is open solely to actors that "the Council determines can contribute to its work" and that have demonstrated their Arctic "expertise relevant to the work of the Arctic Council" (Arctic Council, 2013). In practice, that oftentimes requires extensive scientific involvement for a country that intends to apply for the AC observer status, and most Observer states to the AC, including China, seek to maintain and develop their scientific credentials and presence in the Far North.

In exploring China's role in Arctic science, the chapter proceeds as follows. First, it delves into the beginnings of China's interest in the polar regions and

1 The IGY had a strong focus on Antarctica and, as a form of its legacy, the International Council of Scientific Unions (ICSU, today's International Council for Science) established in 1958 the Scientific Committee on Antarctic Research (SCAR), which later came to serve as a model for scientific cooperation in the Arctic (Smieszek, 2015: 2).

the country's gradual development of its scientific capacities up to the present day. Second, seeing the central position of the Arctic Council in discussions pertaining to the region, the chapter concentrates on Chinese involvement within the AC working groups, which conduct most of the work delivered by the Council. In addition, the same section explores China's involvement with the Agreement to prevent unregulated high seas fisheries in the Central Arctic Ocean. Third, in order to provide a broader perspective for China's engagement in polar science, the following section offers a picture at large of research and development in China, including the sector's structural organization and China's unparalleled rise in terms of its global science position. Next, the chapter elaborates on the bilateral linkages that China has been systematically developing with Arctic countries. Finally, the chapter concludes with the most recent political developments on the circumpolar arena, in particular the shift of the United States administration concerning the behavior of China and Russia in the Arctic, which might affect not only the future course of relations between these countries but also the shape of circumpolar collaboration as such, including its scientific dimension.

4.3 History of China's Arctic Science

According to Wang and Zhang, although China did not send any participants to the polar expeditions, it was involved in both the first and second International Polar Years (IPY) in 1882–83 and 1932–33 by providing data for international collaboration from geomagnetic stations located in the country's territory. They note that as the second IPY coincided with a significant buildup of Chinese scientific potential under the new nationalist government, China was able to expand its participation in international efforts by carrying out measurements related to the determination of longitudes and latitudes, as well as conducting meteorological measurements from the newly established stations in Shandong and Sichuan – even if, in general, the scale of those contributions remained marginal (Wang & Zhang, 2010).

In the period between the second and the third IPYs, between the 1930s and 1950s, the world underwent a fundamental transformation and the international environment changed dramatically, also with regard to scientific cooperation. As a result, the third International Polar Year, the history of China's initial participation and the later withdrawal from it, served perhaps as the most vivid illustration of the intertwined relations between science and politics at that time.

Following the victory of the communists under the leadership of Mao Zedong in the civil war against the nationalist government of Chiang Kai-shek in 1949, the latter, with the support of the United States, retreated to Taiwan, leading ultimately to the country's split into mainland China (i.e. the People's Republic of China, PRC) ruled by the Communist Party of China, and Taiwan (i.e. the Republic of China, ROC) governed by the Nationalist Party of China. The situation had obviously far-reaching international consequences as both sides – the PRC and the ROC – claimed rights to legitimate representation of China on international science and began vying for China's seat in international institutions. The situation was further complicated by the position of the United States which, in armed conflict with China in Korea, actively backed the ROC in the United Nations and other international fora, including scientific international bodies.

Consequently, in 1951–52, when the International Council of Scientific Unions (ICSU) approved the proposal for the IGY, China's participation in the next international polar year came to be considered not only in terms of its scientific merits, but it turned into a contentious and sensitive political issue. Whereas any investigation of the Earth's geophysics would not be comprehensive without the inclusion of China's vast territory and Chinese scientists were eager to join the major international scientific endeavor, China's involvement in the IGY depended in the first place on the decision of the Soviet Union to access the IGY, and second, on the resolution of the situation with Taiwan – more precisely, on the exclusion of Taiwan from the IGY (Wang & Zhang, 2010). The events of 1953–1955 – the end of the Korean War and the death of Stalin – seemed to serve a relaxation of Cold War tension, and in 1955 the Soviet Union decided to join the IGY, paving the way for a similar decision of the Chinese Academy of Sciences (CAS) and a consequent buildup over the following two years of scientific capacities and infrastructure that China aimed to contribute within the IGY. The PRC and CAS behaved as they did in the belief that the matter of Taiwan's participation in the IGY was resolved in their favor when Taiwan failed to respond to the invitation from ICSU in 1955. It proved, however, not to be the case, as, with the backing of the U.S. State Department, Taiwan applied late for participation in the IGY, and its application was accepted. The situation was ultimately unacceptable to the PRC, which informed the ICSU accordingly that "China will join [the] IGY only on [the] condition Taiwan should not be admitted. Otherwise China will withdraw from [the] IGY" (Sullivan, fn. 36 in: Wang & Zhang, 2010: 150). Despite the ICSU's continuous reassurances of the unpolitical nature of the entire collaborative scientific endeavor and the efforts of the Council's Special Committee to keep both China and Taiwan onboard, the PRC held its promise – when it was confirmed that the Taiwanese delegation would take part in the science meetings of the International Polar Year, China withdrew from the IGY. Nevertheless, the withdrawal of China from the IGY did not result in the complete abandonment of the planned IGY activities, and the collection of data continued, albeit in a much less coordinated and urgent manner as would have likely been the case under the aegis of the IGY. The situation illustrated as well the ultimately political nature of the international scientific interactions at the height of the Cold War, even when it concerned the furthermost regions of the world (Wang & Zhang, 2010; Barr & Luedecke, 2010).

With respect to more focused institutional developments oriented toward the Earth's poles, China's involvement in polar science originated in Antarctica and only later moved into the Arctic. The State Oceanic Administration (SOA) was established in 1964 under a mission that included to "engage in polar expeditions in the future" and in 1985 the SOA purchased the first ice-capable vessel from Finland to launch China's annual Antarctic expeditions. The ship *Jidi*(极地), or *Polar*, ferried supplies for China's Antarctic mission from 1986 to 1994, when it was replaced by an icebreaker research vessel *Xuelong*(雪龙), or *Snow Dragon* (Nong, 2014), a Ukraine-built cargo vessel converted into a polar research and re-supply vessel. *Xuelong* was dispatched for its first Arctic voyage to the Bering and Chukchi seas in 1999 and later in 2003, and since then has been regularly operating in the North as well as in the waters off Antarctica.

To date, *Xuelong* has completed nine Arctic expeditions (named CHINARE), with the most recent operating from July until September 2018. In addition to the scientific studies carried out during the expeditions, each departure and return of *Xuelong* has served to popularize China's polar activities and has received some coverage in the Chinese media.[2] In a similar vein, the operations of the *Xuelong* also served as a platform for tightening bonds between Chinese and Arctic states. In 2012, during its first visit to an Arctic country on the 5th Chinese National Arctic Research Expedition, the *Xuelong* anchored in Iceland to enhance the cooperation of Chinese and Icelandic scientists on polar and marine sciences. At the occasion of CHINARE5 in 2012, *Xuelong* also became the first Chinese-flagged vessel to transit the North-East Passage on its way between Qingdao and Reykjavik, and then the first vessel to transit the Arctic Ocean from Akureyri to Shanghai, drawing attention to the possibilities

2 In general, the popularization of science among the Chinese public has been a notable feature of the country's Arctic profile. To that end, China has been investing in the development of education centers as well as in the publication of cultural and educational material for a broader audience.

of operating outside the exclusive economic zones of the Arctic littoral states in the conditions of the rapidly warming Arctic and decreasing Arctic sea ice. Five years later, in 2017, *Xuelong* undertook a voyage through the North-West Passage and consequently became the first vessel to transit all three Arctic passages. In 2018, the 9th CHINARE expedition showcased China's increasing level of scientific and technological potential when, for the first time, Chinese scientists on the Arctic drift ice floes deployed two Atmosphere-Sea-Ice-Ocean (ASO) unmanned stations developed by the Polar Research Institute of China (*Zhongguo Jidi Yanjiu Zhongxin* 中国极地研究中心) (INTAROS, 2018).

In order to expand its potential for operating in both polar regions, a second icebreaker, *Xuelong 2* (雪龙2), was constructed in partnership with the Finnish ship-building firm Aker Arctic to commence operations in 2019, with its first voyage planned for the occasion of the 36th Chinese national Antarctic Research Expedition in the latter part of 2019.[3] Moreover, Beijing has also expressed interest in constructing a nuclear-powered icebreaker, using either domestic technology or pursuing a project in cooperation with Russia. Currently, Russia is the only country that operates nuclear-powered icebreakers, while other countries are in the planning stages (Eiterjord, 2018). China's Arctic research expeditions were further expanded in 2019 with the oceanographic research vessel *Xiangyanghong 01* departing for the 10th Arctic expedition in August 2019, covering areas of the Bering Sea and the Bering Strait, as well as the Chukchi Sea and other seasonally open waters in the Arctic Ocean during a 50-day mission.

In parallel to its logistics capacities, China has been building institutional infrastructure necessary to organize and support the country's growing polar interests and expertise. In 1989, China established the Polar Research Institute of China (PRIC) in Shanghai under the SOA, which marked the country's rising interest in polar affairs beyond Antarctica. In 1990, Chinese scientists visited the North Pole for the first time and planted a flag there, and in 1996 the National Antarctic Expedition Committee Office was renamed to the Chinese Arctic and Antarctic Administration (CAA). Also in 1996, China joined the International Arctic Science Committee (IASC), a leading non-governmental international organization supporting scientific research and collaboration in the Arctic, and in 2005, it hosted the Arctic Science Summit Week (ASSW) in the city of Kunming, becoming the first Asian country to host the event. In 2007–2008 it participated in the fourth International Polar Year (IPY).

3 Practically, the vessel was given a 'soft launch' in September 2018 (Straits Times/Xinhua, 11 September 2018).

In 2004, China built its first Arctic research station, the Yellow River Station (*Huanghe zhan*黄河站), in the research village of Ny-Ålesund in the Spitsbergen Archipelago. In 2012, Iceland and China signed a comprehensive Framework Agreement on Arctic Cooperation for the occasion of an official visit of then-Premier Wen Jiabao to Iceland, and in 2013 the Polar Research Institute of China and the Icelandic Centre for Research (RANNIS) agreed to build a joint aurora observatory (CIAO) at Kárhóll in northern Iceland (Karholl.is). In 2017, the PRIC and RANNIS decided to expand the scope of cooperation, which would consequently enable observations of not only auroras but also research on atmosphere, oceanography, glaciers, geophysics, remote sensing and biology. This new mandate was confirmed when the facility was officially renamed into the China-Iceland Arctic Science Observatory during its official inauguration in October 2018 (*Xinhua*, 19 October 2018). The CIAO is now the second science station, after Ny-Ålesund, administered by China in the Arctic. More recently, there has been some discussion about a third Chinese research station in the Arctic, to be located in Greenland, but that project remains in the early planning stages.

As outlined in the White Paper, "the availability of technical equipment is essential to understanding, utilizing and protecting the Arctic" (PRC State Council, 2018). Consequently, China both "actively participates in the building of infrastructure for Arctic development" while also encouraging the development of environment-friendly polar technical equipment. As listed in the White Paper, it also "pushes for the upgrade of equipment in the fields of deep sea exploration, ice zone prospecting, (...) atmosphere and biology observation, (...) promotes technology innovation in Arctic oil and gas drilling and exploitation, renewable energy development, navigation and monitoring in ice zones, and construction of new-type icebreakers" (*ibid.*). Simultaneously, all these areas of interest should be read – next to their scientific relevance – within the broader setting of China's policies and in conjunction with the prioritized aspects of China's Arctic policy, which include both protecting the environment and utilizing Arctic resources (see Chapters 5 and 6 in this volume).

4.4 China's Scientific Engagement with the Arctic Council

China participated for the first time in the meetings of the Arctic Council in 2007 and it was officially admitted as a formal Observer to the Council in 2013. As the Arctic Council Rules of Procedure stipulate, the Observers' primary role is to observe the work of the Arctic Council and to contribute to it primarily at the level of working groups. Whereas the six working groups of the Council vary in their areas of focus, most of them have a strong science orientation and serve to inform decision-making with the best available scientific knowledge. Up to now, it appears fair to say that Chinese involvement with the AC's working groups has been fairly limited, while most attention has concentrated on the political level of the Senior Arctic Officials (SAO). Part of the reason behind this situation might be the learning curve that all new Observers to the Council face in a novel organizational environment, norms and procedures. As most of the WGs are attended by experts in their respective fields, the identification of the appropriate representatives – both on the side of Member States as well as Observers – is critical to the provision of meaningful input to the working group projects and discussions.

After the initial period of little visibility, inconsistent attendance and a high rotation among its representatives, China has begun to slowly mark its areas of interest and engage in selected activities of the AC working groups. The projects that it has been most invested in have included the Arctic Migratory Birds Initiative (AMBI) of the Conservation of Arctic Flora and Fauna (CAFF) working group of the AC. The project aims at improving the status and securing the long-term sustainability of declining Arctic migratory bird populations and, since many species of Arctic birds move from Arctic breeding grounds to overwintering or stopover sites at lower latitudes, the cooperation between countries along their flyways is vital to any conservation efforts.

The AMBI has been very successful in terms of bringing together the Observers and Member States of the Council. Whereas two previous workshops were held in the Netherlands (April 2016) and in Singapore (January 2017), the third took place in Hainan, China, in December 2018 (CAFF, 2018a). China is a critical partner when it comes to the East Asian-Australasian Flyway, where much of the cause for concern lies in the migration bottleneck of the Yellow Sea region, where birds rest and feed in this densely populated region on the coasts of China, North Korea and South Korea. Over the past fifty years, half of those vital intertidal areas have disappeared and today they are shrinking faster than tropical forests due to the pursued land reclamation policy. To address this issue, in early 2018 the Chinese government announced dramatic changes to their land reclamation policy, stating much enhanced conservation measures in relation to its coastal development and cooperation with the Arctic Council CAFF on that matter (CAFF, 2018b).

Regarding other working groups, at the meeting of the Protection of Arctic Marine Environment (PAME) in Malmö, Sweden in February 2019, China gave a presentation on its areas of interest in the work of PAME as well as its capacities and potential contributions to them. The presentation is a part of efforts undertaken by all the AC working groups to engage more closely with the

Council's Observers. Apart from those, China has previously attended some meetings of the other working groups too: Emergency Preparation, Preparedness and Response (EPPR); the Arctic Contaminants Action Program (ACAP); and the Arctic Monitoring and Assessment Program (AMAP) but so far has not been actively engaged in their projects. It has also not engaged up to now with the Sustainable Development Working Group (SDWG).

From a broader perspective, Chinese engagement with the Arctic Council's working groups reflects a more general pattern of the gradual development of Chinese scientific presence in the polar regions (Lasserre, Alexeeva and Huang, 2017). Both in the Antarctic and the Arctic, Chinese presence was marked first by a strong focus on the foundational construction and set-up of infrastructure and only in the second phase by shifting priorities to formulating a meaningful polar scientific research program. This situation is not surprising, seeing that China, as a developing country that went through long periods of international isolation, needed time to build its capacities and expertise in those areas, also through international collaborations and partnerships. One of the most recent examples of China's involvement with Arctic governance initiatives has been its participation in the negotiations and the signing of the 2018 Agreement on unregulated fishing in the Central Arctic Ocean (CAO) adopted in the so-called 'A5 + 5' format: the "Arctic Five" – Canada, Denmark (Greenland and the Faroe Islands), Norway, Russia, the United States – and five major distant fishing powers – China, Iceland,[4] Japan, South Korea and the European Union (EU) (Arctic Fisheries Agreement, 2018). Among others, the agreement provides for the creation of the Joint Program of Scientific Research and Monitoring, in which China intends to actively participate and which would allow it, along with the other parties, to keep track of changes in the range and distribution of fish stocks in the Central Arctic Ocean area over the coming decades. Beyond that, however, it is too early to speak about the details or a specific format of the scientific collaboration under the CAOF Agreement – in order for it to enter into force, all ten parties must first ratify it and so far, at the moment of this writing, Canada, the EU, the Russian Federation and the United States have done so. Furthermore, the Agreement does not require its parties to establish the Joint Program until two years after the entry into force.[5]

4 Iceland as a coastal Arctic state but not an Arctic Ocean coastal state was not invited to the initial talks in 2013, but later joined the negotiations with the European Union and the Asian stakeholders.

5 The Agreement on unregulated fishing in the Central Arctic Ocean stands out among other recently-signed, legally-binding agreements pertaining to the Arctic – the Agreement on Cooperation on Aeronautical and Maritime Search and Rescue in the Arctic (Arctic SAR Agreement) signed in 2011, the Agreement on Cooperation on Marine Oil Pollution, Preparedness

In discussing China's increasing polar science capacities and potential, it is still important to note a larger picture of the Chinese approach to research and development (R&D) and, in particular, its unprecedented leap forward in the last decade.

4.5 China's Science at Large

In keeping with Chinese President Xi Jinping's motto of the 'Chinese Dream', China has set a goal of becoming a world-class innovator by 2050, further confirmed by the Minister of Science and Technology, Wan Gang, in 2017 (Han and Appelbaum, 2018; Reuters, 2018, February 27). Toward that goal over the past decades, China's spending on research and development has been steadily growing, with annual increases of three or more times compared to the rest of the world, including the United States (Global R&D Funding Forecast, 2018). In comparison, even if China's spending on science in 2017 amounted to around 2.1 percent of the total gross domestic product (compared with around 2.8 percent in the United States, 2.9 percent in Germany and 3.3 percent in Japan), between 2000 and 2015, R&D investments in China have soared annually by an average of 18%, whereas U.S. spending rose in the same period by about 4% annually. China's annual R&D spending has risen 70.9 percent from 2012 and, based on data from 2015, China's R&D investments have now surpassed those of the European Union with its US$386 billion expenditure on research and development and remain second only to the United States (Showstack, 2018; "China spends $279 bln on R&D in 2017: science minister", 2018).

Science has also been considered by President Xi Jinping as one of the central pillars of the Belt and Road Initiative (BRI), China's mega-plan for global infrastructure announced in 2013. Whereas most of the BRI has been centered around industrial developments aimed at increasing trade through

and Response in the Arctic (Arctic MOSPA) signed in 2013, and the Agreement on Enhancing International Arctic Scientific Cooperation signed in 2017 – as the first circumpolar treaty concluded not exclusively among Arctic states, but with non-Arctic states and entities as parties to the Agreement. Under the terms of the Agreement on Enhancing International Arctic Scientific Cooperation, the cooperation of its parties – eight Arctic states – with non-Arctic states such as China is regulated by Article 17, which stipulates that the "Parties may continue to enhance and facilitate cooperation with non-Parties with regard to Arctic science (...), [and] Parties may in their discretion undertake with non-Parties cooperation described in this Agreement and apply measures consistent with those described in this Agreement in cooperation with non-Parties" ("Agreement on Enhancing International Arctic Scientific Cooperation", 2017). Both the realization of the Agreement and its effects in practice are yet to transpire.

transforming global trade networks that both supply China and provide a market for its products, science, technology and innovation play an extremely important, if sometimes overlooked, role in the BRI and are viewed as amongst the key driving forces behind its development (Masood, 2019). In particular, when it comes to cooperation with developing countries, China views science as a central element in building bridges with them through offering scientific assistance and signing collaborative agreements. To provide a scale of this assistance "not seen since the United States and the former Soviet Union vied with each other to fund researchers in allied nations during the Cold War" (*ibid.*, 21), in April 2019 the Chinese Academy of Sciences (CAS) announced that up to now it has invested nearly US$268 million in the science and technology parts of the BRI, involving tens of thousands of researchers and students, and hundreds of universities. Viewed from a science perspective, next to its infrastructure dimension, the goal of the BRI appears to be the restoration of "China's place as one of the world's great civilizations, and that includes being seen by all other nations as a source of scientific power, too" (*ibid*).

Science in China is conducted in five main institutional sectors. The first comprises around 120 institutes overseen by the Chinese Academy of Sciences (*Zhongguo Kexueyuan*中国科学院), or CAS. They include "big science" facilities, and today many of their labs engage in word-class research across a wide range of disciplines, including quantum physics, mathematics and neuroscience. The second is universities, which have emerged as important centers of basic and applied research, and which also serve to support high-tech entrepreneurship. Government research institutes under civilian ministries – among them public health, environmental protection and natural resources – are the third system, whereas R&D dedicated to serving military needs is the fourth.

Finally, China's industrial enterprises constitute the last system. It is in this sector that the most significant changes have taken place over the past two decades, with an emergence of market-owned, non-state-owned high-tech firms and a surge of company-based research and development, especially in the fields of information and communication technology. For instance, Alibaba, China's leading e-commerce company, has recently announced plans to invest US$15 billion in new R&D projects, including the opening of seven new research labs in such locations as Moscow and Silicon Valley, amongst others. The research in those labs will be focused on foundational and disruptive technologies such as the Internet of Things, data analysis, artificial intelligence, and quantum computing. In general, expenditures for research and development in the enterprise sector now amount to approximately 80% of the nation's total (Suttmeier, 2018).

China's continued emphasis on, and investments in, research and development have brought outstanding results and have placed China among the world's leading science powers. China has completed numerous large-scale science projects (Bloomberg, 2018, June 19) and has risen to the forefront of science at a global scale with an improved scholarly rating impact, manpower (it has more scientists and engineers than any other country), a dynamic space program, and also an increasing share of the world's research articles (even if their quality, judged by the number of citations, still remains below average) (Global R&D Funding Forecast, 2018). Whereas some of the Chinese accomplishments and progress in the fields of research and technology have been disputed as results of violation of intellectual property rights and forced technology transfers (Office of the United States Trade Representative, 2018), as well as of misconduct in research publishing (Cyranoski, 2018), and there still remain structural challenges in the country's education and research environment that might interfere with its aim of successfully transforming into a knowledge-based economy (Han and Appelbaum, 2018), the country's improvement in its science and innovation capacities have been dramatic and unprecedented.

This emphasis has also been reflected in Chinese investments into, and development of, its polar capacities. Since 2003, China has been building new infrastructure and refurbishing older assets (among others, it has twice refitted *Xuelong* and constructed a dedicated berth and warehouse space in Shanghai) and has also been increasing its budget for polar research. While the economic crisis in 2008 forced other countries to cut or suspend their spending on R&D, and institutions in the United States and in the European Union saw decreasing budgets to support their research infrastructure, China has been advancing its polar capacities, even if at a slower pace because of its own recent economic slowdown. Chinese Arctic research funders include: the Ministry of Science and Technology (*Kexue Jishubu*科学技术部), or MOST; the Ministry of Natural Resources (*Ziran Ziyuanbu*自然资源部), or MNR, and its subordinate agency, the State Oceanic Administration (SOA); the National Natural Science Foundation of China (*Guojia Ziran Kexue Jijin Weiyuanhui*国家自然科学基金委员会); the Ministry of Education (*Jiaoyubu*教育部); and the China Meteorological Administration (*Zhongguo Qixiangju*中国气象局) (2nd Arctic Science Ministerial, 2018).

Whereas providing exact numbers for China's spending on polar research is very difficult because spending is allocated via those various ministries and agencies, it can be assessed that most of the budget is spent on investments in the infrastructure and on annual expeditions to the Antarctic and the Arctic under the SOA; much less, however, is spent on scientific research itself.

According to a statement provided by China to the second Arctic Science Ministerial Meeting in Berlin in October 2018, "NSF funds about 40 Arctic research projects per year, at a level of up to 18 million RMB (circa $2,7 million) US in 2015". (2nd Arctic Science Ministerial, 2018:92). Together with Russia, China will also provide fuel and key logistical support to *R/V Polarstern* during MOSAiC (The International Multidisciplinary drifting Observatory for the study of the Arctic Climate), the largest international Arctic cooperation project ever funded and the first year-around expedition in the central Arctic Ocean planned from September 2019 until September 2020 (*ibid.*).

4.6 Bilateral Arctic Science Collaboration

Next to involvement in multilateral bodies such as the IASC[6] or major projects such as MOSAiC, China has also been seeking to enhance its bilateral scientific cooperation with Arctic states. In light of the costs of operating and conducting scientific research in the North – a recent study found them eight times more expensive than similar studies in southern locations, and with Svalbard and Nunavut in Canada being on the top of the list (Hoag, 2018) – the interest for scientific partnerships with China has been increasing on their side, even if Arctic countries have taken a varied stance on this cooperation. Concurrently, polar scientific collaborations can be seen as part of broader and more strategic bilateral relationships between China and the Arctic countries.

Among them, Iceland has been the most proactive and, as mentioned earlier, has been consequently developing its closer relations with China for around a decade, including a bilateral Arctic science exchange that commenced in 2011. In the case of Norway, following the restoration of relations between the two countries in December 2016, in April 2018 Norway's Minister of Research and Education led a delegation of 250 of the country's heads of universities and scientists to strengthen Chinese-Norwegian research collaboration (Myklebust, 2018).[7] The program of the visit, hosted by China's Minister of Science and Technology, was organized by the Norwegian Centre for International Cooperation in Education (SIU)[8] and the Research Council of Norway

6 At present, Chinese representative, Dr. Yang Huigen, Director-General of PRIC, serves as IASC's Vice-President and a member of IASC 6-person Executive Committee.

7 Following the awarding of the Nobel Peace Prize to Chinese dissident Liu Xiaobo in 2010, diplomatic relations between China and Norway were frozen for six years and fully restored only since 2017 (Watts and Weaver, 2011).

8 In October 2018, following its organizational changes, SIU was renamed to the Norwegian Agency for International Cooperation and Quality Enhancement in Higher Education (Diku).

on behalf of the Ministry of Education and Research, and included such topics for cooperation as digitalization, climate, environmental and polar research. It was also accompanied by a roadmap for cooperation on research and education with China 2018–2020, drawing attention to the fact that at present China has the world's largest education system with a stated goal to increase both incoming and outgoing student mobility (Forskningsrådet, 2018). With respect to polar science, Chinese scientists are likewise encouraged to conduct international academic exchanges and the involvement with the University of the Arctic – whose international secretariat is located at the University of Lapland in Rovaniemi, Finland – is strongly promoted among Chinese higher education and research institutions (PRC State Council, 2018). Given Finland's expertise and focus on meteorological cooperation and icebreaking capabilities, Chinese partners cooperate with the Finnish Meteorological Institute's Arctic Space Centre in Sodankylä on meteorological data and, as mentioned earlier, it contracted the concept and basic design of its second research icebreaker from the Finnish company Aker Arctic. Finally, a new series of collaboration agreements between the two countries were signed during President Xi's visit to Finland in April 2017, including the memorandum of understanding between Universities Finland (UNIFI) and the Chinese Academy of Social Sciences.

Beyond strictly bilateral relations, in order to facilitate and provide a platform for academic cooperation with the Nordic states on the Arctic, in December 2013 four Chinese and six Nordic institutions established the China-Nordic Arctic Research Centre (CNARC), located in Shanghai and dedicated to Arctic research. Since its inception, the CNARC has convened the annual China-Nordic Arctic Cooperation Symposia that rotate between Chinese and Nordic members of the network and attract an increasing number of attendees and participants.[9] In accordance with the adopted formula, CNARC symposia consist of two parts: an academic conference and a business roundtable, which is open only to invited participants and brings together relevant partners from China and Nordic countries (in the case of conferences held in the Nordics, invited guests come from China and the organizing country). In this model,

9 Up to now, seven symposia have taken place: "Sustainable Development in the Arctic: Human Activity and Environmental Change" in June 2013 in Shanghai; "North meets East" in June 2014 in Akureyri, Iceland; "Arctic Synergies: Policies and Best Practices" in May 2015 in Shanghai; "The Sustainable Arctic – Opportunities and Challenges of Globalization" in June 2016 in Rovaniemi, Finland; "Towards the Future: Transregional Cooperation in the Arctic Development and Protection" in May 2017 in Dalian, China; "Integrated Ocean Management in the Arctic" in May 2018 in Tromsø, Norway; and "Arctic Fisheries, Polar Silk Road, and Sustainable Development Practices" again in Shanghai, China, in May 2019.

CNARC conferences serve not only as academic exchanges but also aim to enhance bilateral linkages between the involved countries.[10]

In the case of the United States, science and technology have been primary vehicles for enhancing the bilateral relationship with China since the opening of relations between the two countries in the late 1970s. At present, however, this trend appears to be heading towards the reverse. Among other measures, as early as 2011, Congress prohibited the White House Office of Science and Technology Policy (OSTP) and the National Aeronautics and Space Administration (NASA) from coordinating any joint scientific activity with China.[11] Recently, the U.S. began expressing its wariness of China's rise to the position of global research power more explicitly, as reported in January 2018 by the U.S. National Science Board to Congress, where it announced the possibility that Chinese R&D investments might soon catch up with those of the U.S. (Showstack, 2018). The change of tone in relation to increasing Chinese engagement in the global arena in general, and to China's increasing scientific potential and capacities, did not omit the Arctic either, despite the invitation issued for scientists from the U.S. to join the 9th expedition of the *Xuelong* into the Arctic in 2018. Amid rapidly escalating tensions between the two countries, the Trump administration used the occasion of the Arctic Council Ministerial Meeting in May 2019 in Rovaniemi, Finland to manifest not only its hardline opposition to include any reference to climate change in the Arctic ministerial statement, but also to unilaterally single out and criticize, in an unprecedented manner, China and Russia for their activities in the region, marking a sharp contrast with the culture of dialog and cooperative spirit, which have characterized circumpolar Arctic affairs since their institutionalized beginnings in the early 1990s. In his statement delivered on the day preceding the actual Ministerial gathering, Secretary of State Pompeo denounced China for its aggressive behavior in other parts of the world and accused it of repeating the same expansion patterns in the Arctic. Moreover, in direct reference to China's scientific engagement in the North, Pompeo recalled the annual report of the Pentagon

10 Speaking of multilateral fora for collaboration on Arctic matters, among other recent developments has been the emergence of the trilateral high-level dialog on the Arctic formed by China, Japan, and South Korea to discuss their engagement in the region and engage in polar science diplomacy. The first dialog took place in Seoul in April 2016, the second in June 2017, and the third one in Shanghai in June 2018. As noted by Lanteigne, "[t]hus far, these meetings have produced little in terms of concrete regional initiatives beyond pledges for future cooperation" (Lanteigne, 2018).

11 There has been, however, some cooperation between the two countries in areas such as aeronautics and Earth science (Foust, 2018).

to Congress on military developments in China, which in April 2019 included for the first time a section about the Arctic and stated that China's "[c]ivilian research could support a strengthened Chinese military presence in the Arctic Ocean, which could include deploying submarines to the region as a deterrent against nuclear attacks" (Office of the Secretary of Defense, 2019: 114). The report noted as well that "outside potential friction over the Northern Sea Route" (*ibid.*), the Arctic represents an area of opportunity for Sino-Russian commercial cooperation (see Chapter 6 in this volume), the advancements of which were also criticized by Secretary Pompeo (U.S. Department of State, 2019).

Next to enhanced cooperation between China and Russia in the development of Russian energy resources and the Northern Sea Route, two countries have been increasingly working together, also in the research domain. Among others, in 2016, the Far Eastern Federal University in Russia and the Harbin Polytechnic University in China established the Russian-Chinese Polar Engineering and Research Center, dedicated to developing engineering capabilities for polar conditions, such as ice-resistant platforms and more efficient and durable icebreakers (Devyatkin, 2019). More recently, in April 2019 – the same month in which Pentagon issued its report to the U.S. Congress – two major oceanology institutes from both countries, China's Pilot National Laboratory for Marine Science and Technology (QNLM) and the P.P. Shirshov Institute of Oceanology of Russian Academy of Sciences (IO RAS) signed an agreement to form the Chinese-Russian Arctic Research Center to conduct joint research projects in the Arctic (*ibid.*). The new center is aimed to study the Far North's mineral and biological resources, deepen the comprehension of the changing northern ecosystems, and enable the forecasting of ice conditions along the Northern Sea Route. As proclaimed by two founding institutes, the results obtained from conducted research will provide for recommendations for the environmentally-sound economic development of the Arctic region. In August 2019, scientists involved with the newly established Center announced that the goal of their first joint expedition will be a broad study of Russia's Siberian Arctic shelf and of the European part of the Laptev Sea (Quinn, 2019).

4.7 Conclusions

In light of the unprecedented scale and pace of changes unfolding in the socio-ecological systems of the Arctic, their deepened scientific understanding is a matter of primary importance. In addition to the regional consequences of Arctic climate change are its global impacts, which through altering weather patterns, rising sea levels and effects on the ocean circulation matter to countries located in the southern latitudes, among them China. Whereas China's interest and capacities to operate in the polar regions and Earth's poles date back to the middle of the twentieth century, it is over the past decade that the country has exponentially developed its polar expertise, infrastructure and logistics capabilities. This growth in polar domain paralleled China's unprecedented leap forward in research and development in general, reflecting not only country's scientific ambitions, but most of all China's steady rise to the position of a global power capable of operating in all parts of the world and developing its competitive advantage across the whole spectrum of activities, from trade and business to science.

With the launch of its second icebreaker in 2019, China joined the ranks of a handful of countries able to simultaneously operate at both of Earth's poles. Until very recently, the country's scientific engagement has been largely welcomed among Arctic nations, none of which possesses sufficient resources and capacities to conduct research in the North correspondent in its scale and pace to the magnitude of changes observed in the Arctic ocean, climate and biodiversity. At the same time, from the outset, China's involvement in the Arctic has generated unparalleled attention and has been viewed with caution by some Arctic observers, wary of the country's economic interests, potential, and possibly also military motives, even if none of the latter have ever come to the surface. It appears fair to say that the speech of U.S. State Secretary Pompeo, delivered in May 2019 in Rovaniemi, Finland, opened a new chapter in relations between the United States, China and Russia in the Arctic, and in circumpolar collaboration more broadly. In his adopted rhetoric, Secretary Pompeo showcased the Arctic not only as a region of grand economic potential but also an arena for power and competition, where the United States is ready to fortify its strategic and diplomatic actions to secure its interests from Arctic and non-Arctic states alike. Therefore, while many multilateral and bilateral projects including Chinese scientists are ongoing, and even intensifying, as in the case of collaboration with Russia, the extent to which the stance of the United States will affect the shape of relations in the Arctic remains to be seen.

Literature

Arctic Fisheries Agreement. (2018). Agreement to Prevent Unregulated High Seas Fisheries in the Central Arctic Ocean signed in Ilulissat, Greenland on 3 October 2018. Retrieved August 5, 2019 from https://eur-lex.europa.eu/resource.html?uri=cellar:2554f475-6e25-11e8-9483-01aa75ed71a1.0001.02/DOC_2&format=PDF.

2nd Arctic Science Ministerial. (2018, October 25–26). Report of the 2nd Arctic science ministerial. Cooperation in Arctic science – Challenges and joint actions. Berlin, Germany. Retrieved November 20, 2018, from https://www.arcticscienceministerial.org/files/BMBF_ASM2_Broschuere_V1_A4_webRZ_bf.pdf.

Arctic Centre. (2014). Comparing Arctic law and governance in China and Finland. Arctic Centre. Retrieved June 10, 2018, from https://www.arcticcentre.org/EN/research/NIEM/Projects/Arctic-Law-and-Governance-in-Finland-and-China.

Arctic Council. (2013, May 15). *Arctic Council Rules of Procedure*. Revised by the Arctic Council at the Eight Arctic Council Ministerial Meeting. Kiruna, Sweden.

Barr, S. & Luedecke, C. (Eds.). (2010). The History of the International Polar Years (IPYs). Berlin: Springer Verlag.

Bloomberg. (2018, June 19). China is getting ready to take on the world's biggest drugmakers. *Bloomberg*. Retrieved June 25, 2018, from https://www.bloomberg.com/news/features/2018-06-19/china-s-getting-ready-to-take-on-the-world-s-biggest-drugmakers.

Business Finland. (2018, January 18). Finland and China tackle medical AI together. Good News from Finland website (Business Finland promotional website). Retrieved June 15, 2018, from http://www.goodnewsfinland.com/finland-and-china-tackle-medical-ai-together/.

CAFF. (2018a, December 5.–8.). AMBI meeting. Hainan, China. Retrieved October 22, 2018, from https://caff.is/arctic-migratory-birds-initiative-ambi/east-asian-austral asian-flyway/china.

CAFF. (2018b, October 23). Our shared heritage: Arctic breeding birds in the Yellow Sea. Conservation of Arctic Flora and Fauna. Retrieved October 29, 2018, from https://www.youtube.com/watch?v=8HLPGy3hvCk&t=3s.

Cyranoski, D. (2018, June 8). China introduces sweeping reforms to crack down on academic misconduct. *Nature*. Retrieved September 20, 2018, from https://www.nature.com/articles/d41586-018-05359-8.

Devyatkin, P. (2019, April 15). Russian and Chinese Scientists to Establish Arctic Research Center. *High North News*. Retrieved August 31, 2019 from https://www.highnorthnews.com/en/russian-and-chinese-scientists-establish-arctic-research-center.

Eiterjord, T.A. (2018, July 17). China's planned nuclear icebreaker. *The Diplomat*. Retrieved July 20, 2018 from https://thediplomat.com/2018/07/chinas-planned-nuclear-icebreaker/.

Forskningsrådet. (2018). Infoside om Kina-delegasjon 2018. Retrieved December 10, 2018, from https://www.forskningsradet.no/prognett-chinor/Nyheter/Infoside_om_Kinadelegasjon_2018/1254034490994/p1253952407056.

Foust, J. (2018). NASA opens door to additional cooperation with China. *SpaceNews*. Retrieved December 10, 2018, from https://spacenews.com/nasa-opens-door-to-additional-cooperation-with-china/.

Global R&D Funding Forecast. (2018). China plans to be global R&D leader, 22–23. Retrieved November 20, 2018, from http://digital.rdmag.com/researchanddevelopment/2018_global_r_d_funding_forecast?pg=22#pg22.

Han, X., & Appelbaum, R.P. (2018). China's science, technology, engineering, and mathematics (STEM) research environment: A snapshot. *PLoS ONE*, 13(4). Retrieved from https://doi.org/https://doi.org/10.1371/journal.pone.0195347.

Hoag, H. (2018, June 18). Fieldwork in the Arctic is surprisingly costly, limiting the research done there. *Science.* Retrieved June 20, 2018, from http://www.sciencemag.org/news/2018/06/fieldwork-arctic-surprisingly-costly-limiting-research-done-there.

INTAROS. (2018). *Chinese expedition launches unmanned probes in the high Arctic.* Retrieved December 10, 2018, from http://www.intaros.eu/news/recent-news/chinese-expedition-launches-unmanned-probes-in-the-high-arctic/.

Karholl. Retrieved August 20, 2018, from https://karholl.is/en/.

Lanteigne, M. (2018, June 9). 'Three to Get Ready': Northeast Asian Neighbors Discuss Joint Arctic Policies. Retrieved August 20, 2019, from https://overthecircle.com/2018/06/09/three-to-get-ready-northeast-asian-neighbours-discuss-joint-arctic-policies/.

Lasserre, F., Alexeeva, O.V., & Linyan, H. (2017). China's strategy in the Arctic: threatening or opportunistic? *Polar Record*, *53*(1), 31–42.

Masood, E. (2019, May 2). How China is redrawing the map of world science. *Nature,* vol. 569, 20–23.

Myklebust, J.P. (2018, April 17). Norway sends 250-strong research delegation to China. *University World News.* Retrieved June 20, 2018, from http://www.universityworldnews.com/article.php?story=20180417153536424.

Nong, H. (2014). Emerging interests of non-Arctic countries in the Arctic: a Chinese perspective. *Polar Journal*, *4*(2): 271–286.

Office of the Secretary of Defense. (2019). Annual Report to Congress. Military and Security Developments Involving the People's Republic of China 2019. Retrieved August 30, 2019, from https://media.defense.gov/2019/May/02/2002127082/-1/-1/1/2019_CHINA_MILITARY_POWER_REPORT.pdf.

Office of the United States Trade Representative. (2018). 2018 Special 301 Report. Retrieved November 20, 2018, from https://ustr.gov/sites/default/files/files/Press/Reports/2018Special 301.pdf.

PRC State Council. (2018, January 26). *Full text: China's Arctic policy.* Beijing, China: The State Council Information Office of the People's Republic of China. Retrieved March 12, 2018, from http://english.gov.cn/archive/white_paper/2018/01/26/content_281476026660336.htm.

Quinn, E. (2019, August 7). Russia, China to do joint research in Arctic Siberia. *Eye on the Arctic.* Retrieved August 31, 2019 from https://www.rcinet.ca/eye-on-the-arctic/2019/08/07/russia-china-to-do-joint-research-in-arctic-siberia/.

Reuters. (2018, February 27). China spends $279 bln on R&D in 2017: science minister. *The Reuters.* Retrieved December 12, 2018, from https://www.reuters.com/article/us-china-economy-r-d/china-spends-279-bln-on-rd-in-2017-science-minister-idUSKCN1GB018.

Showstack, R. (2018, January 24). China catching up to United States in research and development. *EOS*. Retrieved August 20, 2018, from https://eos.org/articles/china-catching-up-to-united-states-in-research-and-development.

Smieszek, M. (2017). The Agreement on Enhancing International Arctic Scientific Cooperation: From Paper to Practice. In L. Heininen, H. Exner-Pirot, & J. Plouffe (Eds.), *Arctic Yearbook 2015*. Akureyri, Iceland: Northern Research Forum. Retrieved August 15, 2019 from https://arcticyearbook.com/images/yearbook/2017/Briefing_Notes/6_The_Agreement_on_Enhancing_International_Arctic_Scientific_Cooperation.pdf.

Smieszek, M. (2015). 25 Years of the International Arctic Science Committee (IASC). In L. Heininen, H. Exner-Pirot, & J. Plouffe (Eds.), *Arctic Yearbook 2015*. Akureyri, Iceland: Northern Research Forum. Retrieved August 15, 2019 from https://arcticyearbook.com/images/yearbook/2015/Briefing_Notes/5.BN_M_Smieszek.pdf

Straits Times / Xinhua. (2018, September 11). *China launches first homemade polar icebreaker Xuelong 2.* Retrieved October 20, 2018, from https://www.straitstimes.com/asia/east-asia/china-launches-first-homemade-polar-icebreaker-xuelong-2.

Suttmeier, R.P. (2018, June 29). How China is trying to invent the future as a science superpower. *Scientific American*. Retrieved October 7, 2019, from https://www.scientificamerican.com/article/how-china-is-trying-to-invent-the-future-as-a-science-superpower/.

U.S. Department of State. (2019). Looking North: Sharpening America's Arctic Focus. Remarks by Michael R. Pompeo, Secretary of State, Rovaniemi, Finland, May 6, 2019. Retrieved August 30, 2019 from https://www.state.gov/looking-north-sharpening-americas-arctic-focus/.

Wang, Z., & Zhang, J. (2010). China and the International Geophysical Year. In R.D Launius, , J.R. Fleming & D.H. DeVorkin (eds.), *Globalizing Polar Science. Reconsidering the International Polar and Geophysical Years.* New York: Palgrave Macmillan, 143–155.

Watts, J., & Weaver, M. (2010, October 11). China Cancels Meeting with Norwegian Minister after Nobel Peace Prize Row. *The Guardian.* Retrieved November 25, 2018, from https://www.theguardian.com/world/2010/oct/11/china-cancels-norway-meeting.

Xinhua Agency. (2018, October 19). China-Iceland Arctic science observatory inaugurated in Northern Iceland. *Xinhuanet.* Retrieved October 20, 2018, from http://www.xinhuanet.com/english/2018-10/19/c_137542493_2.htm.

CHAPTER 5

China, Climate Change and the Arctic Environment

Sanna Kopra, Karoliina Hurri, Liisa Kauppila, Adam Stepien and Yulia Yamineva

5.1 Introduction

In recent decades, the Arctic region has faced major environmental changes. In particular, there is growing scientific evidence that Arctic climate change is proceeding much faster than expected earlier: the Arctic Ocean may be ice-free in summer as early as the late 2030s (AMAP, 2017: 3). At the same time, the melting of ice and permafrost in the High North is accelerating climate change and altering ecosystems globally, including in China (ACIA, 2004; AMAP, 2017). Climate change is a complex global problem that cannot be solved through regional actions by Arctic states and hence, global efforts are necessary to respond to climate change. China, the world's biggest greenhouse gas (GHG) emitter, plays a crucial role in those efforts – without its participation, any effort to prevent dangerous climate change from happening will fail. For China, climate change is also an important driver of the state's Arctic engagement: the Chinese government argues that due to the adverse effects of climate change, it has special interests in the Arctic and it must have a chance to be involved in Arctic governance. In this chapter, we investigate China's role and interests in international climate politics, and discuss their implications for the Arctic. We offer a short historical overview of China's role in the United Nations (UN) negotiations on climate change as well as its domestic climate mitigation policies. Since the very beginning in the late 1980s, China has taken an active part – if not always with enthusiasm – in international negotiations on climate change. Today, China is party to the United Nations Framework Convention on Climate Change (UNFCCC), the Kyoto Protocol, and the Paris Agreement, which establish the keystones of international climate regime. In addition, we study the extent to which China's Arctic policy addresses climate change. We also take a look at China's broader ecological footprint in the High North.

5.2 China's Contribution to Arctic Environmental Change

Today, it is evident that human activities such as burning fossil fuels have increased the concentration of greenhouse gas emissions in the atmosphere and

© KONINKLIJKE BRILL NV, LEIDEN, 2020 | DOI:10.1163/9789004408425_006

hence caused climate change (Intergovernmental Panel on Climate Change, 2014). In October 2018, the Intergovernmental Panel on Climate Change made very clear that to prevent the most dangerous climate change from happening, we must reduce global net carbon dioxide (CO_2) emissions from 2010 levels by 45 percent before 2030 (Intergovernmental Panel on Climate Change, 2018). Although only a small proportion of global greenhouse gas emissions originate in the Arctic, the region has emerged as a showcase of global warming and its impacts. In the Arctic, temperatures have risen more rapidly than in any other region on earth during the last 30 years. As a result, sea ice, permafrost and snow cover have decreased dramatically, which hampers the livelihoods of local people and threatens the survival of many Arctic species such as the polar bear, the walrus and the seal, for instance (see, for example, ACIA, 2004; AMAP, 2017; Serreze, 2018). Arctic environmental change also has significant global impacts, and it may have an influence on Southeast Asian monsoon and winter haze in China, for instance (ibid.; Wang, Chen & Liu, 2015.). At the same time, the warming climate brings new economic opportunities for resource exploitation, fisheries, shipping, and tourism – further intensifying the already high pressure on the Arctic environment.

In line with China's rapid economic growth, its total greenhouse gas emissions have grown at extraordinary speed during the past couple of decades. Between 1990 and 2013, China's carbon dioxide emissions increased by 80 percent (Olivier et al., 2015: 10). In brief, China's total energy consumption and carbon dioxide emissions started to grow significantly from 2001 onwards when China joined the World Trade Organization, which directed the nation towards heavy and chemical industries instead of centralizing to modern technologies (Chen, 2012). China's emissions also grew because of huge infrastructure projects such as the Three Gorges Dam (ibid.). Today, China is the world's biggest contributor to climate change – in 2017, its greenhouse gas emissions accounted for 27 percent of global emissions (Olivier & Peters, 2018). In terms of per capita emissions, however, China's emissions are much lower than those of the United States, Canada and the Arab states of the Persian Gulf, for example (EDGAR, 2017). In addition, China's non-CO_2 GHG emissions,[1] especially methane and hydrofluorocarbons (HFCs), are high and are projected to nearly double by 2030 under existing policies (Yao et al., 2016).

China further impacts global and regional climate change through its emissions of black carbon. Black carbon, which also contributes to air pollution, has recently emerged as a key climate-warming agent and is as such referred to

1 The remaining GHGs covered by the Kyoto Protocol include: methane (CH_4), nitrous oxide (N_2O), hydrofluorocarbons (HFCs), perfluorocarbons (PFCs), sulfur hexafluoride (SF_6), and nitrogen trifluoride (NF_3).

as one of the short-lived climate pollutants (SLCPs)[2] (Bond et al., 2013). It is formed as a result of the incomplete combustion of fossil fuels and biomass, and co-emitted with GHGs and other aerosols. Black carbon accelerates global warming directly and indirectly through reducing the albedo effect (the ability to reflect sunlight) of the surface of the earth. Its emissions have a stronger warming effect on glaciated regions including the Arctic (AMAP, 2015: 9), where about 20–25 percent of warming and snow-ice cover loss is attributed to the reduction of the albedo effect caused by black carbon (Koch et al., 2011). China's emissions of black carbon have been estimated at 20–24 percent of global emissions for the period of 1990–2007 (UNEP, 2015: 11); however, these emissions reportedly fell by 27 percent in 2010–2017 due to pollution reduction policies (Zheng et al., 2018). Using biomass, coal or oil for cooking and heating in residential and industrial sectors as well as the use of diesel fuel for transportation are the main causes of black carbon emissions in China (Zheng et al., 2018). It has been shown that two-thirds of black carbon's warming effects in the Arctic come from non-Arctic countries (AMAP, 2015: 9), which highlights the role of China's emissions in Arctic warming.

China's role in driving climate change through its emissions of long-lived GHGs and SLCPs is part of the country's broader environmental footprint in the Arctic. China is a source of a variety of pollutants (e.g. persistent organic pollutants and mercury) reaching the Arctic, and Chinese policies aimed at controlling such pollutants – if implemented effectively – benefit the Arctic environment. The picture of Chinese environmental footprint is complemented by the more direct impacts, namely through Chinese investments in Arctic locations. Moreover, China has an indirect influence on the Arctic environment and Arctic communities via driving the demand for Arctic resources and actions, such as contracts with Arctic states, aimed at securing China's access to these resources.

Persistent organic pollutants (POPs) and other long-range pollutants such as mercury can be transported by wind or ocean currents into the Arctic. POPs are deposited in the tissue of animals and humans and have noticeable health implications, especially in utilizing traditional sources of food (AMAP, 2009a; 2009b). While the global emissions of some POPs have decreased significantly, partly due to the adoption of the Stockholm POPs Convention[3] – ratified by China in 2004 – other pollutants are still of major concern.

It is very difficult to assess the amount of pollution coming to the Arctic specifically from China. However, a few examples of the level of impact

2 Others include methane, tropospheric ozone and some hydrofluorocarbons.

3 The Stockholm Convention on Persistent Organic Pollutants, 23 May 2001, in force 17 May 2004, 40 ILM 532 (2001).

referring to East Asia or Asia (with China clearly the largest contributor due to the size of its manufacturing sector) can be given (data for 2000–2014). South-Eastern Asia is responsible for 12% of hexachlorobenzene (HCB) depositions over the Arctic (compared to a contribution of 35% by the European continent), and East Asia is a source region for 11% of sulfur dioxide (SO_2) and 21% of nitrogen oxides (NO_x) depositions. Lindane (y-HCH) pollution reaching the Arctic from outside of the region comes mainly from China, which is responsible for 59% of global emissions. Brominated flame retardants (BFRS) come to the Arctic primarily from Asia (69% of depositions in the Arctic) (Cavalieri et al., 2010).

According to Travnikov (2005), "about half the mercury deposition to the Arctic is due to the atmospheric transport from anthropogenic emission sources, of which the greatest contribution is made by Asian (33%) and European sources (22%)". South-East Asia is responsible for 39% of global mercury emissions (equal to 685–1430 tonnes of mercury) (UNEP, 2018). The recently adopted Minamata Mercury Convention[4] – ratified by China in 2016 – gives hope for the gradual decrease in the presence of mercury in the environment; however, the effects will be visible only in the long-term.

Historically, a crucial pollutant impacting the Arctic – and to a much greater extent, the Antarctic – were ozone-depleting substances (ODSs), in particular chlorofluorocarbons (CFCs). Following the entry into adoption (1982) and entry into force (1989) of the Montreal Protocol, global emissions of CFCs have fallen significantly. However, emissions of trichlorofluoromethane (CFC-11), the second-most abundant CFC, began to rise after 2012. According to recent findings, one of the key sources of new emissions is probably located in North-East China (likely due to foam production) (Rigby et al., 2019).

An environmental issue currently in focus in the Arctic is pollution with marine litter – primarily plastics – and microplastics. Sources of plastic in the Arctic Ocean include shipping, fisheries, Arctic rivers, as well as long-range transport via sea currents. Due to limited inflow of waters from the Pacific Ocean via cold currents passing the Bering Strait, Chinese litter sources are of secondary importance for the Arctic Ocean (PAME, 2019). However, microplastics may be airborne and transported long distances (Allen et al., 2019) and thus, China may constitute an important source of such airborne pollutants.

Apart from pollutants emitted within China's territory – and policies aimed at controlling these pollutants – China and Chinese economic operators may affect Arctic habitats in a more direct manner through the investments of Chinese companies in Greenland, northern Canada or Siberia, for example.

---

4 Minamata Convention on Mercury, 19 January 2013, in force 16 August 2017, 55 ILM 582 (2016).

Chinese demand for resources is a key contributor to the extractive industries investment potential in the Arctic. For instance, in 2013, China imported more than 60% within the international iron ore trade, and the country accounted for 44% of global nickel demand in 2011. China is also a major and growing market for pulp derived from boreal forests. Moreover, Chinese shipping activities have marine and air quality impacts in the Arctic, which are bound to increase with the growing presence of Chinese vessels in the Arctic Ocean and adjacent waters.

In contrast to the European Union, which has attempted to assess its environmental footprint on the Arctic region (Cavalieri et al., 2010), China has thus far not undertaken such an evaluation.

5.3 China's National Goals and Environmental Challenges in a Nutshell

China is a one-party state without such democratic institutions as general elections. This does not, however, mean that the Chinese government can overlook the needs of its citizens. In other words, Chinese leaders must consider the question of legitimacy – the right to rule the country – in its decision-making. In practice, this means that the government's policies must address the key concern of the Chinese people, which arguably is the maintaining of social stability (Kopra & Kauppila, 2018; cf. Kallio, 2016). Ever since the beginning of the Reform and Opening Up period (*gaige kaifang* 改革开放) in 1978, one of the core prerequisites for reaching social stability has been material well-being – the sufficient wealth and health of Chinese people. For this reason, maintaining rapid economic growth has been a core priority of the Chinese government for the past forty years. As a consequence, China has lifted millions of people out of absolute poverty and has simultaneously become the world's second-largest economy, with a nominal gross domestic product (GDP) of USD13,616 billion in 2018, with continued 6.6% year-on-year growth (National Bureau of Statistics China, 2019).

The Chinese growth story is remarkable on both national and global scales, but it has also made the country's carbon dioxide emissions the highest in the world and created severe environmental problems domestically. The country's rapid industrialization has been a double-edged sword, as providing material well-being through improved standards of living and employment, the high GDP share of the manufacturing sector (29% in 2017) (World Bank, 2019) has also contributed negatively to the state of the country's environment. Furthermore, the growth of heavy industry in particular has been largely fueled by coal, whose largest global producer and consumer is China. In 2018, the industrial sector's overall contribution continued to account for approximately 34% of the GDP (National Bureau of Statistics China, 2019), despite the fact that China's new economic policy is to shake off the status of being the "world's factory" and to prioritize quality over quantity through the Made in China strategy (State Council of the People's Republic of China, 2015). In addition, unbalanced and fast-paced urbanization has further deteriorated the environment by creating some of the world's most polluted megacities.

Given the structure of the country's economy and considerable population of 1.4 billion people, it is clear that China's energy demand is equally vast. Despite recent investments in renewable energy, energy production continues to be a key source of China's carbon emissions. At present, coal accounts for around 59 percent of the country's energy mix (National Bureau of Statistics of China, 2019), causing severe environmental degradation around the country. Given the fact that not only the air but also water and soil are largely contaminated by decades of burning coal (among other factors), Chinese people have been exposed to various kinds of pollution-related health problems, varying from respiratory to cardiovascular and mental health issues (e.g. Liu, Xu & Yang, 2018). Indeed, numerous scientific studies have shown that fine particulate matter (PM2.5) causes adverse environmental and health impacts in China. In 2010, a million premature deaths in China annually were attributed to air pollution (Gu et al., 2018). A growing awareness of this linkage between pollution and personal health and wellbeing has provoked numerous pollution-related riots and demonstrations across China, (see, for example, Albert & Xu, 2016; Babones, 2017; Kennedy, 2012) to an extent that is hard to estimate in the absence of trustworthy and transparent reporting.

Since the early 2000s, thus, it has became increasingly clear that the government's pursuit to build a *harmonious society* (*hexie shehui* 和谐社会) will not be successful without paying more attention to environmental protection (e.g. Pan, 2006). In 2007, then-President Hu Jintao officially proposed the building of an *ecological civilization* (*shengtai wenming* 生态文明) as a new guideline for the building up of a moderately well-off society. Although Hu did not offer a clear definition of the concept, his report to the 17th National Congress of the Communist Party of China indicated that the government had redefined its development model by putting more emphasis on sustainable development (Hu, 2007). The concept of an ecological civilization was quickly incorporated into the government's overall policy plans, and it was added to the Constitution of the Communist Party of China in 2012 (the 18th National Congress of the Communist Party of China, 2012). This development put the Chinese government in a position in which it must increasingly find a balance between maintaining steady economic growth and reducing the health impacts of pollution and other environmental hazards and catastrophes affecting China.

It is clear that there are strong domestic incentives for China to decrease the use of coal in order to improve air quality and public health, and such reductions undoubtedly decrease both GHGs and air pollutant emissions as well. To some extent, the Chinese government's participation in the pioneering Arctic liquefied natural gas (LNG) project in Northern Siberia's Yamal Peninsula can also be connected to this trend: LNG is viewed as a rising, greener alternative to coal burning. The Arctic region is estimated to possess 30% of the world's undiscovered natural gas (U.S. Geological Survey, 2008), making it too lucrative a frontier for China to ignore, especially with the current plan to increase the use of LNG to 10% by 2020 and 15% by 2030 (Xinhua, 2019).

Not only domestic but also global environmental issues affect social stability in China. The Chinese government must equally respond to these challenges in order to prevent instances of civil disorder. Out of such global challenges, climate change can be seen to pose the most severe risks. In the future, climate change is expected to cause floods, drought and extreme weather events in China, all of which can potentially affect not only the everyday life of Chinese citizens but also the country's agriculture and food production, security of supply and military strategies. There seems to be no apparent dispute about these impacts, let alone climate change itself, in China. On the contrary, the Chinese government has openly acknowledged that global warming threatens the country's national security. Most tellingly, China's Arctic strategy and most major policy speeches all emphasize the severe consequences of climate change on China (State Council Information Office of the People's Republic of China, 2018; e.g. Zhang, 2015).

In addition to finding a balance between growth and its costs, another factor that is crucial to the legitimacy of the Chinese government is its prowess on the international stage. Due to the growing environmental awareness of the Chinese people, taking responsibility for global climate change in such contexts as the Arctic high-level meetings is likely to promote a better image of the Chinese government and the ruling party among the domestic audience. Indeed, as China rises to the status of a global power and the Chinese society becomes increasingly open and integrated with the rest of the world, Chinese people are likely to evaluate their government's worth in terms of both domestic and international achievements, a fact that is recognized by the party-state in its portrayal of China's participation in Arctic science activities, for example at the National Museum of China in Beijing (Kopra & Kauppila, 2018). This creates a strong incentive to replenish China's international image in environmental issues and gain a stronger foothold in international climate politics.

5.4 From Rio to Paris: China's Changing Role in International Climate Politics

The United Nations Framework Convention on Climate Change (UNFCCC) was adopted in Rio de Janeiro in 1992 and entered into force in 1994. As of 2019, it has been ratified by 197 countries that are often referred to as 'the Parties to the Convention' (UNFCCC, 2019). The Convention marks an important step for international climate politics because, for the first time, countries agreed to stabilize GHGs at a non-hazardous level in order to prevent climate change. China ratified the Convention in January 1993. However, for a long time, China refused to shoulder any responsibility in the UN negotiations for climate change mitigation and highlighted the historic responsibility of developed countries to reduce emissions as well as to aid developing countries to handle the adverse effects of climate change.

The legally-binding Kyoto Protocol was negotiated in 1997 and entered into force as late as 2005. The burden-sharing of the Kyoto Protocol for 2008–2012 set quantitative emission reductions only for developed countries, including the members of the Organization for Economic Co-operation and Development (OECD) in 1992 and the Economies in Transition including the Russian Federation, the Baltic States, and a number of Central and Eastern European States (UNFCCC, 2019). The rest of the Parties were not required to reduce their emissions, as they were seen as developing countries. This group included emerging powers such as China, South Africa, Brazil and India. The Protocol covered only some 30 percent of global emissions because, amongst other factors, the United States (U.S.) never ratified it, and the growing emissions of emerging nations were excluded from the quotas (Durand, 2012; Syri et al., 2013). In reality, the number is ambiguous since, for example, in 2011 Japan and Russia announced that they would withdraw from the protocol (Korhola, 2014). In 2012, only 19 out of 41 countries were expected to achieve the given reductions, and on the contrary, emissions actually continued to grow in many of the OECD countries (Hurrell, 2012; Napoli, 2012). Developing countries' position of not having binding emission obligations in the Protocol is suggested to be a merit of China for its role as the leading negotiator in the developing country group G-77 (Chen, 2012). G-77 represents one major group in climate politics and is an important negotiation coalition for China to be included in with its 133 members covering ⅔ of the world's nations. However, the group of developing countries has become more diverse, the interests of the group conflict more, and the common identity has moderately deteriorated, thereby putting into question the practicality of the group in climate negotiations (Blaxekjær & Nielsen, 2015).

China's first National Program on Climate Change was published in 2007, clearing awareness of climate change and promising to agree on voluntary targets for energy consumption. At that stage, China was unable to commit to binding emission targets because of its coal-dominated energy structure and low per capita income levels (Chen, 2012). In COP13 (conference of parties) in Bali in 2007, climate action was requested from all Parties for the first time – mitigation commitments from developed countries and mitigation actions from developing countries (Brunnée & Streck, 2013). The outcome of COP13 also urged the Parties to come to an agreement by 2009, which led to the high expectations for COP15 in 2009 in Copenhagen. In COP15, Parties disagreed whether to format the agreement to extend the mandate of the Kyoto Protocol or negotiate a new agreement (Christoff, 2010). In the end, the conference came out only with a weak Copenhagen Accord, from which many blame the emerging powers' negative attitude, especially that of China and India (Hallding et al., 2011; Hurrell, 2012; Brunnée & Streck, 2013). Despite the weak outcome, the legacy of Copenhagen can be seen in the strengthening position of the emerging powers within climate politics (Hallding et al., 2011). In 2009, the emerging powers Brazil, South Africa, India and China founded an annual negotiation coalition, called the BASIC Countries, as a subgroup for the developing country bloc G-77 with motivation to strengthen the position of developing countries (ibid.)

Until the 2011 COP17 in Durban, China had determinedly refused to agree to any binding climate obligations, preferring voluntary national objectives. However, in Durban, the Parties agreed to commit to a new legally-binding climate agreement by 2015 to be entered into force in 2020 (Roberts, 2016). At this point, all eyes turned to Paris COP21 with expectations as great they were before Copenhagen's meeting in 2009. After Durban, China took a more constructive role in international climate negotiations. The remarkable difference in China's role in 2009 in Copenhagen in comparison to Paris in 2015 results from the prioritization shift in economic development in China's 12th Five-Year Plan from energy-intensive growth to innovation and low-carbon technologies (Hilton & Kerr, 2017). This change enabled China to reformulate its international climate priorities before COP21. For instance, in 2013, the government stated that "Since 2012, the Chinese government has taken positive action in enhancing its capability across major sectors to adapt to climate change and respond to extreme weather and climate-related events" (National Development and Reform Commission, 2013: 27).

In particular, China began to cooperate with the United States on climate change – a crucial development that can be seen as a critical driver to the adoption of a new international climate agreement at the COP21 held in Paris in 2015. The Sino-American climate cooperation flourished in particular during the Obama administration, and between 2013 and 2016, China and the United States issued several joint statements in which the two nations agreed on their shared urgency to solve climate change (e.g. National Development and Reform Commission, 2014, 2015, 2016). In 2014, China and the U.S. made an emission-cutting agreement which has been acknowledged as significant also on the global level. In the agreement, China pledged to halt carbon emissions growth around 2030. Also, it pledged 3.1 billion USD to developing countries to address climate change (National Development and Reform Commission, 2015). The deal gained widespread international attention prior to COP21, and the text directly encouraged other Parties to be inspired by the Sino-American effort and to submit their own contributions. The image of an uncooperative country, as China was accused of being in the negotiations in 2009, was at least partly gone in Paris in 2015.

5.5 China and International Climate Politics in the Paris Era

In COP21, Parties delivered the Paris Agreement on the 12th December 2015 with the main targets of halting the global average temperature increase to below 2°C whilst also attempting to limit it to 1.5°C and reaching net zero emissions after 2050 (Ge et al., 2019). The Paris Agreement was opened for ratifications on 22nd April 2016 and entered into force on 4th November 2016 after reaching the threshold of being ratified by 55 Parties accounting for a minimum of 55% of global emissions on 5th October 2016 (UNFCCC, 2019). It requires 55% of all global emissions, while in comparison, the Kyoto Protocol covered only 55% of the emissions of industrialized countries. In Paris, China agreed for the first time to an absolute cap on emissions, dependent on international measurements, reporting and verification (MRV) (Hilton & Kerr, 2017). The Paris Agreement is based on states' voluntary, nationally-determined contributions that were first called Intended Nationally Determined Contributions (INDC) as nations were submitting their first ones prior to the finalization of the Agreement. INDCs changed to Nationally Determined Contributions (NDCs) without the prefix "intended" when a Party ratified the Paris Agreement. NDCs are drafted at the national level, considering the domestic circumstances and capabilities (Dalby, 2016). At the same time, the Paris Agreement contains several procedural obligations, including that each NDC should reflect the highest possible ambition and progress beyond the existing pledge. A further important element of the Paris Agreement is its international reporting and transparency framework.

Nationally-determined contributions support the climate negotiation process to shift further towards a bottom-up approach and currently represent the public prime channel between the international and national climate politics. Thus, the long-term success of the agreement depends on the NDCs' ability and ambition to respond to the targets of the Paris Agreement.

NDCs were an important source of encouragement for China's positive attitude towards the Paris Agreement since they represent an important bottom-up and voluntary option to traditional reduction quotas (Hilton & Kerr, 2017). China submitted its comprehensive 40-page long NDC to the UNFCCC in June 2015, which promises by 2030:

a) to achieve the peak of carbon dioxide emissions around 2030 and to conduct their best efforts to peak early;
b) to lower carbon dioxide emissions per unit of GDP by 60% to 65% from the 2005 level;
c) to increase the share of non-fossil fuels in primary energy consumption to around 20%; and
d) to increase the forest stock volume by around 4.5 billion cubic meters on the 2005 level
(China's National Development and Reform Commission, 2015).

To achieve these 2020 and 2030 targets, the NDC document of China introduces a number of actions, of which the majority have already been implemented (den Elzen et al., 2016). The document highlights the significant impact that developed countries have had on the emissions and defines China as a responsible developing country. The contribution also explains China's will to increase the South-South climate cooperation and China's wish to assist other developing countries facing climate change, including small island nations, the least developed countries and African countries. The document describes China as motivated to act on climate change because of the domestic need for sustainable development and the will to ensure economic, energy, ecological and food security and people's health in addition to China's willingness for global cooperation. However, the NDC document does not mention China or climate change in the context of the Arctic region. The document is in agreement with the ideas of the 13th Five-Year Plan as China is said to aim for a "moderately prosperous society in an all-around way by 2020 and to create prosperous, strong, democratic, culturally developed and harmonious modern socialist country by the middle of this century" (China's NDC, 2015: 4).

The Paris Agreement is credited for its symbolic value of Parties coming into an agreement of legally-binding terms but criticized for the wide gap between the ambition of the NDCs and the actual targets of the agreement. For example,

China's NDC is 'little more than business as usual' (Harris, 2017: 102) and "highly insufficient" in order to reach the goal to limit the global temperature rise to 2°C unless other states do not implement much more ambitious emissions reduction measures (Climate Action Tracker, 2018).

In 2016, the Sino-American climate cooperation was influenced by the U.S. political situation as the Republican Party in the U.S. has, at least until this far, not supported active international climate policy (Kemp, 2016). A few days after the Paris Agreement had entered into force, climate sceptic Republican Donald J. Trump was elected U.S. president. During his election campaign, several times Trump called climate change a 'Chinese hoax' as well as announced to nullify the climate policies made by the Obama administration. Therefore, Trump's election instantly elevated China into a new position as a global climate leader – whether or not it wanted it or was ready for that in practice (Kopra, 2019). The Chinese government seemed to respond to international expectations of its leadership role positively, and many officials convinced the international community that China would not change its approach to international climate policy despite Trump's negative approach. In June 2017, Trump indeed decided to withdraw the U.S. from the Paris Agreement, which caused harsh criticism around the world and ended the Sino-American cooperation on climate change. As a leadership vacuum in international climate negotiations emerged, the international society began to expect China to step in. Notably, the Chinese government did not stand to oppose these expectations, but pledged to increase cooperation with the European Union instead. Remarkably, president Xi Jinping declared in his speech to the 19th National Congress of the Communist Party of China that China had taken a "driving seat" in international climate negotiations and hence had "become an important participant, contributor, and torchbearer in the global endeavor for ecological civilization" (Xi, 2017: 4).

In COP24 in Katowice in 2018, Parties were urged to agree on implementation, and the conference finally delivered a rulebook for the Paris Agreement. In the Paris Agreement, Parties committed to an ambition mechanism regarding the NDC documents: approximately every five years, Parties must submit a new, more ambitious, nationally-determined contribution to UNFCCC. Critics to the 2018 Paris rulebook were quick to point out that the commitment for increased ambition is not defined clearly enough in the key chapter of the rulebook. Hence, the expectations vary for the second round of NDCs. The Marshall Islands were the first country to submit their second NDC in November 2018 but the other Parties, including China, are expected to submit theirs during 2020 (UNFCCC INDC Submission Portal, 2019). The ambition mechanism was meant to make the Paris Agreement responsive to the message of the 2018

Intergovernmental Panel on Climate Change (IPCC) special report and to enable Parties to scale up their commitments to reach the 1.5°C target. However, at present, it remains unclear whether China is willing to enhance its NDC under the Paris Agreement in an ambitious manner or whether it will more determinately emphasize the historic responsibility of developed countries – as it and other BASIC (Brazil, South Africa, India and China) countries did in the UN climate negotiations in Bonn in 2017. China's historical emissions will soon override the other Parties' but China can still argue for its lower per capita emissions which will still be, thanks to the great population, a real argument in the near future (Woon, 2018). With the business-as-usual model, also the per capita emissions of China will reach the average of the developed countries by 2030 (IEA, 2011).

The increased cooperation between the EU and China especially from 2018 onwards could support China to submit a more ambitious pledge. In particular, the agreement that China and the EU made in July 2018 to intensify their cooperation on climate change and clean energy is a positive sign, and there are many opportunities for collaboration in the fields of emissions trading systems, energy efficiency, clean energy and technology, low-emission transportation, and low-carbon cities, etc. In April 2019, the two nations published the EU-China Summit Joint Statement (2019) in which they express the will to a deeper cooperation in addressing global environmental challenges such as pollution and marine litter. The statement was viewed "promising" by Europe's largest coalition of non-governmental organizations working on climate and energy issues (CAN Europe, 2019).

5.6 China's Arctic Strategy and Climate Change

In January 2018, China's State Council Information Office published its long-awaited Arctic white paper. According to the paper, the state's goals in the region include "to understand, protect, develop and participate in the governance of the Arctic, so as to safeguard the common interests of all countries and the international community in the Arctic, and promote sustainable development of the Arctic". "While pursuing its own interests", the white paper explains, "China will pay due regard to the interests of other countries and the broader international community, bear in mind the importance of the protection and development of the Arctic, and of keeping in proper balance its current and long-term interests, so as to promote the sustainable development of the Arctic". The white paper identifies "sustainability" as "the fundamental goal" of China's Arctic engagement, which, in turn, "means promoting the sustainable development of the Arctic by ensuring the sustainability of environmental protection, resource utilization and human activities in the area". Furthermore, it "means realizing harmonious coexistence between man and nature, better coordination between ecological protection, economic growth and social progress, better balance between utilization, management and protection, and intergenerational equity" (State Council Information Office of the People's Republic of China, 2018). Notably, the white paper does not mention the concept of ecological civilization at all.

Defining China as a 'near-Arctic state', China's Arctic white paper emphasizes that the "natural conditions of the Arctic and their changes have a direct impact on China's climate system and ecological environment, and, in turn, on its economic interests in agriculture, forestry, fishery, the marine industry and other sectors" (State Council Information Office of the People's Republic of China, 2018). Scientific findings do indeed show that Arctic climate change causes risks to human security and ecosystems in China. For example, many of China's coastal mega-cities, such as Shanghai, Tianjin and Hong Kong, are expected to suffer from flooding due to rising sea levels caused by the melting of sea ice in the Arctic. Moreover, Arctic climate change is also expected to increase haze pollution in eastern China (Wang, Chen & Liu, 2015) as well as alter many global natural processes, causing changes likely to hamper China's agricultural production. As discussed above, air pollution and food security are critical factors of the legitimacy of the Chinese Communist Party. Therefore, it is unsurprising that scientific research on climate change is one of the key interests of China's Arctic policy, and the Chinese government wants to learn more about the linkages between Arctic climate change, natural cycles, domestic interests, and social stability in China (for more information, see Chapter 4 in this volume).

Although China's Arctic white paper notes that "China's emission reduction measures have a positive impact on the climatic and ecological environment of the Arctic", it does not introduce additional measures to reduce greenhouse gas emissions in China. Thus, China's Arctic strategy pays more attention to the link between Arctic climate change and the adverse effects of climate change in China than to the ways in which the world's largest carbon emitter could mitigate Arctic climate change. A key reason for this may be that China uses "climate change as a key justification for its Arctic engagement" (Kopra, 2020: 47), and it argues that due to Arctic climate change's adverse effects on the Chinese society, the Chinese government has special interests in the region and it should be accepted as a legitimate participant in the regional governance. However, China could also legitimate its growing regional role by announcing additional, ambitious measures to cut greenhouse gas emissions, a move that China's Arctic strategy fails to take. In broader terms, such tightening of domestic climate policy measures would prove to the world that China is ready to play a leadership role in international climate policy (Kopra, 2019).

5.7 China and Global Cooperation on SLCPS

Global cooperation efforts have expanded recently to cover emissions of SLCPS, the reduction of which helps mitigate short-term climate change and, in some cases, air pollution.[5] As explained above, SLCPS refer to GHGS such as methane, some HFCS and tropospheric ozone as well as black carbon, which is an aerosol. What unites them under one label – apart from their climate impact – is their relatively short lifetime in the atmosphere compared to CO2. This implies that rapid reduction in SCLPS will lead to relatively quick gains in terms of climate change mitigation. That said, reducing SLCPS is viewed as only complementary to CO2 reductions, which are essential for addressing long-term global climate change (Intergovernmental Panel on Climate Change, 2014: 20). In addition, methane, tropospheric ozone and black carbon contribute to air pollution, which implies that there are significant co-benefits of their reductions for public health and the environment.

Many international regimes and institutions are relevant for reducing SLCPS and hence the related legal and governance regime is complex and fragmented. Methane and HFC emissions have traditionally been discussed under the UNFCCC. The latter have also recently been designated to be phased out under the Kigali amendment to the Montreal Protocol on Substances that Deplete the Ozone Layer.

In addition to these, in the last decade global initiatives have emerged to draw attention specifically to SLCPS and the co-benefits of their reductions. The main initiative is the Climate and Clean Air Coalition (CCAC), a voluntary government-led partnership that was launched in 2011 with the goal to raise awareness and improve scientific understanding of SLCPS, build capacities, strengthen national and regional actions, and promote best practices. The Coalition has been successful in generating support from 64 states and 73 intergovernmental and non-governmental organizations thus far. China is not a member of the CCAC but participates in its meetings as an observer state.

The Arctic Council has also been proactive in addressing SLCPS, specifically black carbon and methane emissions. It has done so through scientific assessments and the adoption of the Framework for Action on Enhanced Black

5 This section draws on Yamineva & Liu 2019; and Yamineva & Kulovesi 2018.

Carbon and Methane Emission Reductions (Arctic Council, 2015a). Under the Framework, the Arctic States committed themselves to taking national mitigation actions and to a collective goal to limit black carbon emissions to between 25% and 33% below 2013 levels by 2025 (Arctic Council, 2017). The Framework also aims to raise awareness of SLCPs among observer states whose emissions impact the Arctic and to welcome their participation in the implementation of the Framework, for instance in the development and improvement of emissions inventories. Indeed, seven observer states, including France, Poland, Japan, Korea, and India, along with the EU have voluntarily submitted their national reports on black carbon and methane emissions reductions (Arctic Council, 2015b). As of May 2019, China has not submitted its national report.

China's passive stance when it comes to participating in global cooperation on SLCPs is partly explained by the immaturity of its domestic discussion and policy approach to the subject. There has been limited attention on the part of policy-makers to methane and black carbon emissions, although there are signs of that changing. China's domestic climate policy has primarily focused on CO2, and this approach is reflected in its NDC to the UNFCCC, which includes only CO2 targets. In principle, as CO2, methane and black carbon are often co-emitted by the same sources, measures to reduce CO2 emissions will lead to reductions in SLCPs; however, the degree of such reductions is unclear. China's 13th FYP highlights the importance of tackling non-CO2 GHGs but specific policy measures are yet to be developed. On black carbon, the main challenge is insufficient data on emissions and limited understanding of their sources, impacts and mitigation pathways. There are no policies targeting black carbon emissions per se; however, black carbon is a component of PM2.5, which is covered by quantified air quality targets. Overall, synergies between climate and air quality goals have been receiving more and more recognition in recent policies, for instance in the new Three-year Action Plan for Winning the Blue Sky War (2018–2020); however, related actions are still short on detail.

5.8 China's Domestic Climate, Air Quality and Energy Policies

China is the largest energy consumer and largest emitter of CO2 emissions in the world; Between 1978–2014, China's total energy production increased annually by 4.83% and its total energy consumption by 5.58% (Zhang et al., 2017). Since the late 2000s, China has formulated various domestic policies to reduce the growth of greenhouse gas emissions. Its climate mitigation policies have mostly focused on CO2 emissions, as explained above. However, China has not indicated how much its emissions will grow before they peak. Between 2014 and 2016, it seemed that the peak had already been reached. In 2017, however, China's carbon dioxide emissions grew again to 9.1 Gt, which is a 1% increase from the 2014 emission level (IEA, 2018). Despite this negative trend towards peaking, in 2017 China's economy grew by 7%, which could have caused emissions to increase more, but thanks to the deployment of renewables and accelerating the switch from coal to gas, overall emissions grew only by 1.7% (ibid.). Though coal demand seemed to peak in China in 2013, the growing energy demand has increased energy-related emissions by raising the demand for oil and gas (ibid.). The scenarios of the possible peak in Chinese emissions vary considerably depending on GDP growth assumptions and the development of policy implementation, amongst other factors (den Elzen et al., 2016). All these scenarios agree that reaching the peak before 2030 would require China to implement new, more ambitious climate policies (ibid.)

Like elsewhere, energy policy plays an especially important role in China's climate policy. To decrease reliance on coal and other (imported) fossil fuels, China's 13th Five-Year Plan orders an increase in the proportion of non-fossil fuel energy to 15 percent of total energy consumption and a decrease in the consumption of coal to below 55 percent. In efforts to promote the production of non-fossil fuel energy, hydropower and nuclear energy are important. China is the biggest source of hydropower in the world, and the installed capacity of hydropower exceeded 100,000 megawatts in 2004, 200,000 megawatts in 2010 and 300,000 megawatts in 2015 (Li et al., 2018). Still, China's huge hydropower projects such as the Three Gorges Dam (*Sanxia Daba* 三峡大坝) have caused severe social and environmental damage on a local scale. In April 2019, there were 45 nuclear plants in operation, about 15 under construction, plus more about to start construction on mainland China, meaning that the number of nuclear power plants has increased more than tenfold since 2000 (World Nuclear Association, 2019).

Furthermore, China has invested heavily in renewable energy and is unquestionably the leader of renewable growth – Chinese renewables now account for 16.7% of the global total (IEA, 2017; Zhang et al., 2017). It is the world leader in solar energy by manufacturing about 60 percent of global solar cell capacity and by using about half of global solar power per year. In 2017 alone, China installed at least 50 gigawatts of solar power capacity, which means that it already exceeded the 13th Five-Year Plan's target of 105 gigawatts (Buckley, Nicholas & Brown, 2018). Solar power will affect China's energy mixture dramatically in the future (Zhang et al., 2017).

Moreover, China has abundant wind energy resources and it is able to develop wind power on a large scale (Sahu, 2018). In 2016, China represented 35 percent of global cumulative wind power installations. The objective of the

13th Five-Year Plan for wind power is at least 210 gigawatts, and China is expected to achieve the target in 2019 (IEA, 2017). China's Arctic white paper defines the region as a source of "clean" energy:

> The Arctic region boasts an abundance of geothermal, wind, and other clean energy resources. China will work with the Arctic States to strengthen clean energy cooperation, increase exchanges in respect of technology, personnel and experience in this field, explore the supply of clean energy and energy substitution, and pursue low-carbon development.
>
> State Council of the People's Republic of China, 2018

The government has made serious efforts to decrease energy demand by promoting energy conservation and energy efficiency. The growth of renewables is still challenged by the lack of adequate technology and innovation, as for instance a remarkable share of the renewable generation capacity is currently wasted because of insufficient electricity grids (Zhang et al., 2017). The government has closed ineffective power plants and small or outdated industrial factories, promoted the development of modern, energy-saving technology and products and has also established national standards to improve automotive fuel economy, for instance. The Chinese government also employs market approaches to reducing emissions although these are viewed as mostly complementary to traditional command-and-control policies (Duan, 2015). A national carbon market was launched in 2017 with the initial focus on the power sector (Pike & Zhe, 2017). The market was designed to be the world's largest emissions trading system, accounting for about 30% of national emissions with a coverage of 1700 power companies and three billion tonnes in total greenhouse gas emissions (ICAP, 2019).

Despite the growth of renewables and the launching of the carbon market, coal represents an important role in China's economic development and currently accounts for 70% of the primary supply (Zhang et al., 2017). Hence, the total energy mixture requires a greater change in order to be able to reach peak emissions by 2030.

The number of cars is expected to more than triple by the end of the next decade in China, which could cause severe air pollution locally and inhibit the state from reaching peak emissions by 2030 (Zheng et al., 2015). In order to boost the development of electric vehicles, the Chinese government has launched many plans and policies, the most influential being the announcement to ban the production and sale of fossil fuel cars in the near future. In 2018, China also issued the China VI Emission Standard (*Guoliu Paifang Biaozhun* 国六排放标准) that orders all new diesel heavy-duty vehicles introduced to the market after July 2021 to have diesel particulate filters. If efficiently implemented, this means that all new heavy duty vehicles in China will be soot-free after 2021 (Cui & Minjares, 2018).

Furthermore, the development of green technologies plays an important role in China's efforts towards the 'greenization' of its society as well as developing the country as a 'knowledge power'. China's participation in Arctic LNG projects supports these goals by increasing (technical) knowhow, and the government is making efforts to replace coal and oil with natural gas, a less environmentally-harmful fossil fuel. A good example of linkages between Chinese and Arctic partners in the area of renewable energy is a large-scale joint geothermal project between Sinopec (*Zhongguo Shihua* 中国石化) and the Arctic Green Energy Corporation, with the latter partner being focused on utilising Icelandic geothermal energy expertise internationally (Arctic Green Energy Corporation, n.d.).

Due to public discontent caused by 'Airpocalypses' (severe haze and smog episodes in many Chinese megacities), the Chinese government has taken the issue of air pollution seriously. For example, in 2014 it declared a 'War Against Pollution', a major campaign targeted at altering energy production and consumption (State Council of the People's Republic of China, 2014), whereas in 2016, the government issued a "Healthy China 2030 Plan", which underlined the efforts to tackle the health impacts of the country's environmental challenges (Central Committee of the People's Republic of China, 2016). For instance, the Air Pollution Action Plan (2013–2017) forced key regions to significantly decrease PM2.5 levels, resulting in dramatic improvements of air quality in Beijing (Zheng et al., 2018). Moreover, the 13th Five-Year Plan (2016–2020) (*Shisanwu Guihua* "十三五"规划) pledges to "ensure that the concentration of fine particulate matter is reduced by at least 25%" and sets key indicators for air quality: the percentage of days experiencing "good" or "excellent" air quality in cities at and above the prefectural level, with the target being 80 percent. The cities that fail to meet the target percentage should reduce PM2.5 intensity by 18 percent. These targets were reiterated by the Three-Year Action Plan (*Sannian Xingdong Jihua* 三年行动计划) for Winning the Blue Sky War (2018–2020) (*Daying Lantian Baoweizhan* 打赢蓝天保卫战), published in July 2018.

China's efforts to move away from coal-based energy production domestically stand somewhat in contrast to its investments abroad. A recent report by the Institute for Energy Economics and Financial Analysis highlighted that a significant percentage of Chinese offshore investments – including primary financing provided by China's state-controlled financial institutions – go into coal projects in South-East Asia, the Indian Ocean basin and in Africa in general. The report states that "Chinese finance continues to play a significant role in global coal development, supporting over one-quarter of all coal plants currently under development outside China" (Shearer, Brown & Buckley, 2019). This comes at a time when many other financial institutions, including the World Bank, multilateral development banks, or OECD countries' financial institutions, among others, are pulling out of such investments due to both climate and environmental goals as well as poor long-term economic assessments of coal energy projects. Chinese investments in coal projects lock in a significant amount of carbon emissions for 40 to 50 years. Simultaneously, Chinese companies are being provided with contracts related to construction and management of coal power plants, which partly explains the continued willingness of Chinese financial institutions to engage in such projects.

Other Chinese foreign investments can also be considered from the viewpoint of their long-term climate impacts, in particular in reference to resource extraction projects. The recent Global Resources Outlook (International Resource Panel, 2019) highlighted that around 17% of global emissions are related to the extraction and refining of non-energy resources before these are used in manufacturing. A further 17% of emissions are connected to the extraction and refining of fossil fuels, even before these are burned for energy. Therefore, Chinese mining projects abroad – as with all other foreign resource extraction financing – should be a part of the evaluation of the climate impacts of overseas investments.

5.9 Conclusions

China is the world's biggest CO2 emitter and a significant contributor of SLCPs and other pollutants that cause environmental harm in the Arctic and beyond. In addition, the ecological footprint of China's BRI continues to be large, especially due to investments in the coal industry. Hence, China plays a crucial role in climate and environmental protection in the High North. Given the state's 'highly insufficient' ambition to limit the global temperature rise to 2C or 1.5C (Climate Action Tracker, 2018), raising the level of ambition of China's climate mitigation pledged in the second NDC would clearly be necessary for a resilient future of the region (and the whole planet). However, China is not likely to commit itself to a very ambitious emissions reductions target in the future; such a commitment would cause a high risk of 'losing face' in the case of failing to reach the target. Yet climate change mitigation and adaptation are in China's domestic interest, as is engagement in global cooperation, and it will continue to play an active role in the implementation of the Paris Agreement. This is also important for preventing environment-related protests at home and, thus, maintaining social stability and the communist party's ruling position in the country.

Although it is unlikely that China can commit to a significantly more ambitious mitigation target in the near future, there are several openings that can be explored to strengthen the involvement of China in global cooperation on climate change. For instance, though China has made great progress with renewable energy production, the share of renewables in China's energy mix still remains below the world average because of the high energy demand. The increase in the share of renewable energy offers China a good option to enhance the ambition level of its climate policy in the near future. Another opportunity for China arises in emphasizing interconnections between air quality, public health and climate policies in such cases as through the focus on SLCPs. Opportunities should be explored to engage China more closely in the related work under the Arctic Council and the CCAC. Given that adequate scientific knowledge and emission inventories are a prerequisite to stronger actions, scientific cooperation also needs to be strengthened through both scientific organizations and science-policy bodies such as the IPCC. Moreover, the "greenification" of the BRI projects would be necessary in order to reach the goals of the Paris agreement. Chinese financing institutions should assess and be transparent about the climate and environmental footprint of the investments they support, in particular those related to resource extraction, fossil fuels and coal power.

Beyond climate change, it would be important to assess the Arctic footprint of China's domestic emissions of pollutants that are prone to long-range transport into the Arctic environment, including persistent organic pollutants and mercury. The understanding of such impacts should be taken into account in future policymaking aimed at emissions reductions. In this way, China could show that it carries out domestic environmental policies in a way that contributes to the sustainability principles stated in the country's Arctic white paper.

Literature

ACIA. (Arctic Climate Impact Assessment). (2004). *Impacts of a warming Arctic: Arctic climate impact assessment.* Retrieved August 14, 2019, from http://amap.no/acia/.

Albert, E., & Xu, B. (2016). China's environmental crisis. Backgrounder. *Council on Foreign Relations.* Retrieved August 14, 2019, from https://www.cfr.org/backgrounder/chinas-environmental-crisis.

Allen, S., Allen, D., Phoenix, V.R., Le Roux, G., Durántez Jiménez, P., Simonneau, A., … Galop, D. (2019). Atmospheric transport and deposition of microplastics in a remote mountain catchment. *Nature Geoscience*, 12, 339–344.

AMAP. (Arctic Monitoring and Assessment Programme). (2009a). *AMAP Assessment 2009: Human health in the Arctic.*

AMAP. (Arctic Monitoring and Assessment Programme). (2009b). *Arctic pollution 2009: Persistent organic pollutants, radioactivity, human health.* Oslo, Norway.

AMAP. (Arctic Monitoring and Assessment Programme). (2015). *Summary for policy-makers: Arctic climate issues 2015.* Oslo, Norway.

AMAP. (Arctic Monitoring and Assessment Programme). (2017). *Snow, water, ice and permafrost in the Arctic (SWIPA) 2017.* Retrieved August 14, 2019, from https://www.amap.no/documents/doc/Snow-Water-Ice-and-Permafrost-in-the-Arctic-SWIPA-2017/1610.

Arctic Council. (2015a). Annex 4. Iqaluit 2015 SAO Report to Ministers. Enhanced black carbon and methane emission reductions: An arctic council framework for action. Retrieved August 14, 2019, from https://oaarchive.arctic-council.org/handle/11374/610.

Arctic Council. (2015b). *Arctic Council observer states 2015 national reports on enhanced black carbon and methane emissions reductions.* Retrieved October 20, 2018, from https://oaarchive.arctic-council.org/handle/11374/1169.

Arctic Council. (2017, May 11). *Fairbanks Declaration.* Retrieved August 14, 2019, from https://oaarchive.arctic-council.org/handle/11374/1910.

Arctic Green Energy Corporation. (n.d.). *Arctic green energy corporation.* Retrieved November 9, 2018, from http://arcticgreencorp.com.

Babones, S. (2017). Red alert for China's pollution protesters. *AlJazeera.* Retrieved August 14, 2019, from https://www.aljazeera.com/indepth/opinion/2017/02/red-alert-china-pollution-protesters-170217111717375.html.

Blaxekjær L., & Nielsen, T. (2015). Mapping the narrative positions of new political groups under the UNFCCC. *Climate Policy, 15*(6), 751–766.

Bond, T.C., Doherty, S.J., Fahey, D.W., Forster, P.M., Berntsen, T., DeAngelo, B.J., … Zender, C.S. (2013, June 16). Bounding the role of black carbon in the climate system: A scientific assessment. *Journal of Geophysical Research: Atmospheres, 118*(11), 5380–5552.

Brunnée, J., & Streck, C. (2013). The UNFCCC as a negotiation forum: Towards common but more differentiated responsibilities. *Climate Policy, 13*(5), 589–607.

Buckley, T., Nicholas, S., & Brown, M. (2018). *China 2017 review. World's second-biggest economy continues to drive global trends in energy investment.* Cleveland, OH: Institute for Energy Economics and Financial Analysis.

CAN Europe. (2019, May 9). EU and China point to the UN Secretary General's climate summit as an important milestone. *Climate Action Network Europe.* Retrieved

August 14, 2019, from http://www.caneurope.org/publications/press-releases/1756-eu-and-china-point-to-the-un-secretary-general-s-climate-summit-as-an-important-milestone.

Cavalieri, S., McGlynn, E., Stoessel, S., Stuke, F., Bruckner, M., Polzin, C., ... Nilsson, A.E. (2010). *The EU Arctic footprint and policy assessment.* Report summary. Retrieved June 20, 2018, from https://arctic-footprint.eu/sites/default/files/AFPA_Summary_Report.pdf.

Central Committee of the People's Republic of China. (2016). 健康中国2030" 规划纲要 [Healthy China Plan 2030]. Retrieved August 14, 2019, from http://www.gov.cn/zhengce/2016-10/25/content_5124174.htm.

Chen, G. (2012). China's climate policy. *China Policy Series* (pp. 144). London, England: Routledge.

China's National Development and Reform Commission. (2015, June 30). *Enhanced action on climate change: China's intended nationally determined contributions.* Retrieved June 20, 2018, from http://www4.unfccc.int/ndcregistry/PublishedDocuments/China%20First/China%27s%20First%20NDC%20Submission.pdf.

China's NDC. (2015). Enhanced actions on climate change: China' s intended nationally determined contributions. Unofficial translation. Retrieved August 14, 2019, from https://www4.unfccc.int/sites/ndcstaging/PublishedDocuments/China%20First/China's%20First%20NDC%20Submission.pdf.

Christoff, P. (2010). Cold climate in Copenhagen: China and the United States at COP15. *Environmental Politics, 19*(4), 637–656.

Climate Action Tracker. (2018). *China.* Retrieved August 14, 2019 from https://climateactiontracker.org/countries/china/.

Cui, H., & Minjares, R. (2018). *China VI: A milestone for the world's transition to soot-free vehicles.* International Council on Clean Transportation. Retrieved November 20, 2018, from https://www.theicct.org/blog/staff/china-vi-milestone-world%E2%80%99s-transition-soot-free-vehicles.

Dalby, S. (2016). Interpreting climate geopolitics: Knowledge, power, and security. *Geopolitics, 21*(1), 236–241.

Duan, M. (2015). From carbon emissions trading pilots to national system: The road map for China. *Carbon & Climate Law Review, 9*(3), 231–242.

Durand, A. (2012). Common responsibility: The failure of Kyoto. *Harvard International Review, 34*(1), 8–9.

EDGAR. (2017). Fossil CO2 & GHG emissions of all world countries, 2017. Retrieved August 14, 2019, from https://edgar.jrc.ec.europa.eu/overview.php?v=CO2andGHG1970-2016&dst=CO2pc.

den Elzen, M., Feketeb, H., Höhneb, N., Admiraala, A., Forselld, N., Hof, A.F., ... van Soes, H. (2016). Greenhouse gas emissions from current and enhanced policies of China until 2030: Can emissions peak before 2030? *Energy Policy, 89*, 224–236.

EU-China Summit Joint Statement. (2019). Outcome statement. Retrieved August 14, 2019, from https://www.consilium.europa.eu/media/39020/euchina-joint-statement-9april2019.pdf.

Ge, M., Lebling, K., Levin, K., & J. Friedrich (2019). Tracking Progress of the 2020 Climate Turning Point. World Resources Institute. Working Paper. Retrieved August 14, 2019, from <https://wriorg.s3.amazonaws.com/s3fs-public/2020-turning-point-progress_2.pdf?_ga=2.77395413.191076062.1560251648-569271310.1556197040>.

Gu, Y., Wong, T.W., Law, C.K., Dong, G.H., Ho, K.F., Yang, Y., & Yim, S.H.L. (2018). Impacts of sectoral emissions in China and the implications: Air quality, public health, crop production, and economic costs. *Environmental Research Letters, 13*(8).

Hallding, K., Olsson, M., Atteridge, A., Vihma, A., Carson, M., & Román, M. (2011). Together alone: BASIC countries and the climate change conundrum. (pp. 123). Copenhagen, Denmark: Nordic Council of Ministers.

Harris, P.G. (2017). China's Paris pledge on climate change: inadequate and irresponsible. *Journal of Environmental Studies and Sciences, 7*(1), 102–107.

Hilton, I., & Kerr, O. (2017). The Paris agreement: China's 'New normal' role in international climate negotiations. *Climate Policy, 17*(1), 48–58.

Hu, J. (2007). Report at the 17th Party Congress of the Communist Party of China. Retrieved August 14, 2019, from http://www.chinadaily.com.cn/china/2007-10/24/content_6204564_14.htm.

Hurrell, A. (2012). Emerging powers, North-South relations and global climate politics. International Affairs, *88*(3).

ICAP. (2019). China National ETS. *International Carbon Action Partnership. ETS Detailed Information.* Retrieved August 14, 2019, from https://icapcarbonaction.com/en/?option=com_etsmap&task=export&format=pdf&layout=list&systems[]=55.

IEA. (International Energy Agency). (2011). *China's per capita emissions match the OECD average in 2035. World Energy Outlook 2011.* Retrieved August 14, 2019, from http://www.climate-change.ch/4DCGI/energie/detail_all?2146.

IEA. (International Energy Agency). (2017). *Renewables 2017: Analysis and Forecasts to 2022.* [Executive summary]. Retrieved February 3, 2018, from https://www.iea.org/Textbase/npsum/renew2017MRSsum.pdf.

IEA. (International Energy Agency). (2018). *Global Energy and Co2 Status Report 2017.* Retrieved August 14, 2019, from https://www.iea.org/publications/freepublications/publication/GECO2017.pdf.

International Resource Panel. (2019). *Global Resources Outlook 2019: Natural Resources for the Future We Want.* A Report of the International Resource Panel. Nairobi, Kenya: United Nations Environment Programme.

Intergovernmental Panel on Climate Change. (2014). Climate Change 2014 Synthesis Report. Retrieved August 14, 2019, from https://www.ipcc.ch/report/ar5/syr/.

Intergovernmental Panel on Climate Change. (2018). *Global Warming of 1.5°C. An IPCC Special Report on the impacts of global warming of 1.5°C above pre-industrial levels and related global greenhouse gas emission pathways, in the context of strengthening the global response to the threat of climate change, sustainable development, and efforts to eradicate poverty*. Geneva, Switzerland: World Meteorological Organization.

Kallio, J. (2016). *Towards China's Strategic Narrative. On the Construction of the Historico-Cultural Roots of China's National Identity in the Light of the Chinese Debate Relating to the Rise of Traditional Schools of Thought* [Doctoral dissertation]. Acta Universitatis Lapponiensis, 339.

Kemp, L. (2016). US-Proofing the Paris climate agreement. *Climate Policy*, 1–16.

Kennedy. (2012). Environmental protests in China on dramatic rise, expert says. *SCMP*. Retrieved August 14, 2019, from https://www.scmp.com/news/china/article/1072407/environmental-protests-china-rise-expert-says.

Koch, D., Bauer, S.E., Del Genio, A., Faluvegi, G., McConnell, J.R., Menon, S., … Shindell, D. (2011). Coupled aerosol-chemistry-climate twentieth-century transient model investigation: Trends in short-lived species and climate responses. *Journal of Climate, 24*, 2693–2714.

Kopra, S., & Kauppila, L. (2018). China, fundamental responsibility and Arctic regionalisation. Presented at the International Studies Association Annual Convention, San Francisco, CA.

Kopra, S. (2019). *China and great power responsibility for climate change.* London, England and New York, NY: Routledge.

Kopra, S. (2020). China, great power responsibility and Arctic security. In L. Heininen & H. Exner-Pirot (Eds), *Climate Change and Arctic Security. Searching for a Paradigm Shift*. London, England: Palgrave Pivot.

Korhola, E. (2014). The rise and fall of the Kyoto protocol: Climate change as a political process. [Academic Dissertation]. Retrieved August 14, 2019, from https://helda.helsinki.fi/bitstream/handle/10138/136507/Therisea.pdf.

Kyoto Protocol. (1998). Kyoto protocol to the United Nations framework convention on climate change. Text of Kyoto Protocol in English, United Nations.

Li, X., Chen, Z., Fan, X., & Cheng, Z. (2018). Hydropower development situation and prospects in China. *Renewable and Sustainable Energy Reviews, 82*, 232–239.

Liu, W., Xu, Z., & Yang, T. (2018). Health effects of air pollution in China. *International Journal of Environmental Research and Public Health, 15*(7), 1471. doi: 10.3390/ijerph15071471.

Napoli, C. (2012). Understanding Kyoto's failure. *SAIS Review, 32*(2), 183–196.

National Bureau of Statistics of China. (2019). Statistical communiqué of the People's Republic of China on the 2018 national economic and social development. Retrieved August 14, 2019, from http://www.stats.gov.cn/english/PressRelease/201902/t20190228_1651335.html.

National Development and Reform Commission. (2013). China's Policies and Actions for Addressing Climate Change. Policy Paper. The People's Republic of China. Retrieved August 14, 2019, from http://en.ndrc.gov.cn/newsrelease/201311/P020131108611533042884.pdf.

National Development and Reform Commission. (2014). U.S.-China joint statement on climate change. Retrieved August 14, 2019, from http://en.ndrc.gov.cn/newsrelease/201402/t20140218_579304.html.

National Development and Reform Commission. (2015). China-U.S. joint Presidential statement on climate change. Retrieved August 14, 2019, from http://en.ndrc.gov.cn/newsrelease/201511/t20151109_757957.html.

National Development and Reform Commission. (2016). China-U.S. joint Presidential statement on climate change. Retrieved August 14, 2019, from http://en.ndrc.gov.cn/newsrelease/201604/t20160401_797242.html.

Olivier, J.G.J., Janssens-Maenhout, G., Muntean, M., & Peters, J.A.H.W. (2015). Trends in global CO2 emissions: 2015 report. Retrieved August 14, 2019, from https://www.pbl.nl/sites/default/files/cms/publicaties/pbl-2015-trends-in-global-co2-emisions_2015-report_01803.pdf.

Olivier, J.G.J., & Peters, J.A.H.W. (2018). Trends in global CO2 and total greenhouse gas emissions: 2018 report. Retrieved August 14, 2019, from https://www.pbl.nl/sites/default/files/cms/publicaties/pbl-2018-trends-in-global-co2-and-total-greenhouse-gas-emissons-2018-report_3125.pdf.

PAME. (Protection of Arctic Marine Environment). (2019, May 7). Desktop study on marine litter including microplastics in the Arctic. Rovaniemi, Finland: 11th Arctic Council Ministerial Meeting.

Pan, Y. (2006). Evolution of an ecological civilization. *Beijing Review*, 45. Retrieved August 14, 2019, from http://www.bjreview.cn/EN/06-45-e/point-1.htm.

Paris Agreement. (2015). The English text of the Paris agreement. United Nations framework on climate change.

Pike, L., & Zhe, Y. (2017, December). Five things to know about China's national carbon market. Retrieved August 14, 2019, from https://www.chinadialogue.net/blog/10303-Five-things-to-know-about-China-s-national-carbon-market/en.

Rigby, M., Park, S., Saito, T., Western, L.M., Redington, A.L., Fang, X., … Young, D. (2019). Increase in CFC-11 emissions from eastern China based on atmospheric observations. *Nature*, 569, 546–550.

Roberts, D. (2016). A global roadmap for climate change action: From COP17 in Durban to COP21 in Paris. *South African Journal of Science*, *112*(5), 9.

Sahu, B.K. (2018). Wind energy developments and policies in China: A short review. *Renewable and Sustainable Energy Review*, *81*(1), 1393–1405.

Serreze, M.C. (2018). *Brave new Arctic. The untold story of the melting North.* Princeton, NJ: Princeton University Press.

Shearer, C., Brown, M., & Buckley, T. (2019, January). China at a crossroads: Continued support for coal power erodes country's clean energy leadership. *Institute for Energy Economics and Financial Analysis.* Retrieved August 14, 2019, from http://ieefa.org/wp-content/uploads/2019/01/China-at-a-Crossroads_January-2019.pdf.

State Council of the People's Republic of China. (2014, March 5). China declares war against pollution. Retrieved August 14, 2019, from http://english.gov.cn/premier/news/2014/08/23/content_281474983008687.htm.

State Council of the People's Republic of China. (2015, May 8) 国务院关于印发《中国制造2025》的通知 (Announcement on the publication of 'Made in China 2025' report). Retrieved August 14, 2019, from http://www.gov.cn/zhengce/content/2015-05/19/content_9784.htm.

State Council of the People's Republic of China. (2018). *China's Arctic Policy.* Retrieved August 14, 2019, from http://english.gov.cn/archive/white_paper/2018/01/26/content_281476026660336.htm.

State Council Information Office of the People's Republic of China. (2018). *China's Arctic policy.* Retrieved August 14, 2019, from http://english.gov.cn/archive/white_paper/2018/01/26/content_281476026660336.htm.

Syri, S., Vihma, A., Airaksinen, M., Hast A., Järvelä, M., Ollikainen, M., ... Soimakallio, S. (2013). *Suomen ilmastopaneeli: Kansainvälisen ja EU:n ilmastopolitiikan ajankohtaisia teemoja.* [Report] Suomen Ilmastopaneeli, Raportti (6th ed.). Retrieved August 14, 2019, from http://www.ilmastopaneeli.fi/uploads/selvitykset_lausunnot/ilmastopaneelin_raportti6. pdf.

The 18th National Congress of the Communist Party of China. (2012). Constitution of the CCP (revised). Retrieved August 14, 2019, from http://www.china.org.cn/chinese/18da/2012-11/19/content_27156212_2.htm.

Travnikov, O. (2005). Contribution of the intercontinental atmospheric transport to mercury pollution in the Northern Hemisphere. *Atmospheric Environment, 39*, 7541.

UNEP. (2015). The climate and environmental benefits of controlling SLCPs in P.R. China. Nairobi, Kenya: UN Environment Programme.

UNEP. (2018). Global Mercury Assessment 2018. Geneva, Switzerland: UN Environment Programme. Retrieved May 20, 2019, from https://wedocs.unep.org/bitstream/handle/20.500.11822/27579/GMA2018.pdf?sequence=1&isAllowed=y.

UNFCCC. (2019). United Nations framework convention on climate change. *United Nations.* Retrieved August 14, 2019, from http://unfccc.int/2860.php.

UNFCCC INDC Submission Portal. (2019). *INDC submissions of Parties. United Nations.* Retrieved August 14, 2019, from http://www4.unfccc.int/submissions/indc/Submission%20Pages/submissions.aspx.

U.S. Geological Survey. (2008). Circum-Arctic resource appraisal: Estimates of undiscovered oil and gas north of the Arctic Circle. *U.S. Department of the Interior.* Retrieved August 14, 2019, from http://pubs.usgs.gov/fs/2008/3049/fs2008-3049.pdf.

Wang, H-J., Chen, H-P., & Liu, J. (2015). Arctic sea ice decline intensified haze pollution in Eastern China. *Atmospheric and Oceanic Science Letters, 8*(1), 1–9.

Woon, C.Y. (2018). China's contingencies: Critical geopolitics, Chinese exceptionalism and the uses of history. *Geopolitics,* 23(1), 67–95.

World Bank. (2019). Data. Manufacturing, value added (% of GDP). Retrieved from https://data.worldbank.org/indicator/nv.ind.manf.zs.

World Nuclear Association. (2019). *Nuclear power in China.* Retrieved May 24, 2019, from http://www.world-nuclear.org/information-library/country-profiles/countries-a-f/china-nuclear-power.aspx.

Xi, J. (2017). *Secure a decisive victory in building a moderately prosperous society in all respects and strive for the great success of socialism with Chinese characteristics for a new era.* Retrieved August 14, 2019, from http://www.xinhuanet.com/english/download/Xi_Jinping's_report_at_19th_CPC_National_Congress.pdf.

Xinhua. (2019). Natural gas consumption surges in China in 2018. Retrieved August 14, 2019, from http://www.xinhuanet.com/english/2019-02/04/c_137798876.htm.

Yamineva, Y., & Kulovesi, K. (2018). Keeping the Arctic white: The legal and governance landscape for reducing short-lived climate pollutants in the Arctic region. *Transnational Environmental Law, 7*(2), 201–227.

Yamineva, Y., & Liu, Z. (2019). Cleaning the air, protecting the climate: Policy, legal and institutional nexus to reduce black carbon emissions in China. *Environmental Science and Policy,* 95 (May), 1–10.

Yao, B., Ross, K., Zhu, J., Igusky, K., Song, R., & Damassa, T. (2016). Opportunities to enhance non-carbon dioxide greenhouse gas mitigation in China. [Working Paper]. Washington, DC: World Resources Institute. Retrieved August 14, 2019, from http://www.wri.org/publication/greenhouse-gasmitigation-in-china.

Zhang, D., Wang, J., Yonggang, L., Si, Y., Huang, C., Yang, J., ... Li, W. (2017). Present situation and future prospect of renewable energy in China. *Renewable and Sustainable Energy Reviews,* 76, 865–871.

Zhang, M. (2015, October 17). China in the Arctic – Practices and policies, China country session. [Keynote speech]. Iceland, Reykjavik. Retrieved August 14, 2019, from https://www.fmprc.gov.cn/mfa_eng/wjbxw/t1306858.shtml.

Zheng, B., Zhang, Q., Borken-Kleefeld, J., Huo, H., Guan, D., Klimont, Z., ... He, K. (2015). How will greenhouse gas emissions from motor vehicles be constrained in China around 2030?. *Applied Energy, 156*, 230–240.

Zheng, B., Tong, D., Li, M., Liu, F., Hong, C., Geng, G., ... Zhang, Q. (2018). Trends in China's anthropogenic emissions since 2010 as the consequence of clean air actions. *Atmos. Chem. Phys., 18*, 14095–14111. doi.org/10.5194/acp-18-14095-2018.

CHAPTER 6

China's Economic Presence in the Arctic: Realities, Expectations and Concerns

Adam Stepien, Liisa Kauppila, Sanna Kopra, Juha Käpylä, Marc Lanteigne, Harri Mikkola and Matti Nojonen

6.1 Introduction

This chapter focuses on the economic presence of China in the Arctic regions. First, we consider the economic relations between China and the Nordic states, the North American Arctic and Russia, as Chinese activities have different characteristics in different parts of the Arctic. Second, the chapter looks at the key Arctic industries in which China's role is or may become relevant: shipping, oil and gas, minerals extraction, and tourism. Finally, we consider various concerns related to Chinese economic activities: the anxiety related to the economic and political influence gained through investments, the apprehension regarding the environment and social performance of Chinese actors, as well as doubts about the reliability of Chinese companies. Many of these concerns – related to a great extent to Chinese actions in regions such as Africa or South-East Asia – have not yet materialized in the Arctic context. Nonetheless, such anxieties have themselves led to the termination of some proposed investments. The chapter does not make predictions as to whether these concerns may materialize as the role of Chinese actors becomes more prominent in the future.

The definition of Arctic regions in the chapter is based on the Arctic Human Development Reports from 2004 and 2014. The overall economic relations pertaining to the Arctic states as a whole are not discussed. Certainly, economic activities are at the core of China's presence in the Arctic. Chinese companies are present in a number of sectors, in particular in resource extraction, transport and tourism. Chinese public and private investors are carefully monitoring various developments in the Arctic. The Chinese market is an important destination for a variety of Arctic products, including mineral resources, pulp from boreal forests and fish. Chinese companies are likely to be important users of future Arctic shipping lanes and China will be one of the main places either of origin or destination of products transported through the northern seaways. Including the Arctic maritime shipping lanes in the Belt and Road

© KONINKLIJKE BRILL NV, LEIDEN, 2020 | DOI:10.1163/9789004408425_007

Initiative is testament to these predictions. Companies based in Arctic regions buy from China, sell to China and establish production facilities in China. The numbers of Chinese tourists have also been on the increase across the circumpolar North.

Overall, Chinese economic actors are increasingly active in the region, especially in the Russian Arctic. However, these activities remain relatively limited, and many developments expected or proposed in the last few years, especially in the Nordic countries and North America, have not taken place or have been significantly delayed.

6.2 Arctic Economies

There is a wide difference between Arctic regions in terms or their economic profiles. In some parts of the North there is a high level of economic diversity. Yet, the northern regions of Arctic states share a number of characteristics relevant to the role that Chinese actors can take in economic developments and the perception of Chinese investments in the Arctic states. A cold and often harsh climate, low population density and sparsity, remoteness, great distances, a vulnerable environment and the presence of traditional subsistence livelihoods determine the conditions for economic activities. The subsistence economy, including traditional fishing, gathering, hunting or pastoralism, remains important across the circumpolar North, although the character and role of traditional activities differs greatly from region to region. Many Arctic residents combine cash employment or entrepreneurship with subsistence activities, which results in the emergence of mixed economic systems. The small size of settlements and, in some regions, relatively low income levels – when compared to other parts of the Arctic states – results in many inhabitants being dependent on public welfare. Many communities experience challenges such as high outmigration (especially of youth and women) and the resulting depopulation of the countryside, in addition to unemployment and high suicide rates. Moreover, the public sector, including administration, constitutes a major component of employment and regional GDP. The service sector is on the rise across the North, mirroring global trends.

Arctic regions are usually associated with resource extraction, including hydrocarbons, minerals, forestry and living resources. Primary sectors are indeed of central importance. The need to address the aforementioned socio-economic challenges often results in positive attitudes towards new extractive activities, which are seen as an opportunity to boost local economies. On the other hand, there are problematic issues related to the expansion of resource extraction, including environmental impacts, land-use tensions, interaction with other industries such as tourism, and impacts on traditional livelihoods. The fair distribution of benefits from extractives remains a challenge, and the legacy of past expropriation increases anxieties related to new projects. In some regions, there is an increasing realization that excessive dependence on extractive industries can be problematic in the long term, as these activities are prone to fluctuations in global resource prices. Efforts are therefore made to diversify northern economies and increase local processing of resources extracted in the North. These latter objectives are, however, challenging due to a lack of critical mass in terms of the number, diversity and concentration of companies and clients. Other barriers include the small size of northern markets, gaps in human capital, and difficulties in securing financing for new projects or for the expansion of activities (Glomsrød and Aslaksen, 2009; Huskey et al., 2014; Stepien et al., 2016 – several chapters in an edited volume).

Economic actors from outside the Arctic regions and the Arctic states play an increasingly important role in shaping economic developments in the North. Their presence may bring both benefits and problems, support or hinder desired development pathways, and bring wealth to some interest groups while adversely impacting others. There are fears that more wealth originating from resource extraction would flow out of the Arctic regions. China and Chinese economic operators are particular objects of these concerns due to the size of the Middle Kingdom's economy and the financial resources Chinese investors are capable of mobilizing. Additional factors are the high level of activity of Chinese actors around the globe and the controversies related to these activities in other parts of the world.

6.3 The Economic Dimension of China's Arctic Policy

For many analysts, the main purpose of an external economic actor's interest is profit-generation or, more generally, national welfare. For instance, Aki Tonami (2019) believes that the general goal of Chinese involvement in the Arctic – as an extrapolation of China's overall foreign policy – is to support internal economic development and prosperity, with other interests being of secondary nature. This appears to be confirmed by Rosen and Thuringen (2017: 61), who define the purpose of most Chinese investments in the regions as follows:

> As one of the last remaining sources of unexploited resources, the Arctic is an attractive source of the raw materials that China needs to fuel its

> development. Beyond resources, the Arctic is the potential launching pad for Chinese state owned enterprises (SOEs) seeking profit and market dominance. The Arctic is also a location where many Chinese laborers could find employment and possibly residence. For China, the Arctic is a vast landscape of opportunity.

In the White Paper on China's Arctic Policy from January 2018, Beijing sought to explain the role of economic interests in Chinese engagement in the Arctic, including in the areas of energy, resources and shipping, as well as bilateral cooperation with the 'Arctic Eight' through various routes. Through 2017 and 2018, the Northern Sea Route was included in the Belt and Road Initiative. What remains unclear, however, is what sort of new projects beyond existing ones such as Yamal LNG might form a part of this new wing of the Belt and Road Initiative (BRI), and which Arctic countries might be the beneficiaries of Chinese BRI investment.

Many Arctic economic and political decision-makers perceive China's increasing presence and interest in the region as an opportunity for regional economic growth, new or better jobs and additional income for local and regional budgets, supporting the mitigation of numerous socio-economic challenges that trouble sparsely-populated Arctic regions. A number of investment gaps, challenges and obstacles have been identified for Arctic regions (for the European Arctic, see e.g. Arctic Investment Platform 2019: 13). China could, in principle, contribute to addressing these gaps by providing additional sources of financing for developments in the Arctic regions, but also via increased demand for Arctic resources and products, affecting prices and levels of production, offering lower costs for construction, etc. Other stakeholders, however, view the Chinese economic presence with a degree of anxiety. Various concerns are discussed at the end of this chapter.

6.4 Chinese Investments Overseas in General

The expansion of the Chinese economy has been one of the most important global socio-economic developments in the past few decades. The spectacular growth has not only lifted more than 600 million people out of poverty and created a large middle class, but it has also turned China into the world's de facto manufacturing house.

China is deeply integrated into the world economy. After the U.S., the country is the second-largest recipient of foreign direct investments (FDI) in the world. However, Chinese Outward Direct Investment (ODI) has also increased dramatically. In 2015, Chinese ODI surpassed the incoming FDI for the first time. In 2016, China became the second-largest ODI actor in the world, a position that it has since held (UNCTAD website).

The Chinese government has provided long-standing support for outbound investments. In order to facilitate overseas activities, the banking sector was reformed and a number of financial institutions were established. Among these are the Silk Road Fund and Asia Infrastructure Bank, which actively provide finance for Chinese companies overseas. Two Chinese policy banks – China Export and Import Bank and China Development Bank – and their provincial subsidiaries have become significant global financial institutions that offer funding for Chinese companies investing abroad.

The history of Chinese ODI policies can be divided into four periods. The first stage covers the period between 1982 and 1991, during which the ODI was strictly controlled and around 100 companies managed to acquire approval for overseas activities. The country did not adopt its first ODI regulations until 1984. In 1992, the reform wing of the Communist party won the intra-party power struggle, which launched the second phase of Chinese ODI development. Beijing cut some of the ODI red-tape and the limited restrictions on access to foreign exchange. However, the Chinese ODI remained rather modest. In 1999, China ranked only 23rd in the world with a stock of US$27 billion for ODI, representing a mere 0.4 percent of the global total.

In 2001, China joined the World Trade Organization. That resulted in the gradual loosening of ODI regulations and improved access to capital. What followed was a rapid growth of ODI from 2004 onwards. Chinese companies were particularly eager to grasp the investment opportunities in the aftermath of the global economic crisis in 2008. In 2008, the value of global FDI fell by 14 percent, while simultaneously the Chinese ODI more than doubled to US$60 billion. This growth accelerated rapidly until 2017, when the central government issued "Guiding Opinions on Further Guiding and Regulating Outbound Investment" (Guiding Opinions) (*Guanyu Jinyibu Yindao he Guifan Jingwai Touzi Fangxiang de Zhidao Yijian* 关于进一步引导和规范境外投资方向的指导意见) (NDRC, 2017). The adoption of this legally-binding document marks the beginning of the current period in Chinese ODI, characterized by the attempt to mainstream investments and by an increased focus on the Belt and Road Initiative (BRI). Due to the new regulations, China's ODI saw a dramatic drop from US$196 billion in 2016 to US$158 billion in 2017, and further to US$130 billion in 2018 (UNCTAD Fact sheets, n.d.).

The Guiding Opinions is a set of regulations that provides a list of restricted or prohibited illegal and "irrational" investments such as sport clubs, culture and entertainment business. It also lists priority projects related to the BRI. The Guiding Opinions highlight the following sectors:

- Infrastructure projects related to the construction of the BRI, including the surrounding and interconnecting infrastructure.
- Investments facilitating the utilization of China's industrial capacity and export of China's high quality equipment and technology standards.
- High-tech, advanced manufacturing enterprises, and overseas research and development (R&D) centers.
- Oil, gas, mineral, and energy resource projects that are based on a careful assessment of economic benefits and national interests.
- Industries such as agriculture, forestry, animal husbandry, side-line production, and fishery.
- Investments in service sectors such as commerce, culture, and logistics, as well as investments that help qualified Chinese financial institutions to establish offshore branches and service networks.

The Guiding Opinions document was issued at the central government level by four ministry level units: the National Development and Reform Commission (NDRC) (*Guojia Fazhan he Gaige Weiyuanhui* 国家发展和改革委员会), the Ministry of Commerce (MOFCOM), the People's Bank of China, and the Ministry of Foreign Affairs. These four ministry-level bodies have subsidiaries at each provincial, prefecture and county level. These subsidiaries are the actual decision-making entities in the bureaucratic application process that companies have to get through before they acquire the final approval for their planned ODI operations. The implementation of the Guiding Opinions at the lower levels will determine the direction of the Chinese ODI and will likely have a significant influence on the success of the BRI. Among the challenges is the availability and reliability of ODI statistics. There is no centralized process or a responsible institution that approves the BRI projects, so there is no clear understanding of the actual value of BRI projects that are carried out in all corners of the world. Furthermore, the performance of local level bureaucrats, party cadres and businesses is currently measured by their ability to deliver BRI projects. As a result, local level actors eagerly label all possible international-bound projects as components of the BRI. This has induced some local actors to even fabricate their BRI activities. One recent example of such dynamics was the case of the China Railway Corporation, which was reported to have sent empty railway cargo-cars to Europe in order to present a BRI success story (Leng, 2019, August 20).

Notwithstanding the aforementioned bureaucratic challenges and recent decrease in the value of Chinese ODI, and despite China being the second largest ODI actor, there is still much untapped potential for growth. Measured in ODI stock as a percentage of GDP, the proportion for China was at 14.5% in 2018. Keeping in mind that China is the world's second-largest economy with

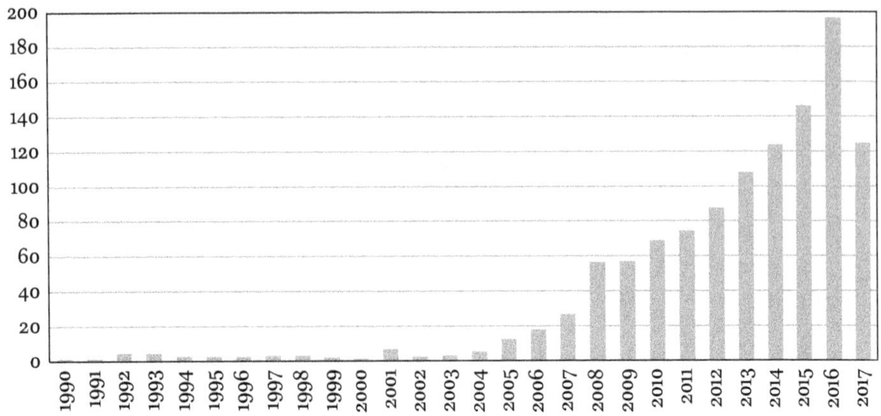

FIGURE 6.1 Mainland China's ODI 1990–2017
SOURCE: UNCTAD'S FDI DATABASE

the biggest foreign exchange reserves, the country is lagging far behind the U.S. (31.6%), Japan (33.5%), Germany (41.1%) and the UK (60%) (UNCTAD Fact Sheets, n.d.) in terms of the value of the ODI as a percentage of the GDP. While the economic structures and histories of these economies vary significantly, China has room for growth in its outbound investments. Beijing can therefore be expected to continue encouraging the Chinese economy to internationalize – including via activities in the Arctic, as was clearly confirmed in the 2018 White Paper (PRC State Council, 2018).

6.5 China's Economic Relations with Arctic States

There are substantial differences in regards to governance systems and economic characteristics between the Arctic regions of Russia, the Nordics and North America. Correspondingly, the presence of China, the type of investments and the nature of economic relations will differ as we move across the circumpolar North. The focus in this chapter is on Chinese economic activities in circumpolar regions of the eight Arctic states. Nonetheless, in order to provide some background, we present below the national trade (figures 6.2–6.4) – which show trade balance as well as the relative role of the national trade with China from the perspective of the Arctic states' overall international trade volumes as well as within the Chinese overall trade, which suggests the level of respective importance of these markets for one another – and offshore direct investments (ODI) statistics (see figure 6.5).

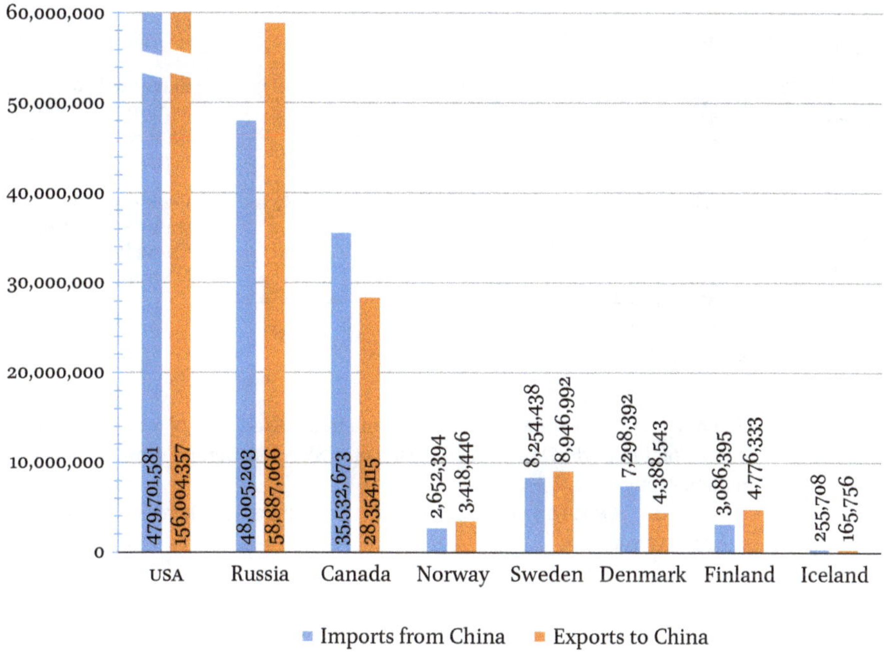

FIGURE 6.2 Arctic states' imports from and exports to China. Data for 2018 in US$thousands. Compilation by Adam Stepien, Arctic Centre
SOURCE: INTERNATIONAL TRADE CENTRE STATISTICS AT HTTPS://WWW.TRADEMAP.ORG

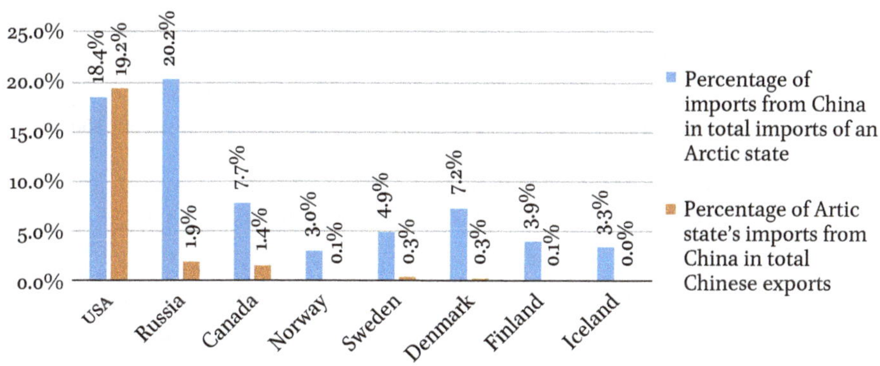

FIGURE 6.3 Percentage of Arctic states' imports from China in the Arctic states' total imports and China's total exports. Data for 2018 based on US$ value. Compilation by Adam Stepien, Arctic Centre
SOURCE: INTERNATIONAL TRADE CENTRE STATISTICS AT HTTPS://WWW.TRADEMAP.ORG

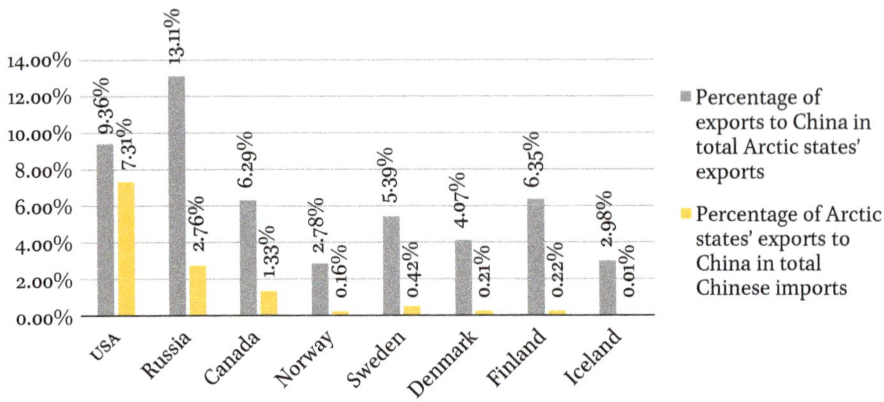

FIGURE 6.4 Percentage of Arctic states' exports to China in the Arctic states' total exports and China's total imports. Data for 2018 based on US$ value. Compilation by Adam Stepien, Arctic Centre
SOURCE: INTERNATIONAL TRADE CENTRE STATISTICS AT HTTPS://WWW.TRADEMAP.ORG

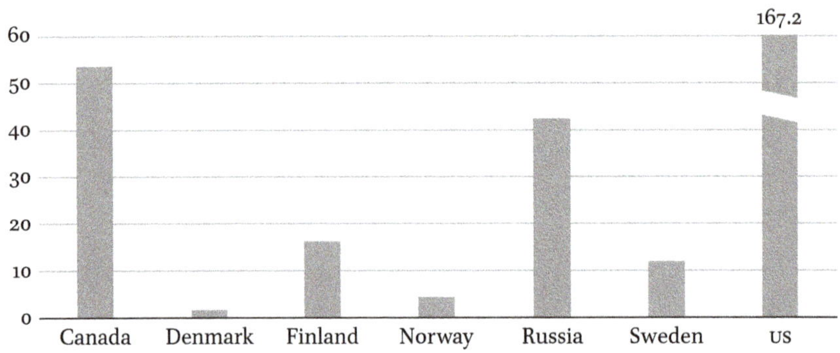

FIGURE 6.5 Chinese (mainland) offshore direct investment towards (whole) Arctic states, 2009–2018 in US$bln. No data for Iceland
SOURCE: AMERICAN ENTERPRISE INSTITUTE AT HTTPS://WWW.AEI.ORG/CHINA-GLOBAL-INVESTMENT-TRACKER/, DATA RETRIEVED 8 OCTOBER 2019

6.5.1 *Russia as a Key Partner in the Arctic*

Among Arctic states, Russia has had the greatest number of Chinese economic cooperation initiatives located above the Arctic Circle. After the fall of the Soviet Union, Chinese-Russian relations went through upturn and downturn phases and were characterized by a degree of distrust, especially on the Russian side. In resource exports, Russia was focused on Europe, and it did not take the potential of the Chinese energy market seriously. Until 2013/2014, there were informal barriers for Chinese investments and market access in different sectors, including infrastructure, resources and cars. The Russian government feared that China could become a senior partner in bilateral relations – Russia becoming a source of raw materials and a market for Chinese goods – and that China would advance strategic interests via economic presence. Nonetheless, already by that time, China was Russia's second-largest trading partner after the European Union (Gabuev, 2015).

The gradual intensification of economic relations started from 2012, when the Putin government began a policy of 'turning to the East' after the Asia-Pacific Economic Cooperation summit in Vladivostok (APEC summit, *Yatai Jingji Hezuo Zuzhi* 亚太经济合作组织). This process was accelerated in the wake of the 2014 Crimea/Donbas crisis and subsequent U.S. and Western European sanctions, which left China as the primary partner for numerous Russian energy and infrastructure initiatives that involved the Siberian and Russian Far Eastern regions. Until a few years prior, activities in the Russian North and the Far East were not an economic priority for China, with the exception of Chinese provinces bordering Russia, such as Heilongjiang, which engaged in stronger cooperation. In April 2014, then-Vice-Premier Wang Yang (汪洋) suggested during a meeting in Vladivostok that the Russian Far East was becoming increasingly attractive to Chinese business interests. Wang was also a keynote attendee at the fourth annual Arctic forum at Arkhangelsk in March 2017, where he discussed various potential Sino-Russian cooperation projects taking place in the Arctic or being of potential relevance for the Arctic.

Energy cooperation has dominated Beijing's interests in the Russian Arctic, including a July 2013 agreement between the China National Petroleum Corporation (CNPC)(*Zhongguo Shiyou Tianranqi Jituan Gongsi* 中国石油天然气集团公司) and Rosneft (worth approximately US$270 billion) to supply Russian petroleum for a twenty-five year period. An even more ambitious natural gas partnership, worth an estimated US$400 billion, was struck between the CNPC and Gazprom. As a result, the CNPC (as well as China's Silk Road Fund) are major stakeholders in the Yamal liquefied natural gas (LNG) project in Siberia. The project, overseen by Russia's Novatek, officially came online in December 2017. Its second phase became operational in August 2018. Novatek delivered the first shipment of LNG to China via the Northern Sea Route (NSR), with the CNPC seeking to commence exports of three million tonnes of gas out of Yamal from 2019. China's activities in regards to Arctic shipping, with a focus on the Northern Sea Route, are discussed in Section 6.6. below.

6.5.2 *Nordic States: Investments and Trade*

Three of the Nordic states – Finland, Sweden and Denmark – are members of the European Union (EU) (although EU legislation and trade agreements do not apply to Greenland and the Faroe Islands). The EU has not commenced free trade agreement (FTA) negotiations with China, as the Union believes that there are still barriers for such an agreement on the Chinese side, including a lack of transparency, industrial policies discriminating against foreign companies, strong governmental intervention in the economy and poor protection and enforcement of intellectual property rights (European Commission website, n.d.). Despite recent progress in regard to industrial subsidies (Blenkinsop and Emmott, 2019, April 9), the chances of adopting a comprehensive trade agreement remain slim. However, in 2013, the two parties started negotiations on an agreement on investments. While these negotiations are ongoing, the concerns about Chinese investments in Europe are on the rise. This led to the cancelation of several Chinese investment projects, including a port in southern Sweden (Suokas, 2018, January 31). The anxieties also resulted in the adoption of legislation (Regulation (EU) 2019/452) that gives the European Commission power to screen major investments of strategic importance for the whole EU (European Commission, 2019, April 10).

After trying unsuccessfully to commence formal free trade talks with the EU, China sought to engage non-EU European economies in bilateral trade talks. The best candidates were the European Free Trade Area (EFTA) countries: Iceland, Liechtenstein, Norway, and Switzerland. Since China was unsure about negotiating with all four EFTA members at once, Beijing decided to commence talks with one state at a time. The asymmetry between China and individual EFTA countries might make it an attractive choice for Beijing to engage these small countries separately. Iceland was the first Arctic state to enter an advanced negotiation phase (Lanteigne, 2010). There was a pause in the talks due to Iceland's application to join the EU (within which the country would not be able to negotiate a separate FTA), and at the same time Iceland was attempting to recover from the post-2008 banking crisis (*kreppa*). By the time the FTA meetings resumed in 2012, Iceland was seen by China as an essential partner in Beijing's Arctic policy development. The free trade agreement was finalised in 2013, with Sino-Icelandic relations remaining strong ever since. They were further augmented by tourism and other services. China is Iceland's largest trading partner in the Asia-Pacific, and there has been discussion about possible Chinese investment in Icelandic ports, including Akureyri and Finnafjörður (Kynge, 2017). Switzerland (and by extension Liechtenstein via a customs union between the two countries) also signed an FTA with China in 2013 (Lanteigne, 2014; Switzerland Federal Department of Foreign Affairs, 2018).

The situation proved more complicated for Norway. Although the initial round of talks proved successful, further negotiations were abruptly severed by Beijing in the wake of the decision by the Norwegian Nobel Committee to award the 2010 Peace Prize to Chinese dissident Liu Xiaobo (刘晓波). Anger at this perceived "insult to the Chinese nation" resulted in a severing of high-level ties, including any further economic talks, until an agreement to restore relations was struck in December 2016. In December 2016, both governments released a document that confirmed the *normalization* of relations, including a promise by the Norwegian government to "do its best to avoid any future damage to bilateral relations" (*Statement…*, 2016). The resolution was welcomed by the Norwegian government but some experts assessed (and criticized) the agreement as an example of a small country submitting to Beijing's pressure (ChinaFile, 2016, December 21).

However, even during the six-year diplomatic freeze between China and Norway, there were still contacts between the two states in multilateral forums, including in the Arctic context, via conferences such as the Arctic Frontiers conference in Tromsø and the China-Nordic Arctic Research Center (CNARC) (*Zhongguo Beiou Beiji Yanjiu Zhongxin* 中国-北欧北极研究中心), based in Shanghai. Norway also chose not to block Beijing's application to become an Observer in the Arctic Council in 2013, affirming that Arctic cooperation would be, to a degree, shielded from the poor bilateral relations. In March 2015, Beijing did not prevent Norway from becoming a member in the Asian Infrastructure Investment Bank (AIIB) (*Yazhou Jichu Sheshi Touzi Yinhang* 亚洲基础设施投资银行), which China oversees (Government of Norway, 2015). At present, all Arctic states, with the exception of the United States, have shares in the AIIB.

With regard to economic relations, Chinese-Norwegian trade actually grew during the period of diplomatic freeze, although there were some problematic issues such as periodic stoppages of Norwegian salmon imports to China on the pretext of health concerns. Norwegian energy and shipping interests found it difficult to discuss new partnerships with their Chinese counterparts. With full diplomatic relations restored, Norwegian companies today are eager to make up for lost time, especially given the growing interest in China to develop Arctic shipping. One example of a possible Chinese investment is the option of financing port facilities in the Norwegian city of Kirkenes (Breum, 2018).

The Sino-Norwegian FTA negotiations have not been finalized at the time of completing this book. However, the outlook for a final agreement appears promising. At a conference in Singapore in August 2018, Chinese Foreign Minister Wang Yi (王毅) suggested to his counterpart, Ine Eriksen Søreide, that the final stages of the trade talks should be accelerated (Reuters, 2018, August 2). Several Norwegian sectors, especially the fishing and shipping industries, have been interested in a deepened trade relationship with Beijing.

Greenland, a country within the Kingdom of Denmark, has also been on China's economic radar. A controversial issue in the recent history of relations between China and Denmark was the expansion of Greenland's airports at Nuuk, the capital, as well as Ilulissat and Qaqortoq. The airport expansion project ran into political headwind when it was revealed that a Chinese firm, the

China Communications Construction Company (CCCC) (*Zhongguo Jiaotong Jianshe Youxiangongsi* 中国交通建设有限公司) was interested in bidding on the contract to overhaul and renovate the airports. This caused concerns in Copenhagen about economic sovereignty and raised security questions (including the relations with the U.S. and the possibility of double-use infrastructure). Analysts were alarmed with the excessive increase in Chinese influence and the possibility of Greenland being caught in a debt trap (McGwin, 2018). In September 2018, the Danish government offered to underwrite the airport project, and the U.S. government also offered, during the same month, to offer financial support for Greenland infrastructure (McPherson, 2018; Ministry of Foreign Affairs Denmark, 2018; Lim, 2018). These moves appeared to be designed to prevent the CCCC bid from going forward, a prospect that was worrisome to both Denmark and the United States.

6.5.3 *North American Arctic: Politicized Resources*

China is, the key trade and investment partner for both Canada and the U.S. However, the Chinese presence in Alaska and in the Canadian Arctic territories has been limited so far. There are Chinese investment plans related to oil and gas and raw materials in Alaska and northern Canada, but they have been shelved at this point.

In general, China is the main international trade partner for Alaska, with the state's exports reaching almost USD1.2bln in 2016 (Lee Falsey, 2017, April 8). In April 2017, following a meeting with the U.S. president, Xi Jinping paid a visit to Alaska. The stopover underlined the importance of the Arctic and the investment interest in the Alaskan LNG project that was to supply the Chinese energy market. However, the current Chinese-U.S. trade war led to the suspension of that project (as of September 2019). In a speech given in Rovaniemi in May 2019 before the Arctic Council Ministerial Meeting, the U.S. Secretary of State strongly warned against Chinese investments in the Arctic, even if underlining that "transparent" investments are welcome (Department of State, 2019, May 6). This indicates that the above-mentioned Alaskan projects may have little support in Washington.

In Canada, Chinese investors, originally interested in more strongly entering mineral extraction – a major sector of Canadian economy – appeared to be partly discouraged by the challenging procedures related to obtaining local consent and permitting processes. These developments are discussed in greater detail in the following sections dedicated to the extraction of hydrocarbons and minerals (Sections 6.7. and 6.8.). Overall, Canadian-Chinese relations have significantly worsened following the arrest of Meng Wanzhou, a Huawei executive (e.g., Zhou, 2019, August 3). However, it is yet to be seen whether this will have long-term implications for economic relations between the two countries.

6.6 Maritime Transport and Shipbuilding

In its policy statement from January 2018, the Chinese government puts emphasis on Arctic shipping as a key element of its Arctic engagement. China wishes "to work with all parties to build a 'Polar Silk Road' through developing the Arctic shipping routes" (PRC State Council, 2018). The Northern Sea Route (NSR) (or, more broadly, the Northeast Passage (NEP)),[1] which follows the coast of Siberia, is not mentioned in the document. However, due to more favourable (as compared to other Arctic waters) navigational and ice conditions as well as China's exchanges with Russia before 2018, it is the use and development of the NSR that is of greatest interest. That was clearly confirmed later in 2018, when a credit line for Chinese investments in Russia included the NSR as a priority in the context of the BRI (Moe and Stokke, 2018).

The Chinese government believes that "[t]he utilisation of sea routes and the development of resources in the Arctic may have a huge impact on the energy strategy and economic development of China". On the other hand, China's "capital, technology, market, knowledge and experience is expected to play a major role in expanding the network of shipping routes in the Arctic" (PRC State Council, 2018). While perhaps overly optimistic, these statements argue that China is important for Arctic shipping just as Arctic maritime transport should be important for China. What is, then, the actual role of Chinese actors in Arctic shipping against the background of the current status of maritime transport in northern waters? As is often in the case of Arctic economic developments, high future expectations contrast with a very limited level of current activities, both in regard to the overall assessment of the situation and specifically for Chinese activities.

---

1 The Northern Sea Route constitutes the part of the Northeast Passage between the Kara Gate Strait and the Bering Strait, while the Northeast passage includes the Bering Sea and the Barents Sea, and it connects Asia and Europe. Russia considers the straits through which the NSR passes (between the coast of Siberia and Russian archipelagos) close to the Siberian coast to constitute internal waters, while the whole area within Russia's Exclusive Economic Zone is subject to legislation (2012) based on Art.234 of the UN Convention on the Law of the Sea. Art.234 allows coastal states to adopt additional non-discriminatory measures for navigation in the ice-covered waters within their EEZ (normally, shipping in exclusive economic zones enjoys almost full freedom of navigation).

Elevated global interest in Arctic shipping goes back to the mid-2000s, following the broader realization that the climate change-driven diminishing of the Arctic Ocean ice cover may lead to increased maritime traffic in the Arctic and in particular to the opening of new shipping lanes between Europe and Asia (Zellen, 2009). The NEP/NSR, the Northwest Passage, which crosses the Canadian Arctic archipelago, and the Polar Route are distinguished as three potential future routes. The latter, which crosses the Central Arctic Ocean, is projected to be traversable only in the very distant future. The navigation on the North American side of the Arctic Ocean is difficult due to the prevalence of thick, multiyear ice and the particularly high variability of ice conditions from year to year. In contrast, the NSR enjoys a relatively long – and, given the effect of climate change, most likely an increasingly longer – navigational season. The waters of the NSR are characterized by the dominance of thinner and weaker one-year ice. The route was used extensively by the Soviet Union until the end of the 1980s. Since the 2000s, it has been promoted by Russia as an international shipping route (Sander et al., 2016).

While there was an expectation of rapid expansion of maritime activity, the developments thus far present a less optimistic and certainly more complex picture. As early as in the 2009 Arctic Marine Shipping Assessment (AMSA), it was outlined that Arctic shipping is likely to remain dominated by destinational shipping[2] for many decades to come. This contrasts with the perception that the Arctic waters would soon become a major transit link between Europe and Asia. As predicted by AMSA, destinational shipping has significantly increased, owing to Russian Arctic resource extraction projects (predominantly onshore) coming online. Recently, the current overall shipping volumes along the NSR have exceeded those at the end of the Soviet era. For these types of shipping, there are, in fact, few or no reasonable alternatives to the NSR. Growing shipping volumes in the past few years confirm this evaluation. In contrast, transit shipping volumes are negligible and, especially in regard to container transport, remain a future prospect. Chinese actors are involved both in Arctic destinational shipping as well as in testing Arctic routes for transit. Chinese maritime traffic related to scientific research supplements these activities (Moe and Stokke, 2019).

The advantages of Arctic shipping routes include decreased shipping distance and, consequently, potentially lower carbon emissions. The NSR in particular can be seen as an alternative or supplementary route if disruptions along the southern routes occur, for instance due to conflicts, blockades or

2 Destinational comprises primarily the exports of Arctic resources, cruise tourism, and voyages related to the development of Arctic construction projects.

piracy around the Malacca Strait, around the Horn of Africa or any problems with the operation of the Suez Canal. However, there are numerous challenges for Arctic maritime navigation that hinder the emergence of the NSR as a significant component of the global transport network. The navigational conditions in Arctic waters will remain difficult, even with less ice and a longer shipping season. Vessels continue to face numerous risks, a concern exacerbated by insufficient search and rescue infrastructure. Many parts of the Arctic also have sparse refueling facilities. In winter, ice, darkness and severe weather conditions will continue to constitute risk factors, even if the ice is thinner and its extent smaller. High year-to-year variability presents challenges for shipping companies' logistical planning, as it is difficult to schedule shipments many months in advance. Moreover, while the distances are shorter than traditional routes, this does not necessarily translate to significant time or cost savings. As ships operate at slower speeds in Arctic waters, travel times are not as short as they would be in ice-free waters. The costs may be inflated by higher fuel expenses, the need to use expensive purpose-designed vessels, as well as fees imposed by Russian authorities in its exclusive economic zone, including for icebreaker assistance. Costs may be further elevated by Polar Code requirements for construction, equipment, the environmental performance of vessels, and crew training. The lack of ports of call for container ships between the Asian and European ports – due to sparse population and limited economic activity in these regions in sectors other than resource extraction – means that container transport would be characterized by point-to-point operations, restricting options for versatility. This constitutes a major difference compared to traditional southern shipping routes, which benefit from complex systems of logistics, cargo diversity and developed infrastructure. In general, the profitability threshold for Arctic shipping – if non-Polar alternatives are available – is high (see e.g., Sander et al., 2016, Humpert, 2014; Sun, 2018). As a result, transit voyages are few and the majority of transits actually involve vessels without any cargo (Kirkenes Nearingshage, 2018: 21–22).

There are additional challenges for container transits as compared to bulk transport transits. The first container did not cross the NSR until the summer of 2018, carrying Korean electronics and Russian fish products (Jacobsen, 2018, August 24). Nonetheless, future predictions are difficult, as the changes in Arctic climate that would allow a significant opening of Arctic Ocean sea lanes – including for low-class vessels or non-Arctic ships – would mean that the changes in global climate are likely to have impacts on all economies around the world. These changes are difficult to model, thus making long-term predictions highly challenging.

Another challenge is the unclear attitude of Russia towards the use of the NSR, at the same time promoting the NSR and introducing restrictions. On the one hand, the Russian government has been promoting the NSR as an international shipping route, with the hope that this would contribute to the development of the Russian North and partly pay for the infrastructure needed to maintain the safety of navigation. In 2012, the bureaucratic procedures for transit voyages were streamlined (Sanders et al., 2016). Recently, parts of the area governed by the law on the NSR have been opened for vessels with lower ice classes (Humpert, 2018, November 26). On the other hand, in the past few years, Russian authorities have banned the use of foreign-built and foreign-registered vessels from exporting Russian hydrocarbons extracted in the Arctic (albeit with exceptions). Furthermore, a new set of stricter rules have been reportedly introduced for vessels entering the Russian ice-covered EEZ. Rhetorically, Russian policy-makers increasingly underline the need for greater self-sufficiency in terms of retaining or acquiring maritime shipping capabilities to transport Russian resources and to develop projects in the Russian Arctic. The governance of the NSR has been transferred to Rosatom, which operates Russia's nuclear icebreakers, underlining the key role of mandatory icebreaker assistance in the management of the Arctic shipping route (Staalesen, 2019, January 2; Humpert, 2019, March 21).

It appears that Chinese experts are aware of the limitations and challenges related to Arctic shipping and they have limited trust in Russian openness to Chinese navigation along the route (Sun, 2018b). At the same time, container shipping flows to and from China may actually be expected to shift further southwards rather than northwards, with China's increasing economic (including resource) relations with Africa and South-East Asia and economic growth in these regions (Erokhin, Tianming & Xinhua, 2018).

After the BRI was formalized by the Xi Jinping government in 2013, there was speculation as to whether the Arctic would form a part of the growing economic links that China was seeking to create between itself and key markets in Africa, Europe and Eurasia. Although the initial stance by Beijing was that although the Arctic, and especially the NSR, was of interest to China for trade in the coming decades, it was not a priority for the BRI. Nonetheless, signs began to appear in 2017 that the official linkage between the Arctic and the BRI would eventually be established. For example, one prominent Beijing academic noted in a report by the *South China Morning Post* in May 2017 that the time had come to add a 'Circle' to the Belt and Road idea (Huang, 2017), and also in the same year, talk began to take shape about potential China-supported port projects in Russia (such as Arkhangelsk) as well as in Iceland and Norway.

The first official government confirmation that Arctic waters would be incorporated into the BRI appeared within a paper co-published by the NDRC and the then-State Oceanic Administration. Entitled "Vision for Maritime Cooperation under the Belt and Road Initiative" (*Yidaiyilu Jianshe Haishang Hezuo Shexiang* 一带一路"建设海上合作设想), the report cited the Arctic, along with the Indian Ocean/Mediterranean and the Pacific Ocean as "blue economic passages" essential for Chinese maritime trade under the auspices of the BRI. This document set the stage for the release of the White Paper in January 2018, which brought together many strands of scientific, economic and political policies into a single document (PRC State Council, 2018), including re-affirming China's identity as a "near-Arctic State" and its interest in developing the Arctic Ocean as an 'Ice Silk Road' as part of the "Maritime Silk Road" within the BRI framework.

With the Arctic officially part of the BRI, there is much anticipation as to how the Arctic economies could benefit from Chinese investments and other forms of economic partnerships. The Arctic is being incorporated into both the maritime 'Road' via proposed port projects as well as the possibility of greater Chinese shipping through the NSR and the land-based 'Belt', including via a proposed railway and other transportation links via Siberia and the Russian Far East (RFE) and as far as the Nordic region. The rail transport between Central Europe and China via Russia and Central Asia constitutes another alternative to the Suez Canal route and competition to Arctic container transport. These rail connections, while growing and being suited for specific goods and situations, involve much smaller volumes and higher costs per unit compared to sea transport.

While Chinese interest is focused on the NSR, some attention has also been given to the Northwest Passage (NWP). In the more distant future, transit shipping between East Asia and the North American east coast can become feasible. Transit routes can reach as far as Iceland and Greenland, especially if mining in the latter country begins to take off in the coming years (Fife & Chase, 2017). In April 2016, China's Maritime Safety Administration released a navigation guide to the NWP in the Canadian Arctic. China has thus far not sent a cargo vessel through the passage, but the icebreaker *Xuelong* has traversed the waterway with Canadian consent.

It is unlikely that the Arctic will be a primary trade route for Chinese goods in the near future. Nonetheless, China appears to have switched towards a more optimistic rhetoric in regards to the prospects of Arctic shipping after the adoption of the 2018 White Paper. This new optimism contrasts with the actual activities in the past few years, as well as with the earlier reluctance to include Arctic sea lanes in the BRI initiative, presumably because the Arctic shipping potential was considered limited compared to other elements of the BRI framework (Moe and Stokke, 2018). In 2017, there were merely five Chinese sailings in both directions through the whole NSR. The more general reasons discussed above play a role. The lack of progress could be partly explained also by the temporary financial problems of China Ocean Shipping Company (COSCO) and its subsidiaries (especially the COSCO Specialized Carriers Company), the main player in the scene of China's Arctic shipping. Also, trade with Northern Europe – where the NSR transits could be competitive – constitutes a mere 2.9% of China's international trade volumes (Moe and Stokke, 2018). Consequently, the main area of Chinese involvement in Arctic shipping is resource extraction projects and exports, which are related to the construction and commencement of production at the Yamal LNG project. The carriers exporting the LNG from the Yamal LNG Sabetta port are co-owned by COSCO and Japanese company Mitsui (Staalesen, 2018, June 29). In 2019, the first Chinese-built LNG carrier for the Yamal LNG project was completed in a Shanghai shipyard, although the vessel, "LNG Dubhe" is not an ice-strengthened unit and is likely to be used for transshipments in Murmansk (Staalesen, 2019, September 27).

Chinese (state-owned) shipping companies have some reserves for investments and are willing to put these resources into projects such as unprofitable trial voyages that are seen as opening the door for future possibilities as well as activities that support governmental agenda, especially the BRI. Against this background, COSCO announced the opening of the regular trial container lane and commissioned three multi-purpose ice-class carriers (Moe and Stokke, 2018).

The development of the infrastructure within the BRI is to be carried out through cooperation between China and individual countries. For the time being, Russia is the only Arctic state that has formally joined the BRI. China's Arctic White Paper emphasises that "[c]oncrete cooperation steps include coordinating development strategies with the Arctic States, encouraging joint efforts to build a blue economic passage linking China and Europe via the Arctic Ocean [...] and building a global infrastructure network". Chinese involvement in ongoing and planned Russian projects, mainly focused on resource extraction and exports, can be seen as contributing to the development of the NSR as a part of the BRI. These include the Belkomur Railway between Siberia and Arkhangelsk, a deep-water port in Arkhangelsk, as well as Yamal LNG, Arctic LNG (planned to be launched on the Gydan peninsula) and associated shipping infrastructure (Soldatkin and Jaganathan, 2019, September 5).

China's overall interest in the NSR is also demonstrated in research activities. Chinese institutes have been engaged in a number of studies dedicated to the feasibility of the NSR (in particular comparing the NSR to the Suez Canal) and the technological solutions needed for operating therein, in particular regarding smaller conventional container vessels (Kirkenes Nearingshage, 2018: 8).

6.7 Oil and Gas Production

The accelerating pace of polar ice erosion has resulted in an increase in the level of international attention to potential fossil fuel (oil and gas) extraction in the circumpolar Arctic. A 2008 survey report by the United States Geological Survey (USGS) evaluated the probability of hydrocarbon occurrence in the Arctic. It concluded that the area within the Arctic Circle, representing six percent of the world's surface, may hold thirteen percent of the globe's unrecovered petroleum supplies (ninety billion barrels), and as much as thirty percent of its natural gas (approximately 47.3 billion cubic meters). A large majority of these fossil fuels, eighty-four percent, would be found offshore, most notably in the Arctic Ocean north of Siberia, in the waters north of Alaska and also between Baffin Island in Nunavut, Canada and Greenland (Bird et al., 2008; Gautier et al., 2009). However, various obstacles have hampered the earlier predicted "scramble" with regard to offshore extraction. First, the rapid drop in oil prices after 2014 made Arctic fossil fuels less attractive from a cost/benefit ratio, considering the difficult operating environment in the North. There are also concerns about the environmental safety of oil and gas drilling in Arctic waters, especially in light of the "Deepwater Horizon" oil spill disaster in the Gulf of Mexico in 2010, as well as the logistical problems of large-scale drilling in the Arctic. Advances in the Russian Arctic – the most prospective region for future development – have been hindered by Western sanctions, which have limited the access of Russian energy companies to international financial markets and have halted most development activities in Russia's northern seas (though not onshore, such as the Yamal peninsula).

For China, the Arctic remains a long-term area of interest considering the country's ongoing need for external energy supplies. Despite the costs of Arctic drilling, the region is attractive to Beijing given its political stability and predictability. A report on the development of China's domestic and overseas oil and gas supplies (*2017 nian guonei wai youqi hangye fazhan baogao* 2017年国内外油气行业发展报告) published in 2017, predicted that China's high dependence on overseas oil would be at around 70 percent in 2018. Meanwhile, the report indicated that China was the second-largest gas importer while global gas consumption in 2017 hit a new high record. China has been seeking to diversify its sources of oil and gas, with a similar situation being faced by its neighbours, Japan and South Korea. The majority of Chinese energy resources are imported from the Middle East, Africa, Central Asia and Oceania (including Australian coal).[3] Arctic resources may play a part in the diversification endeavors, but only to a limited extent. China's dependence on Africa and the Middle East for oil and gas imports will continue in the mid-term.

So far, Russia has been the focus of China's Arctic energy interests (see e.g., Reuters, 2018, August 19). China has been viewed by the Putin government as an emerging energy partner as a result of Moscow's 'Look East' policies and due to Western sanctions. In May 2014, a Sino-Russian natural gas deal, worth approximately US$400 billion, was completed between the Russian energy firm Gazprom and the CNPC. The agreement would lead to regular gas shipments to China via the Russian Far East for approximately thirty years. This was followed by a Sino-Russian liquified natural gas project on the Yamal Peninsula in Siberia (Yamal LNG), valued at US$27 billion, which officially became operational in December 2017, and is financially supported by the CNPC and the Chinese Silk Road Fund. Further energy initiatives may be possible in light of the June 2018 announcement that a US$10 billion development initiative, jointly overseen by the China Development Bank and Russia's Vnesheconombank, would include projects involving the Russian Arctic. A sister-project of Yamal LNG – Arctic LNG 2 with total development costs estimated at US$25.5 billion – has also attracted Chinese investors. The CNPC and the CNOOC have each acquired 10 percent shares in the project (Staalesen, 2019, July 1; Staalesen, 2018, June 14).

Chinese actors have been less successful in pursuing projects in other Arctic jurisdictions. In 2013, Eykon Energy in Iceland created a partnership with the CNOOC and Petoro of Norway to seek out oil and gas in the Jan Mayen/Dreki region of the North Atlantic. However, poor survey results prompted both the Chinese and the Norwegian firms to withdraw from the project in January 2018 (Over the Circle, 2018). However, this does not mean that Beijing has lost interest in the Atlantic Arctic in regards to its energy potential. In October 2018, it was announced that Chinese firms, including the CNPC and the CNOOC, were expressing interest in bidding for exploration contracts in maritime blocks off the coast of Greenland when they become available in 2021 (Daly, 2018).

A Memorandum of Understanding (MoU) was struck between China and the U.S. state of Alaska in 2017 to potentially construct an LNG pipeline and

3 The East China Sea, which has a contested maritime border between China and Japan, also contains a gas field, known in Chinese as the *Chunxiao* (春晓油气田) and in Japanese as the *Shirakaba*, which both governments claim (Kim, 2012).

production facilities. Sinopec (China Petrochemical Corporation), the Bank of China (*Zhongguo Yinhang* 中国银行) and China Investment Corporation (*Zhongguo Touzi Youxian Zeren Gongsi* 中国投资有限责任公司) were negotiating a joint development project with the Alaska Gasline Development Corporation in regards to gas extraction, refining it into LNG and transportation in Alaska. The project, which includes a 1250km pipeline, would cost US$43 billion (press estimates) with 75% of funding coming from the Bank of China and 75% of total capacity being directed to the Chinese market. The final Energy Information Administration (EIA) statement was expected to be issued by the end of 2019 and, in an optimal scenario, the project could go online in 2025 (Graeber, 2018, March 28; Lim, 2018). However, the project experienced problems from the beginning. Before Chinese involvement, major investors (Exxon Mobil, ConocoPhilips and BP) had already abandoned the endeavor (Käpylä and Mikkola, 2018: 217). Currently, the simmering 'trade war' between China and the United States since the beginning of 2018 had limited the likelihood and timeline for that endeavor, despite earlier support from both Presidents Trump and Xi. As of October 2019, the project is effectively on hold.

6.8 Mining

So far, the involvement of Chinese companies in Arctic raw materials mining projects has been limited, especially in contrast to the Chinese presence in Africa or Australia (Lajeunesse & Lackenbauer, 2016).

The most well-known Arctic mining projects related to China involve the extraction of rare earth elements (REEs). China is the world's largest consumer and producer of REEs. REEs are seventeen chemical elements on the periodic table that play vital roles in modern industries and new technologies, including communications, electronics, green technology and national defense. Although many countries have REE deposits, China has taken the lead in their mining and production. Developing the utilization of REEs is an indispensable part of China's 13th Five-Year Plan, which encourages China's corporations to cooperate internationally (Central Committee of the Communist Party of China, 2015). China has also been interested in developing REE mines in the Arctic, starting with Greenland.

One of the most significant and advanced REE projects to be operated is at Kvanefjeld, located in Southern Greenland. The project is estimated to have an after-tax net value of US$1.4 billion. The mining operator is Australia-based Greenland Minerals (formerly Greenland Minerals and Energy), in partnership with Shenghe Resources (*Shenghe Ziyuan* 盛和资源), a Chinese company, which acts as a stakeholder and partner. The two companies signed a MoU in August 2018 for further cooperation on the Kvanefjeld project (Birney, 2018). The project proponents expect the mine to commence operations in the coming years. Furthermore, a zinc mine at Citronen Fjord is planned in Greenland's far north. The project is overseen by Perth-based Ironbark in cooperation with China Nonferrous Metal. Finally, General Nice, a Hong Kong-based company, currently holds the rights to a potential iron mine at Isua in western Greenland (McCrae, 2017; Shi & Lanteigne, 2018). General Nice was the same corporation that fell afoul of the Danish government when it attempted to purchase an abandoned American-built naval facility at Grønnedal. That sale was blocked by Copenhagen, a decision backed by the USA (Matzen, 2017).

The Canadian mining industry is among the most important sectors of the country's economy, and Canada is one of the biggest mining nations globally. Many Canadian mining companies established relationships with Chinese companies, including SOEs, ranging from sources of capital to long-term buyers or active operators. Between 2010 and 2016, there was an elevated interest by Chinese mining companies and investors in Canadian mining industry and resources (Lajeunesse & Lackenbauer, 2016). Most projects, however, took place south of 60°N. For instance, China's CGN Mining Co Ltd bought a nearly 20-percent share in the Fission Uranium Corporation (Canada does not allow foreign investors to have majority shareholding in operating uranium mines). In 2011, Baosteel Resources International Inc, a Chinese state-owned company, invested US$17.7 million in Noront in Northern Ontario's James Bay lowlands, considered one of the largest mineral discoveries in Canada in recent decades. Many Canadian companies received significant Chinese investment, including Teck Resources Ltd, Barrick, Ivanhoe Mines Ltd and Pretium Resources Inc. Moreover, Canadian mining companies partner with Chinese investors in financing and operating projects overseas (see e.g., Friedman, 2018, July 27).

Despite Canada's strong promotion of Chinese investments in its mining sector, the Chinese interest appeared to diminish after 2016. According to media reports (see e.g., Beeby, 2016, June 7), Chinese companies found it challenging to meet complex legal requirements and to manage community relations as well as carry out impact mitigation and negotiate benefit-sharing arrangements. Also, the investment and decision-making processes in Canada turned out to be slower than Chinese actors had wished. For instance, in Nunavut, MMG Ltd (associated with China Minmetals Corp) had long tried to start a zinc project, but without success. In British Columbia, Chinese company HD Mining International Ltd's plan to recruit Chinese labor was met with strong opposition from local communities. Some of the proposed Chinese investment plans did not proceed beyond initial expressions of interest due to restrictions placed by the Canadian government on foreign investments in resources considered highly strategic (e.g. oil sands, uranium).

In Russia, the Nornickel company sought Chinese investment in the exploitation of rare-earth metals, vanadium, molybdenum, and wolframite in the Kola Peninsula, Taimyr Peninsula, and in the Sakha Republic (Ivanov, 2016, as quoted in Erokhin, Tianming & Xinhua, 2018).

There appear to be no Chinese companies or investors actively engaged in mining projects in Northern Fennoscandia beyond initial market surveys.

6.9 Tourism

The growing middle class in China and its increasing prosperity has resulted in increased international travel by Chinese tourists. Chinese travelers are also becoming interested in relatively expensive polar tourist destinations. This resonates with the Chinese attention to both 'green tourism' (often understood as nature tourism, which does not have to imply sustainability) and adventure tourism. The numbers of Chinese tourists to the Arctic and Antarctica have increased steadily in recent years, and China is one of the largest countries of origin of polar tourists (Yang, 2017). In 2012, one year before China was awarded observership in the Arctic Council, China Economic Weekly (*Zhongguo Jingji Zhoukan* 中国经济周刊), an economic journal under the People's Daily Press (*Renmin Ribao She* 人民日报社) published a brief article on Arctic tourism, suggesting possible ways for Chinese tourists to visit the region. Additionally, a look at Chinese online tourism forums reveals various discussions on costs and different kinds of tours in the Arctic. The circumpolar North attracts Chinese tourists with activities including Northern Lights tours, circumpolar fauna and flora watching, experiencing the spectacular Arctic landscape and outdoor activities, especially in winter. Iceland and Finnish Lapland are good examples of increasingly popular destinations. With intensifying media exposure in China, along with a smooth bilateral relationship with the country, Iceland has experienced significant growth in Chinese interest – the number of Chinese passengers at Keflavik airport grew from 9500 passengers in 2007 to 86,000 in 2017 (Icelandic Tourist Board, 2018). Chinese tourism and investments in the sector in Finnish Lapland are discussed in Chapter 7 of this volume.

Parts of the Arctic less accessible compared to the Nordic countries are also attempting to attract Chinese and East Asian travelers. Northern Canada is strongly marketed in China and Japan (Rosen, 2018). However, the sharp downturn in diplomatic relations between Beijing and Ottawa at the beginning of 2019 over the arrest of the Huawei executive resulted in both governments placing travel warnings regarding each of the countries respectively in January (CBC News, 2019, January 26).

Greenland has also been hoping to develop a stronger tourism base with an eye on Chinese guests. One initiative has been to expand Greenland's airports to better attract greater tourist traffic.

Russia is also seeking to cooperate more closely with China to develop Arctic tourism in Siberia and in the Arkhangelsk region (RT, 2018, July 27).

6.10 Concerns Related to Chinese Investments and Economic Cooperation

Many stakeholders in Arctic regions generally welcome foreign, including Chinese, investments. However, analysts have identified risks related to Chinese investments and some actors have expressed concerns. Some of these risks and concerns are specific to China, while many characterize any foreign investments.

First, there is a perception that Chinese investment and economic, scientific and other forms of cooperation may constitute instruments of increasing Chinese influence in the region. The mechanisms which we define as expressions of *sharp power* appear to be of greatest concern among actors in Arctic regions. Simultaneously, high levels of Chinese investments and economic cooperation could increase the exposure of small Arctic countries and sparsely-populated Arctic regions to any future fluctuations in the Chinese economy.

Second, there are concerns related to the performance of Chinese actors as investors or business partners. This refers to environmental impacts and the effects on local socio-economic development, including: social impacts, competition with local businesses, or an adverse influence on the labor market. Moreover, issues related to intellectual property rights or industrial espionage may be problematic for some types of projects. On the other hand, local actors, who are often strongly in favor of Chinese investments, have misgivings that plans announced by Chinese investors, which raise hopes for regional development, may eventually remain unrealized. That may lead to disappointment and the wastage of local human and financial resources mobilized towards the implementation of Chinese investment plans.

6.10.1 *Chinese Political and Economic Influence*

Some analysts, decision-makers and members of the public, both in the Arctic regions and in Arctic capitals, are uneasy about the political and strategic leverage that China can gain via an elevated economic presence. These fears are based on the notion that China is an authoritarian, centralized state with strong governmental control over its economic actors. The Chinese government has proven in the past that it is willing to exercise forceful pressure – also using economic instruments – on countries that it felt had infringed on Chinese core interests or had "offended" China. Two Arctic states – Norway in the aftermath of awarding the Nobel Peace Prize to Liu Xiaobo, and Canada after the arrest of the Huawei executive Meng Wanzhou – experienced the sharp edge of such pressure. It is argued, primarily in the Western media, that closer economic ties with China and greater Chinese economic influence in relatively small Arctic states (apart from Russian and the U.S.) would give China increasing influence over Arctic states' foreign policies and their economic and domestic decision-making, to gradually bring them more in line with Chinese economic and political interests. Such influence could be even more visible in the context of politics and the economies of the sparsely-populated and resource-deficient northernmost regions of the Arctic states.

Deepening interaction with Chinese actors creates new risks with implications for the security policy calculus of small Arctic countries. The concept of *power* helps us scrutinize and anticipate these developments. In the Arctic context, the concept of *sharp power* is particularly useful. In general, power refers to an actor's ability to influence others' behavior to achieve desired outcomes. In addition to the traditional understanding of *hard power*, which is based on the threat or the use of military force, Joseph Nye coined the concept of *soft power* in the 1990s. Soft power builds on the attractiveness of a state's culture and ideals; it seeks to attract other states to voluntarily follow its policies (Nye, 2018). To complement the soft-hard framework,[4] Walker and Ludwig (2017) coined the term *sharp power* that describes the ways in which authoritarian states seek to influence the behavior of other actors by shaping public opinion and perceptions around the globe. Sharp power includes instruments and mechanisms that spread deceptive information, bribe politicians and civil servants, widen socio-political cleavages, weaken the coherence of the targeted society, restrict liberty of speech, and interfere with elections. These instruments are used in order to shape national politics and to silence displeasing

4 Joseph Nye (2009, July/August) also introduced the term "smart power" to describe the cost-effective combination of hard and soft power instruments. Normally, smart power does not necessarily involve deception or clandestine influence methods.

views in other states, as they could prevent an authoritarian state from increasing its global outreach (Walker & Ludwig, 2017; Walker, 2018). In its most extreme form, the use of sharp power may reduce the targeted state's sovereignty. The idea of sharp power is also parallel and interlinked with *hybrid influencing*, a form of power use that has recently attracted attention in Western public debate. Similarly with sharp power, hybrid influencing refers to hidden, non-military methods of exerting power that clearly advance the interests of the influencer by intensifying and creating fissures and polarization in targeted societies (e.g. Cederberg et al., 2017; Mikkola et al., 2018, 24–25; Wigell, 2019). However, unlike with sharp power, hybrid influencing is often – but not always – seen to ultimately rely on the underlying threat of military action (e.g. Salonius-Pasternak, 2017). To a great extent, it is the instruments grouped here under the umbrella of sharp power that appear to be of the greatest concern to Arctic stakeholders, decision-makers and analysts.

Identifying the above-mentioned forms of power helps us to distinguish four ways in which China can exercise power in Arctic affairs and beyond: it can coerce others with threats, induce them with payments, manipulate or deceive them, or it can attract them to voluntarily follow its policies and interests (Nye, 2008; Walker & Ludwig, 2017). In real-life situations, it is not always easy to distinguish between these strategies, as different dimensions of power often overlap. For example, the line between soft power and sharp power can be very thin – while both seek to improve a state's international image, they utilize divergent tools to reach that goal. Economic influence is particularly difficult to categorize; whilst some scholars think it is about hard power, others regard it as a domain of soft power. Nevertheless, an analysis of China's exercise of these three kinds of power (*hard, soft* and *sharp*) helps us scrutinize concerns that China's growing involvement in the Arctic – which remains primarily economic and scientific in nature – causes amongst the regional actors.

First, China's use of hard power refers to the adoption of either military or economic strategies to increase the Middle Kingdom's influence in the Arctic countries. Arguably, global great power competition, especially between the U.S. and an increasingly stronger China, has arguably intensified and is unlikely to subside rapidly. In contrast to the classic realist tendency to believe that the rise of China will evidently cause a hegemonic war (e.g. Mearsheimer, 2001), current evidence gives little reason to believe that the use of armed force by China in the Arctic region would be a likely scenario, at least in the short-term to mid-term future (e.g. Lanteigne & Ping, 2015, but see also Office of the Secretary of Defense, 2019: 114; Brady, 2017). Nonetheless, in the name of mapping all kinds of potential scenarios, it is possible to imagine a situation in which the country's shareholding in Nordic harbour cities – e.g. Kirkenes and

Akureyri – would make it easier for Chinese warships to enter the region and could eventually result in a dual-use of these ports. In a similar vein, the Chinese aurora observatory in Iceland, the research station in Svalbard and the country's new plan to build a nuclear-powered ice-breaker have been linked to dual-use speculations, especially by U.S. observers (Office of the Secretary of Defense, 2019: 114). However, there is no publicly available evidence of current illicit, covert activities.[5]

Outside the Arctic, concerns related to Chinese control over strategic infrastructure and its use in the case of potential tensions have been expressed in particular in the context of Africa or regarding digital infrastructure, especially the deployment of 5G network infrastructure across Europe (see, e.g., Hillman, 2019; Xu Klein, 2018, September 14). Under the current circumstances, rather than via establishing its own infrastructure, it is more likely that China's rapidly modernizing military forces will indirectly shape the dynamics of the Arctic. No region is immune to the impacts of shifts in the balance of power on a global scale.

Second, examples of China's attempts to attract desired partners through the pull effect of the country's culture (i.e. the use of soft power) in the Arctic context include *panda diplomacy* (e.g. Hartig, 2013) in Finland (e.g. Wang, 2018) and the organization of public relations events, such as the China Night Gala at the Arctic Circle Assembly in Reykjavik in 2018 (e.g., Ministry of Foreign Affairs PRC, 2018). In addition to cultural diplomacy, Chinese soft power is strongly based on its economic prowess: its economic model is especially attractive to African and Southeast Asian countries (e.g. Ding, 2008; Percival, 2007). And while China's politico-economic model as such may not be alluring for societies in most (if not all) Arctic states, the visions of investments (from China) or new markets (in China) are easily a part of promotional strategies. As Nye (2018) reminds us, "soft power is not good or bad in itself", but it can be used to advance both positive and negative ends. China's soft power can hence have positive impacts by increasing trust and intercultural understanding – intellectual capital necessary to increase cooperation between China and the

5 However, a new aspect in the broader strategic situation in the circumpolar North is China's ability, in the future, to maintain a continuous sea-based nuclear deterrent through its strategic nuclear submarine force. Some of these assets may also start patrolling in the Arctic Ocean (Stewart and Ali, 2019, May 3). China's military presence could become more visible in the Arctic if great power competition intensifies and this could reflect the growth of China's naval (and other) capabilities. Among others, a related concern is that, over time, dual-use ports and other facilities on the European side of the Arctic could become useful, while in the short term, the Asian side of Arctic/sub-Arctic might be more relevant.

Arctic states. Yet, it may also have negative impacts if Arctic actors seek to please Chinese investors to the extent that China's regional influence increases to the point where Arctic states' national interests – including long-term economic interests – are adversely affected.

Third, the use of sharp power remains the most complex and least discussed form of China's attempts to influence the Arctic countries. In general, the use of sharp power is nothing new in the region – these methods have always been used in politics – but, traditionally, more attention has been paid to Russian attempts, perhaps due to the fact that China's global engagement has only recently reached a notable level (Nye, 2018). Also, the fact that digitalization and globalization have increased the efficiency of these methods makes current instances of sharp power different from the past (Nye, 2018), with Russia's (alleged) Global Positioning System (GPS) jamming attempts during military exercises in Finnish Lapland offering a representative example (BBC, 2018; Mikkola, 2019). So far, there is little publicly available evidence of China's use of sharp power in the Arctic context. As the country's role in the region increases, it may, however, attempt to use questionable methods in Nordic countries. Possibly, this could occur in a similar manner as in Australia, where China has reportedly tried to interfere in the country's domestic politics (e.g. Hamilton, 2018; Walker, 2018). Such attempts may either shape national politics in each country or indirectly affect cohesion within the Nordic region. For instance, differences in China's policy and relations with different Nordic states may prevent these countries from acting as a uniform front on the international stage or from supporting each other.

For the time being, the most likely arena of Chinese sharp power in the Arctic context is academia. Researchers may be influenced both directly or indirectly to produce results that support China's Arctic plans and strategies. China offers generous grants and treats researchers with dinners and gifts in addition to organizing government-funded academic exchange programs and conferences. The aim is primarily to build trust and to strengthen China's status as a legitimate Arctic stakeholder that is interested in more than the region's resources. However, in addition to the positive outcome of increasing Arctic researchers' understanding of the Chinese context, these forums and programmes, and the prospect of future access to such opportunities, may put academics under pressure to censor their words. Although the Arctic context is less sensitive than many other sectors or geographies, it is a priority for the Chinese government to advance the image of China as a responsible Arctic stakeholder. For this reason, it is indeed within the realm of possibility that actions such as refusing to grant a Chinese visa could be taken to silence unwanted voices.

Clearly, China's growing leverage in the Arctic is largely based on its economic prowess, which inevitably increases its influence on the domestic affairs of small Nordic countries or relatively small sub-divisions of Canada, Russia and even in Alaska. The emerging risks are therefore both political and economic. Transport systems in particular are candidates for attracting Chinese investments and thus represent a domain in which countries' security of supply could be affected. Examples of such concerns playing a role in decision-making, in most instances leading to the cancellation of Chinese investment plans, are the aforementioned cases of Greenlandic airport expansions, the Swedish Lysekil port, extensive land purchase proposals in northern Norway, Svalbard and Iceland, as well as the idea of choosing a Chinese operator or a major investor for the railway connection proposed between Rovaniemi and Kirkenes (see Chapter 7 in this volume for details on this project).

Although the Chinese economy has thus far continued to grow according to expectations, disruptions may arise from several sectors, as the Chinese economy is undergoing a challenging process of structural transformation. The growing debt levels of local governments, households and companies, as well as increasing pressure to tackle pollution and inequality, are major risks that the Chinese government currently faces. In addition, external factors such as a trade war with the U.S. may equally upset the balance. In the case of political conflicts, Chinese ownership or control of critical infrastructure would possibly place Chinese operators in a position to decide how it is used and by whom. However, open use of such power is very unlikely, as states generally have the possibility to impose their control on private property in crisis situations. In a similar vein, Chinese economic investments may be used as political leverage in policy disagreements, as was the case in Norway in the aftermath of the Nobel Peace Prize controversy.

Chinese institutions present the decisions of Chinese investment banks and financial institutions as being based primarily on economic evaluation, without requirements related to good governance, human rights, economic restructuring or sustainable development indicators. Such requirements are, at least formally, part of the decision-making process in Western financial institutions such as the World Bank or the European Investment Bank. However, Mattlin and Nojonen (2015) believe that Chinese financing decisions cannot be disentangled from political motives, especially when state-controlled institutions are concerned (this view was also expressed in personal communication, Interviewee 1, June 13, 2018). Therefore, as China wishes to have a gradually stronger presence in the Arctic, many instances of investment and cooperation can serve larger political aims, alongside project-specific business objectives.

There are related concerns that Chinese investments may, in the long-term, result in debt dependence, which may further reinforce the capabilities to influence the policies of investment-recipient countries. Such questions partly arise from the experiences with Chinese activities in Africa, South America and South-East Asia. Cumulative Chinese investments generate tangible development in recipient countries. Yet, on the other hand, they gradually and organically create strong and potentially dangerous path-dependency mechanisms between recipient countries and China. Each investment has its own path-dependency pattern that binds the recipient country to the Chinese supplier through financial obligations, hardware and software, and updating technology and workforce education. Eventually, following the path leads countries to a lock-in phase. The lock-in can emerge either through the cumulative effect of seemingly unrelated Chinese investments or simply through one critical Chinese investment that make it hard or impossible for the recipient country to find alternative suppliers. At this stage, Beijing gains the upper hand and can exert direct or indirect influence over national decision-making. At times, the recipient states' governments actively make concessions in the pursuit of further benefits from China (Mattlin and Nojonen, 2015; see also the recent case of Argentina at Patey, 2019, January 24). These dynamics may be troubling for countries and communities that are just now engaging in investment cooperation with China, as is the case in the Arctic.

While such processes may seem less likely to occur in rich, developed and relatively well-governed Arctic states, various actors express concerns (e.g., Lackenbauer et al., 2018; Lasserre et al., 2017; Department of State, 2019). Rosen and Thuringen (2017) claim that Chinese investments could indeed constitute a security risk, particularly in smaller Arctic jurisdictions:

> Unregulated FDI is a significant, multifaceted security issue. It must be addressed before the influx of unregulated investments, and the soft power politics that come from those investments… We believe that FDI should be tracked carefully, because the impact of large quantities of investment dollars flooding into some Arctic nations (Greenland) or tribally governed land can have an impact on political sovereignty.
>
> ROSEN & THURINGEN, 2017: 2, 53

A good example of how such concerns related to major Chinese investments change legal framework applicable to investments in the Arctic (here, in Sweden and Finland) is a recently adopted EU legislation (Regulation 2019/452). The new regulation gives the European Commission power to scrutinize foreign investments in areas of strategic importance such as infrastructure or energy (i.e., investments that are likely to affect projects or programs of Union interest on the grounds of security or public order). The legislation is perceived as targeting Chinese investors to a great extent, as it was drafted in response to cases such as the Chinese acquisition of the Greek Port of Piraeus. The law was intensely debated in several EU Member States that had benefited from Chinese investments in recent years, such as Portugal or Greece.

The example of the above EU legislation points to a new challenge for Western Arctic states in regards to their relations with China. How should they take account of concerns and possible pressure from their major Western partners – in Brussels and Washington – in regard to enhancing ties with China? Nordic states already need to take heed of the discussion taking place in the EU about China's influence. Moreover, the U.S. Secretary of State in a speech delivered in Rovaniemi, Finland in May 2019 effectively warned Arctic states against Chinese investments (Department of State, 2019). In other contexts, especially regarding the deployment of 5G network in various European countries, the USA openly threatened states considering contracts with Chinese companies that security cooperation with the USA may be limited.

6.10.2 *The Performance and Reliability of Chinese Investors and Partners*

The behavior of some Chinese economic operators in other parts of the world feeds anxieties regarding the reliability of Chinese investors to implement their plans or the social and environmental performance of Chinese companies. This is particularly important in the context of Arctic regions, where land rights, participatory decision-making, broad consultations, and co-management are an important part of any development process – frameworks that often are outcomes of intense conflicts or difficult negotiations. There are also concerns regarding the excessive economic influence of major Chinese players within small Arctic economies.

Rosen and Thuringen (2017) highlight that "China's recent foreign direct investment (FDI) activities in the Arctic are significant in overall dollar value and could be larger than any other country's FDI". The authors, who discuss only the Arctic Ocean littoral states in their paper, not Finland or Sweden, suggest that high levels of the Chinese FDI in the Arctic could mean that there is a "potential that one state could, by enacting low standards, stimulate a race to the bottom in terms of the environmental or labor standards associated with resource extraction". However, the Chinese government usually underlines the company's obligation to adjust to local regulatory frameworks (Stepien, 2017). Therefore, in an operational environment in which regulations are stronger, such as in the Nordic countries, the above-mentioned risks are less likely to turn into actual problems than in states with weaker administrative, regulatory and political systems.

Investments, including Chinese FDI, are always aimed at generating profit or other benefits for the investor, including national access to resources. The authors see many of the Chinese investments in Africa and South America as having a goal to secure resources for the growing Chinese economy.

Various environmental and social impacts of Chinese investments are highlighted in literature and media. For instance, especially in the mid-2000s, there were, allegedly, cases of Chinese mines in Africa having lower labor standards than those run by local or Western companies. There are opinions that the local workforce is treated worse than Chinese expats (which may be characteristic for most foreign investments in developing states) and that the interests and rights of groups such as Indigenous Peoples and minorities are not always observed. At times, Chinese investors pick up projects that have been abandoned by Western investors or international investments banks due to social and environmental challenges (International Rivers, 2012; Cannon, 2019; Canuto, 2019, March 12; Mourdoukoutas, 2018; Marsh, 2015). According to Rosen and Thuringen (2017: 51):

> Widely publicized instances of environmental damage, labor abuse, and violence in South America and Africa have made countries in North America and Europe wary of Chinese direct investment. Had Chinese companies been more attentive to good corporate behavior and had the Chinese government been more effective at managing the behavior of Chinese SOEs, then perhaps China might have a better reputation abroad.

At the same time, analysts highlight that there has been significant improvement in the past decade, both regarding the behavior of Chinese companies and the standards imposed on the Chinese SOEs by the government (Rosen & Thuringen, 2017: 52).

At a general level, international standards and recommendations referring to foreign direct investments (e.g. by the United Nations (UN) or the Organization for Economic Cooperation and Development, OECD) advise the recipient countries and regions to consider both the benefits and disadvantages of particular investments. These include over-dependence on extractive industries, limiting exposure to market volatility, local employment, generation and transfer of technology, eliminating anticompetitive practices, and preventing crowding-out of local investments. The Arctic states and their peripheral Arctic regions – characterized by small economies, populations and limited economic diversification – may be particularly concerned about such risks.

Perhaps being aware of the above concerns and reputational issues, the Chinese government states in its 2018 White Paper (PRC State Council, 2018) that all extractive activities in the Arctic should "proceed in a sustainable way on the condition of properly protecting the eco-environment of the Arctic and respecting the interests and concerns of the indigenous peoples in the region". In general, the Chinese government also advises Chinese companies to abide by local regulatory frameworks (Ministry of Commerce PRC 2013; 2014; China Banking Regulatory Commission, 2013). This commitment is reiterated in the 2018 White Paper:

> [China] requires its enterprises to observe the laws of the relevant States and conduct risk assessments for resource exploration, and encourages them to participate in the exploitation of oil, gas and mineral resources in the Arctic, through cooperation in various forms and on the condition of properly protecting the eco-environment of the Arctic ... respecting the efforts made by the Arctic States to empower the local citizens, foster their social and economic progress, and improve education and medical services, so that the Arctic residents, including the indigenous peoples, will truly benefit from the development of Arctic resources.
>
> PRC State Council, 2018

The latter can be also understood as an encouragement for Chinese companies to engage in corporate social responsibility actions (e.g., community wellbeing support activities) in communities and locations in which they carry out operations. Moreover, in the 2018 White Paper, the Chinese government commits to respecting local and indigenous values and traditions. This is in line with the so-called 'Nuuk Observer rules' (Arctic Council, 2011; Graczyk & Koivurova, 2014; Stepien, 2017), to which China expressed its consent upon applying and taking up an observer status in the Arctic Council.

Such declaratory statements, while not without an intrinsic value, do not necessarily determine the actions of particular Chinese companies or investors, or may not be reflected in actual pressure by the Chinese government on Chinese companies and researchers. They can be, however, used by various Arctic actors in their dealings with Chinese economic operators or investors or in cases when intervention by Chinese authorities is sought with the aim of exerting pressure on Chinese companies that are seen as not meeting the declared standards when conducting activities in the Arctic.

Among key challenges for northern sparsely populated areas is the (mis) match between the skills of the Northerners and the needs of new development projects (Prime Minister's Office, 2013; Stepien & Koivurova, 2017; Olsen et al., 2016). In some northern locations, the existing workforce is too small to meet the labor needs of major investments/developments, especially during the construction phase of projects. The short-term nature of construction activities deters locals from acquiring the skills that would be used for implementing a single project. Therefore, new and expanding businesses often rely on a fly-in workforce. If Chinese construction companies win contracts for major investments in Arctic regions, there is a possibility that Chinese workers will fill a part of the short-term demand for a labor force during the projects' construction phase. In some parts of the Arctic, plans to bring in Chinese workers already proved problematic for local communities. This was the case in Greenland and Canada in which Chinese mining companies planned to use a Chinese workforce. Anxieties related to Chinese subcontractors and a Chinese workforce are related to unfair pricing, a lack of local multiplier effects and undercutting national labor standards. The calculation of the socio-economic benefits and risks may be different for each project, depending on the location, scale and the characteristics of professionals who arrive in the North to support project implementation and operation. Currently, in other parts of the world, the tendency is for highly skilled Chinese professionals to leave after the completion of projects, while unskilled workers tend to remain (Rosen & Thuringen, 2017: 59). The nature of operations in the harsh Arctic climate may result in the dominance of high-skilled professionals among the Chinese workforce. These, usually relatively small groups of expats, may be seen as less problematic or even as desirable newcomers.

Chinese investments related to tourism have proven controversial in some parts of the Arctic. In northeast Iceland, Svalbard and in the Lyngen area in Norway, Chinese billionaire and property tycoon Huang Nubo planned to purchase vast swaths of land with a declared purpose of developing tourist services. However, local resistance and national environmental and security concerns prevented the finalization of these transactions, and in the Lyngen case, the construction of the tourist resort itself (see, e.g., Higgins, 2014, September 27; Staalesen, 2014, October 21).

While many analysts and Arctic residents are concerned about China's increasing economic presence, many actors in Arctic regions look with much hope at Chinese investments, with the belief that it can boost economic development and create much needed jobs (e.g. in Finnish Lapland, personal communication, Interviewee 2, June 12, 2018). For these actors, an important concern is that planned investments and partnerships will ultimately not materialize. This is particularly important if we take into account that social impacts occur from the moment the plans are announced (e.g., Schweitzer et al., 2019; Hansen and Johnstone, 2019). Among other things, local hopes and anxieties are triggered. Conflicts between different interest groups and values may emerge. Local businesses start planning expansion or withhold new investments in line with expected changes in the local economy. Rosen & Thuringen (2017: 32–34, 52) highlight cases in which Chinese investments went bankrupt, leaving local communities and businesses in distress. These failures were often the result of lack of experience and understanding by the Chinese economic actors of local conditions and regulations. However, the same authors also underline that Chinese investments are much better planned nowadays, and investors more carefully consider local conditions and regulations. Investments are more strategic and long-term, with less willingness to engage in risky ventures. In cases of resource extraction in particular, Chinese operators nowadays tend to engage only in secure, promising projects, rather than taking up any opportunity and creating unrealistic expectations.

6.11 Conclusion

The Chinese economic presence in the Arctic region is clearly increasing, and both the current activities and future expectations are related to the expanding role of China in the global economy, the trajectories of Chinese economic development and the changes in global market flows. However, at present the actual Chinese investments and operations are very limited in all major sectors: shipping, energy and non-energy extractive industries or infrastructure. The extension of the Belt and Road Initiative towards the Arctic has not yet produced a tangible increase in the Chinese presence, with the prominent exception is the Chinese involvement in the extraction and shipping of gas from Russia. Moreover, for many sectors such as shipping, extractives and tourism, China is expected to be a major long-term partner, buyer or investor, due to the size of its market and the resources at the disposal of Chinese financial institutions and companies.

Many investments do not come to pass, be it because of economic – as is the case with many mining projects – or political reasons. The latter stem from concerns related to Chinese investors', construction companies' or operators' influence on critical infrastructure (e.g. airport upgrades in Greenland) or are connected to broader economic or geopolitical tensions, as seems to be the case at the moment with the suspended LNG project in Alaska. Apart from strategic concerns, there are also anxieties related to the environmental and social performance of Chinese companies. These concerns are based on past experiences with Chinese activities in other parts of the world. So far, however, no problematic cases have been registered in the Arctic, presumably because Chinese actors tend to adjust to local regulatory frameworks as well as because the number of Chinese investments and operations is still small.

The case of Chinese economic activities in one country – Finland – is discussed in the next chapter, which exemplifies a number of the dynamics discussed above and also provides examples of Chinese investments – or the potential for such investments – outside of the major economic sectors.

Literature

AMSA. (2009). *Arctic Marine Shipping Assessment*. Arctic Council: Protection of Arctic Marine Environment.

Arctic Council. (2011, May). *Senior Arctic Officials (SAO) Report to Ministers*. (pp. 50–51). Nuuk, Greenland.

Arctic Investment Platform. (2019). *Arctic Investment Platform Feasibility Study*. Retrieved August 14, 2019, from https://arcticsmartness.eu/wp-content/uploads/AIP-Feasibility-Study_web.pdf.

BBC. (2018, November 12). Russia suspected of jamming GPS signal in Finland. *BBC News*. Retrieved July 26, 2019, from https://www.bbc.com/news/world-europe-46178940.

BDI. (January 2019). Partner und systemischer Wettbewerber – Wie gehen wir mit Chinas staatlich gelenkter Volkswirtschaft um? BDI Grundsatzpapier China. [A partner and a systemic rival – How do we deal with China's state-controlled economy?, in German] Retrieved July 19, 2019, from https://g8fip1kplyr33r3krz5b97d1-wpengine.netdna-ssl.com/wp-content/uploads/2019/01/BDI-Grundsatzpapier_China.pdf.

Beeby, D. (2016, June 7). Chinese mining companies feel misled by Canada, report says. *CBC News*. Retrieved October 8, 2018, from https://www.cbc.ca/news/politics/china-mining-ambassador-investors-infrastructure-1.3619228.

Bird, K.J., Charpentier, R.R., Gautier, D.L., Houseknecht, D.W., Klett, T.R., Pitman, J.K., … Wandrey, C.J. (2008). Circum-Arctic resource appraisal: Estimates of undiscovered oil and gas North of the Arctic Circle. United States Geological Survey. Retrieved June 10, 2018, from http://pubs.usgs.gov/fs/2008/3049/fs2008-3049.pdf.

Birney, M. (2018, August 21). Greenland minerals sets growth plan with Chinese shareholder. *Business News – Western Australia*. Retrieved August 25, 2018, from https://www.businessnews.com.au/article/Greenland-Minerals-sets-growth-plan-with-Chinese-shareholder.

Blenkinsop, P. & Emmott, R. (2019, April 9). EU hails breakthrough with China on industry subsidies. Reuters. Retrieved September 3, 2019, from https://www.reuters.com/article/us-eu-china/eu-hails-breakthrough-with-china-on-industry-subsidies-idUSKCN1RL0oB.

Brady, A-M. (2017). *China as a polar great power.* Washington, D.C.; Cambridge, United Kingdom: Woodrow Wilson Center Press.

Breum, M. (2018, June 30). How a dispute over China and Greenland's airports worked its way toward a solution. *Arctic Today.* Retrieved July 15, 2018, from https://www.arctictoday.com/dispute-china-greenlands-airports-worked-way-toward-solution/.

Cannon, B.J. (2019). Is China Undermining Its Own Success in Africa?. *The Diplomat.* Retrieved September 10, 2019, from https://thediplomat.com/2019/02/is-china-undermining-its-own-success-in-africa/.

Canuto, O. (2019, March 12). How Chinese Investment in Latin America is Changing. *Americas Quarterly*. Retrieved September 10, 2019, from https://www.americasquarterly.org/content/how-chinese-investment-latin-america-changing.

CBS News (2019, January 25). Huawei arrest: What's happening between Canada and China?. Retrieved September 9, 2019, from https://www.cbc.ca/news/world/huawei-meng-timeline-1.4989139.

Cederberg, A., Eronen, P., & Mustonen, J. (2017). Regional Cooperation to Support National Hybrid Defence Efforts. Working Paper 1. Helsinki: The European Centre of Excellence for Countering Hybrid Threats. Retrieved July 17, 2019, from https://www.hybridcoe.fi/wp-content/uploads/2017/12/hybridcoe_wp1_regional_cooperation.pdf.

Central Committee of the Communist Party of China (2015). 13th Five-Year Plan for Economic and Social Development of the People's Republic of China (2016–2020). Retrieved September 8, 2019, from http://en.ndrc.gov.cn/newsrelease/201612/P020161207645765233498.pdf.

China Banking Regulatory Commission. (2013). Green credit guidelines. (Unofficial translation for internal use). Retrieved June 20, 2018, from pfbc-cbfp.org/docs/news/avril-mai-13/RDP12-Mars-2013/DCC-China%20Banking%20Regulation%20-%20Green%20Credit%20Guidelines.pdf.

ChinaFile (2016, December 21), Did Oslo Kowtow to Beijing? (A ChinaFile Conversation). Retrieved 20 May 2019 from http://www.chinafile.com/conversation/did-oslo-kowtow-beijing.

Creemers, R. (2018). China's Social Credit System: An Evolving Practice of Control. SSRN. Retrieved September, 9, 2019, from https://ssrn.com/abstract=3175792 or http://dx.doi.org/10.2139/ssrn.3175792.

Daly, T. (2018, October 30). Greenland says China oil majors eyeing Arctic island's onshore blocks. *Reuters*. Retrieved November 5, 2018, from https://www.reuters.com/

article/greenland-china-investment/update-1-greenland-says-china-oil-majors-eyeing-arctic-islands-onshore-blocks-idUSL3N1XA33A.

Department of State (US). (2019, May 6). Looking North: Sharpening America's Arctic Focus. Speech by the US Secretary of State Mike Pompeo in Rovaniemi, Finland on 8 May 2019. Retrieved September 26, 2019, from the Department of State website at https://www.state.gov/looking-north-sharpening-americas-arctic-focus/.

Ding, S. (2008). To build a "harmonious world": China's soft power wielding in the Global South. *Journal of Chinese Political Science,* 13(2), 193–213.

Economist. (2018, April 14). China wants to be a polar power. *Economist.* Retrieved June 10, 2018, from https://www.economist.com/china/2018/04/14/china-wants-to-be-a-polar-power.

Erokhin, V., Tianming, G., & Xinhua, Z. (2018). Arctic Blue Economic Corridor: China's Role in the Development of a New Connectivity Paradigm in the North. In L. Heininen & H. Exner-Pirot (Eds.), *Arctic Yearbook 2018.* Akureyri, Iceland: Northern Research Forum.

European Commision (2019, April 10). EU foreign investment screening. Press Release. Retrieved September 3, 2019, from https://europa.eu/rapid/press-release_IP-19-2088_en.htm.

European Commission website (Directorate-General for Trade), "China" (last update 2 August 2019). Retrieved 3 September 2019 from https://ec.europa.eu/trade/policy/countries-and-regions/countries/china/.

Fife, R., & Chase, S. (2017, September 10). China used research mission to test trade route through Canada's Northwest Passage. *Globe and Mail.* Retrieved August 14, 2019, from https://www.theglobeandmail.com/news/politics/china-used-research-mission-to-test-trade-route-through-canadas-northwest-passage/article36223673/.

Friedman, G. (2018, July 27). The world's most insatiable consumer digs deep into Canadian miners. *Financial Post.* Retrieved October 8, 2018, from https://business.financialpost.com/commodities/the-worlds-most-insatiable-consumer-digs-deep-into-canadian-mines.

Gabuev, A. (2015). A "soft alliance"? Russia-China relations after the Ukraine crisis. *European Council on Foreign Relations.* Retrieved May 20, 2019, from https://www.ecfr.eu/page/-/ECFR126_-_A_Soft_Alliance_Russia-China_Relations_After_the_Ukraine_Crisis.pdf.

Gautier, D.L., Bird, K., Charpentier, R.R., Grantz, A., Houseknecht, D., Klett, T.R., … Wandrey, C.J. (2009). Assessment of undiscovered oil and gas in the Arctic. *Science, 324*(5931), 1175–1179.

Global Innovation Policy Centre. (2018). China. *Global Innovation Policy Centre.* Retrieved October 10, 2018, from https://www.theglobalipcenter.com/ipindex2018-details/?country=cn.

Glomsrød, S., & Aslaksen, I. (2009). The Economy of the North 2008. Statistics Norway: Oslo-Kongsvinger.

Government of Norway. (2015, March 31). Norway confirms intention to join Asian infrastructure investment bank. *Government of Norway*. Retrieved June 10, 2018, from https://www.regjeringen.no/en/aktuelt/Norway_intends_AIIB/id2404331/.

Graczyk, P., & Koivurova, T. (2014). A new era in the Arctic Council's external relations? Broader consequences of the Nuuk observer rules for Arctic governance. *Polar Record, 50*(3), 225.

Graeber, D.J. (2018, March 28). Chinese lender gets in line behind Alaska LNG project. *UPI*. Retrieved November 4, 2018, from https://www.upi.com/Chinese-lender-gets-in-line-behind-Alaska-LNG-project/5221522228885/.

Hamilton, C. (2018). *Silent invasion: China's influence in Australia.* Melbourne & Sydney, Australia: Hardie Grant Books.

Hansen, A.M., & Johnstone, R.L. (2019). In the Shadow of the Mountain: Assessing early impacts on community development from two mining prospects in South Greenland. *The Extractive Industries and Society* 6(2): 480–488.

Hartig, F. (2013). Panda diplomacy: The cutest part of China's public diplomacy. *The Hague Journal of Diplomacy*, 8(1). https://doi.org/10.1163/1871191X-12341245.

Higgins, A. (2014, September 27). A rare Arctic land sale stokes worry in Norway. *New York Times*. Retrieved October 10, 2018, from https://www.nytimes.com/2014/09/28/world/europe/a-rare-arctic-land-sale-stirs-concerns-in-norway.html.

Hillman, J.E. (2019). Influence and Infrastructure: The Strategic Stakes of Foreign Projects. Centre for Strategic and International Studies. Retrieved September 10, 2019, from https://csis-prod.s3.amazonaws.com/s3fs-public/publication/190123_Hillman_InfluenceandInfrastructure_WEB_v3.pdf.

Hoffman, S. (2018, June 28). Social credit. *Australian Strategic Policy Institute*. Retrieved July 10, 2018, from https://www.aspi.org.au/report/social-credit.

Huang, K. (2017, May 21). Will the Arctic be the next stop on China's New Silk Road?. *South China Morning Post.* Retrieved October 20, 2018, from https://www.scmp.com/news/china/diplomacy-defence/article/2095078/will-arctic-be-next-stop-chinas-new-silk-road.

Humpert, M. (2014). Arctic Shipping Potential Along the Northern Sea Route. Report. The Arctic Institute. Retrieve September 3, 2019, from https://www.thearcticinstitute.org/arctic-shipping-potential/.

Humpert, M. (2018, November 26). Traffic on Northern Sea Route Doubles as Russia Aims to Reduce Ice-class Requirements. Retrieved September 3, 2019, from https://www.highnorthnews.com/en/traffic-northern-sea-route-doubles-russia-aims-reduce-ice-class-requirements.

Humpert, M. (2019, March 21). Novatek Allowed to Operate Foreign LNG Carriers on Northern Sea Route. High North News. Retrieved September 3, 2019, from https://

www.highnorthnews.com/en/natural-gas-company-novatek-was-granted-exemption-new-law-banning-foreign-flagged-oil-and-gas.

Huskey, L., Mäenpää, I., & Pelyasov, A. (2014). Economic Systems. In J. Nymand Larsen, & G. Fondahl (eds.), Arctic Human Development Report (2): Regional Processes and Global Linkages. Nordic Council of Ministers.

Icelandic Tourist Board. (2018). Numbers of foreign visitors. *Icelandic Tourist Board.* Retrieved November 20, 2018, from https://www.ferdamalastofa.is/en/recearch-and-statistics/numbers-of-foreign-visitors?fbclid=IwAR1WoHzIat2SA4lIKh50_AaC6bdyrNCLhjnrqx5cOaQdSPoa7jLp-uYutMY.

International Rivers (2012). The New Great Walls: A guide to China's Overseas Dam Industry. Retrieved September 9, 2019, from https://www.internationalrivers.org/resources/the-new-great-walls-a-guide-to-china%E2%80%99s-overseas-dam-industry-3962.

Ivanov, S. (ed.). (2016). Asian players in the Arctic: Interests, opportunities, prospects. Moscow, Russia: Russian International Affairs Council.

Jakobsen, S. (2018, August 24). Maersk sends first container ship through Arctic Route. *Reuters.* Retrieved October 21, 2018, from https://www.reuters.com/article/us-arctic-shipping-maersk/maersk-sends-first-container-ship-through-arctic-route-idUSKCN1L91BR.

Kim, S-K. (2012). China and Japan maritime disputes in the East China Sea: A note on recent developments. *Ocean Development & International Law, 43*(3): 296–308.

Kirkenes Nearingshage. (2018, January). An Arctic railway vision. Report for Finnmark Fylkeskommune and Sor-Varanger Utvikling.

Kynge, J. (2017, July 16). Chinese purchases of overseas ports top $20bn in past year. *Financial Times.* Retrieved June 20, 2018, from https://www.ft.com/content/e00fcfd4-6883-11e7-8526-7b38dcaef614.

Kynge, J., Campbell, C., Kazmin, A., & Bokhari, F. (2017, January 13). How China rules the waves. *Financial Times.* Retrieved June 10, 2018, from https://ig.ft.com/sites/china-ports/.

Käpyla, J., & Mikkola, H. (2018). US engagement in the Arctic. In: Aaltola, M., Salonius-Pasternak, Ch., Käpylä, J. & Sinkkonen, V. (eds). Between change and continuity: making sense of America's evolving global engagement. FIIA Report 54, Finnish Institute of International Affairs, 205–225.

Lackenbauer, P.W., Lajeunesse, A., Manicom, J., & Lasserre, F. (2018). *China's Arctic Ambitions and what they mean for Canada.* University of Calgary Press. E-book. Retrieved August 14, 2019, from https://prism.ucalgary.ca/bitstream/handle/1880/106384/9781552389027_web.pdf?sequence=1&isAllowed=y.

Lajeunesse, A., & Lackenbauer, P.W. (2016). Chinese mining interests and the Arctic. In D.A. Berry, N. Bowle & H. Jones (Eds.), *Governing the North American Arctic. St Antony's Series* London, United Kingdom: Palgrave Macmillan.

Lanteigne, M. (2014, February). The Sino-Swiss free trade agreement. *CSS Analyses in Security Policy, 147*. Retrieved June 10, 2018, from http://www.css.ethz.ch/content/dam/ethz/special-interest/gess/cis/center-for-securities-studies/pdfs/CSSAnalyses147-EN.pdf.

Lanteigne, M., & Ping, S. (2015). China's Developing Arctic Policies: Myths and Misconceptions. *Journal of China and International Relations*, 3(1), 1–25.

Lanteigne, M. (2010, June). Northern exposure: Cross-regionalism and the China-Iceland preferential trade negotiations. *China Quarterly, 202*, 362–380. https://doi.org/10.1017/S0305741010000287.

Lasserre, F., Huang, L., & Alexeeva, O. (2017). China's strategy in the Arctic: Threatening or opportunistic? *Polar Record*, 53(1), 31–42.

Lee Falsey, J. (2017, April 8). A surprise guest: Chinese president makes Anchorage stopover, meets Gov. Walker and takes in some sights. Anchorage Daily News. Retrieved September 3, 2019, from https://www.adn.com/alaska-news/2017/04/07/chinese-president-makes-surprise-visit-to-alaska-following-summit-with-trump/.

Leng, S. (2019, August 20). China's belt and road cargo to Europe under scrutiny as operator admits to moving empty containers. *South China Morning Post*. Retrieved October 2, from https://www.scmp.com/economy/china-economy/article/3023574/chinas-belt-and-road-cargo-europe-under-scrutiny-operator.

Lim, K.S. (2018). China's Arctic policy & the Polar Silk Road vision. In L. Heininen & H. Exner-Pirot (Eds.), *Arctic Yearbook 2018*. Akureyri, Iceland: Northern Research Forum.

Marsh, J. (2015). Supplying the World's Factory: Environmental Impacts of Chinese Resource Extraction in Africa. Tulane Environmental Law Journal 28(2): 393–407.

Mattlin, M., & Nojonen, M. (2015). Conditionality and path dependence in Chinese lending. *Journal of Contemporary China*, 24(94), 701–720. DOI: 10.1080/10670564.2014.978154.

Matzen, E. (2017, April 7). Denmark spurned Chinese offer for Greenland base over security: Sources. *Reuters*. Retrieved June 10, 2018, from https://www.reuters.com/article/us-denmark-china-greenland-base/denmark-spurned-chinese-offer-for-greenland-base-over-security-sources-idUSKBN1782EE.

McCrae, M.A. (2017, August 11). Zinc project in Greenland receives Chinese backing. *Mining.com*. Retrieved June 10, 2018, from http://www.mining.com/zinc-project-greenland-receives-chinese-backing/.

McGwin, K. (2018, May 29). As Greenland's plans to build new airports gather momentum, Denmark is struggling to get on board. *Arctic Today*. Retrieved June 10, 2018, from https://www.arctictoday.com/greenlands-plans-build-new-airports-gather-momentum-denmark-struggling-get-board/.

McPherson, R. (2018, September 11). Parliament's 700 million kroner offer to fund Greenland's airports splits Island's coalition. *Copenhagen Post.* Retrieved November 24, 2018, from http://cphpost.dk/news/parliaments-700-million-kroner-offer-to-fund-greenlands-new-airports-splits-islands-coalition.html.

Mearsheimer, J.J. (2001). *The Tragedy of Great Power Politics.* New York: W.W. Norton & Company.

Mikkola, H. (2019, April). The Geostrategic Arctic: Hard Security in the High North. *FIIA Briefing Paper* 259. Helsinki: Finnish Institute of International Affairs. Retrieved July 17, 2019, from https://www.fiia.fi/wp-content/uploads/2019/04/bp259_geostrategic_arctic.pdf.

Mikkola, H., Aaltola, M., Wigell, M., Juntunen, T., & Vihma, A. (2018). Hybridivaikuttaminen ja demokratian resilienssi. Ulkoisen häirinnän mahdollisuudet ja torjuntakyky liberaaleissa demokratioissa. *FIIA Report* 55. Helsinki: Finnish Institute of International Affairs. [Hybrid influencing and the vulnerabilities and resilience of democracy, in Finnish] Retrieved July 17, 2019, from https://www.fiia.fi/wp-content/uploads/2018/05/fiia_report55_web_hybrdivaikuttaminen-ja-resilienssi.pdf.

Ministry of Commerce PRC. (People's Republic of China). (2013). Guidelines on environmental protection in foreign investment and cooperation. *Ministry of Commerce.* Retrieved June 20, 2018, from english.mofcom.gov.cn/article/policyrelease/bbb/201303/20130300043226.shtml.

Ministry of Commerce. (PRC) (2014). *Ministry of commerce introduces newly revised measures for foreign investment management.* Ministry of Commerce People's Republic of China. Retrieved June 20, 2018, from english.mofcom.gov.cn/article/news release/significantnews/201409/20140900729955.shtml.

Ministry of Foreign Affairs Denmark (2018, September 17). The Kingdom of Denmark, including Greenland, welcomes the United States "Statement of Intent on Defense Investments in Greenland". Retrieved September 20, 2018, from http://um.dk/en/news/newsdisplaypage/?newsid=bfc95523-956b-4df9-aba1-6e3f93cfb06d.

Ministry of Foreign Affairs (PRC) (2018). China Night Lights Up 2018 Arctic Circle Assembly. Ministry of Foreign Affairs of the People's Republic of China. Retrieved July 19, 2019, from https://www.fmprc.gov.cn/mfa_eng/wjb_663304/zwjg_665342/zwbd_665378/t1606536.shtml.

Moe, A. & Stokke, O.S. (2019). Asian Countries and Arctic Shipping: Policies, Interests and Footprints on Governance. *Arctic Review on Law and Politics* 10: 24–52.

Mourdoukoutas, P. (2018, Aug 4). What is China doing in Africa? *Forbes.* Retrieved June 5, 2019, from https://www.forbes.com/sites/panosmourdoukoutas/2018/08/04/china-is-treating-africa-the-same-way-european-colonists-did/#6023dac6298b.

Munro, K. (2018, June 27). China's social credit system could interfere in other nations' sovereignty. *The Guardian.* Retrieved July 10, 2018, from https://www.theguardian.com/world/2018/jun/28/chinas-social-credit-system-could-interfere-in-other-nations-sovereignty.

NDRC (2017). Opinions on Further Guiding and Regulating Outbound Investment. [关于进一步引导和规范境外投资方向的指导意见] National Development and Reform Commission. Retrieved October 2, 2019, from http://www.ndrc.gov.cn/gzdt/201708/t20170818_858265.html.

Nye, J.S. Jr. (2008). *The powers to lead.* Oxford, England; New York, NY: Oxford University Press.

Nye, J.S. Jr. (2008, July/August). Combining Hard and Soft Power. *Foreign Affairs.* Retrieved September 9, 2019, from https://www.foreignaffairs.com/articles/2009-07-01/get-smart?page=1.

Nye, J.S. Jr. (2018). How sharp power threatens soft power. *Foreign Affairs.* Retrieved August 14, 2019, from https://www.foreignaffairs.com/articles/china/2018-01-24/how-sharp-power-threatens-soft-power.

Office of the Secretary of Defense. (2019). Annual report to Congress: Military and security developments Involving the People's Republic of China. *Office of the Secretary of Defence.* Retrieved August 14, 2019, from https://media.defense.gov/2019/May/02/2002127082/-1/-1/1/2019_CHINA_MILITARY_POWER_REPORT.pdf.

Olsen, L.S. et al. (2016). Sustainable Business Development in the Nordic Arctic. Stockholm: Nordregio Nordic Centre for Spatial Development.

Over the Circle. (2018, January 24). Stumbling block: China-Iceland oil exploration reaches an impasse. *Over the Circle.* Retrieved June 10, 2018, from https://overthecircle.com/2018/01/24/stumbling-block-china-iceland-oil-exploration-reaches-an-impasse/.

Patey, L. (2017, January 24). China Made Mauricio Macri a Deal He Couldn't Refuse. *Foreign Policy.* Retrieved October 3, 2019, from https://foreignpolicy.com/2017/01/24/china-made-mauricio-macri-a-deal-he-couldnt-refuse/.

Percival, B. (2007). *The Dragon Looks South. China and Southeast Asia in the New Century.* Westport, CT: Praeger Security International.

PRC State Council. (2018, January 26). Full text: China's Arctic policy. Beijing, China: The State Council Information Office of the People's Republic of China. Retrieved March 26, 2018, from http://english.gov.cn/archive/white_paper/2018/01/26/content_281476026660336.htm.

Prime Minister's Office. (2013). Finland's strategy for the Arctic region 2013.

Regulation (EU) 2019/452 of the European Parliament and of the Council of 19 March 2019 establishing a framework for the screening of foreign direct investments into the Union. European Union.

Reuters. (2018, August 2). China says free trade talks with Norway should be accelerated. *Reuters.* Retrieved, August 20, 2018, from https://www.reuters.com/article/asean-singapore-china-norway/china-says-free-trade-talks-with-norway-should-be-accelerated-idUSL4N1UT0O6.

Reuters. (2018, August 19). Russia's Novatek ships first LNG cargo to China via Arctic. *Reuters.* Retrieved August 20, 2018, from https://www.reuters.com/article/

us-novatek-cnpc-lng/russias-novatek-ships-first-lng-cargo-to-china-via-arctic-idUSKBN1K90YN.

Rosen, K. (2018, January 2). N.W.T. needs to get ready for influx of Chinese tourists, says tour operator. *CBC News North*. Retrieved August 20, 2018, from https://www.cbc.ca/news/canada/north/nwt-tourism-chinese-tourists-1.4439402.

Rosen, M.E., & Thuringen, C.B. (2017, November). Unconstrained foreign direct investment: An emerging challenge to Arctic security. *CNA Analysis and Solution*.

Russia Today. (RT). (2018, July 27). China planning to develop tourist routes across Russia's Arctic region. *Russia Today*. Retrieved August 20, 2018, from https://www.rt.com/business/434409-china-tourist-routes-arctic/.

Salonius-Pasternak, C. (2017). An effective antidote: The four components that make Finland more resilient to hybrid campaigns. *FIIA Comment* 19/2017. Helsinki: Finnish Institute of International Affairs. Retrieved July 17, 2019, from https://www.fiia.fi/wp-content/uploads/2017/10/comment19_finland.pdf.

Sander, G., Gille, J., Stępień, A., Koivurova, T., Thomas, J., Gascard, J-C., & Justus, D. (2016). Changes in Arctic maritime transport. In A. Stępień, T. Koivurova & P. Kankaanpää (Eds.), *The Changing Arctic and the European Union*. Leiden, Netherlands; Boston, MA: Brill & Nijhoff.

Schweitzer, P., Stammler, F., Ebsen, C., Ivanova, A., & Litvina, I. (2019). Social Impacts of Non-Renewable Resource Development on Indigenous communities in Alaska, Greenland, and Russia. Resources and Sustainable Development in the Arctic Gap Report #2A. Lakehead University and Yukon College. Retrieved September 10, 2019, from http://yukonresearch.yukoncollege.yk.ca/wpmu/wp-content/uploads/sites/2/2013/09/2-Schweitzer-Gap-analysis-final.pdf.

Shi, M., & Lanteigne, M. (2018, March 30). The (many) roles of Greenland in China's developing Arctic policy. *The Diplomat*. Retrieved June 20, 2018, from https://thediplomat.com/2018/03/the-many-roles-of-greenland-in-chinas-developing-arctic-policy/.

Soldatkin, V., & Jaganathan, J. (2019, September 5). Russia ups LNG race with green light on $21 billion Arctic LNG-2 project. Retrieved October 3, 2019, from https://www.reuters.com/article/us-russia-energy-novatek-lng/russia-ups-lng-race-with-green-light-on-21-billion-arctic-lng-2-project-idUSKCN1VQ0IH.

Staalesen, A. (2014 October 21). No Chinese resort in Svalbard, after all. *The Barents Observer*. Retrieved October 10, 2018, from https://thebarentsObserver.com/en/arctic/2016/10/no-chinese-resort-svalbard-after-all.

Staalesen, A. (2018, June 14). China's National Oil Company looks at Russian Arctic LNG. *The Barents Observer*. Retrieved October 2, 2019, from https://thebarentsobserver.com/en/industry-and-energy/2018/06/chinas-national-oil-company-looks-russian-arctic-lng.

Staalesen, A. (2018, June 29). Arctic LNG carriers sail into deep ice with course for China. *The Barents Observer*. Retrieved October 2, 2019, from https://thebarentsobserver.com/en/industry-and-energy/2018/06/arctic-lng-carriers-sail-deep-ice-course-china.

Staalesen, A. (2019, January 2). It's a law – Russian Arctic shipping to be regulated by Rosatom. *The Barents Observer*. Retrieved September 3, 2019, from https://thebarentsobserver.com/en/arctic/2019/01/its-law-russian-arctic-shipping-be-regulated-rosatom.

Staalesen, A. (2019, July 1, 2019). Japan teams up with Russia in big Arctic LNG. *The Barents Observer*. Retrieved October 2, 2019, from https://thebarentsobserver.com/en/industry-and-energy/2019/07/japan-teams-russia-big-arctic-lng.

Staalesen, A. (2019, September 27). China's first Yamal LNG tanker is soon on its way to Murmansk. *The Barents Observer*. Retrieved October 2, 2019, from https://thebarentsobserver.com/en/industry-and-energy/2019/09/chinas-first-yamal-lng-tanker-sets-course-murmansk.

Statement of the Government of the People's Republic of China and the Government of the Kingdom of Norway on Normalization of Bilateral Relations (2016, December 21). Retrieved September 8, 2019, from https://www.regjeringen.no/globalassets/departementene/ud/vedlegg/statement_kina.pdf.

Stepien, A. (2017). Incentives, practices and opportunities for Arctic external actors' engagement with indigenous peoples: China and the European Union. In T. Koivurova, T. Qin, S. Duyck & T. Nykänen (Eds.), *Arctic Law and Governance: The Role of China and Finland*. Oxford, England: Hart Publishing.

Stępień, A., & Koivurova, T. (2017, February). *Arctic Europe: Bringing together EU Arctic policy and Nordic cooperation.* Publications of the Government's Analysis, Assessment and Research Activities 15/2017. Prime Minister's Office.

Stepien, A., Koivurova, T., & Kankaanpää, P. (2016). The Changing Arctic and the European Union. Brill/Nijhoff.

Stewart, P., & Ali, I. (2019, May 3). Pentagon warns on risk of Chinese submarines in Arctic. *Reuters*. Retrieved October 3, 2019, from https://www.reuters.com/article/us-usa-china-military-arctic/pentagon-warns-on-risk-of-chinese-submarines-in-arctic-idUSKCN1S829H.

Sun, Y. (2018). The Northern Sea Route: The myth of Sino-Russian cooperation. *Stimson Centre*. Retrieved May 15, 2018, from https://www.stimson.org/sites/default/files/file-attachments/Stimson%20-%20The%20Northern%20Sea%20Route%20-%20The%20Myth%20of%20Sino-Russian%20Cooperation.pdf.

Suokas, J. (2018, January 31). Chinese investors cancel plans for massive deepwater port in Sweden. GB Times. Retrieved on September 9, 2019, from https://gbtimes.com/chinese-investors-cancel-plans-for-massive-deep-water-port-in-sweden.

Switzerland Federal Department of Foreign Affairs. (FDFA). (2018). Bilateral relations between Switzerland and Liechtenstein. *Federal Department of Foreign Affairs*. Retrieved September, 2018, from https://www.eda.admin.ch/eda/en/home/representations-and-travel-advice/liechtenstein/switzerland-liechtenstein.html.

Tonami, A. (2019). The rise of Asia and Arctic legal order-making: political-economic settings. In A. Shibata, L. Zou, N. Sellheim, & M. Scopelliti (eds.) *Emerging Legal Orders in the Arctic: The Role of Non-Arctic Actors*. Routledge: New York.

UNCTAD Fact Sheets (n.d.). Country fact sheet: China. UN Conference on Trade and Development. Retrieved October 2, 2019, from https://unctad.org/en/Pages/DIAE/World%20Investment%20Report/Country-Fact-Sheets.aspx.

UNCTAD (UN Conference on Trade and Development) website at www.unctad.org .Retrieved October 2, 2019.

U.S. Geological Survey. (2008). Circum-Arctic resource appraisal: Estimates of undiscovered oil and gas north of the Arctic Circle. *U.S. Department of the Interior.* Retrieved August 14, 2019, from http://pubs.usgs.gov/fs/2008/3049/fs2008-3049.pdf.

Walker, C. (2018). What is "sharp power"? *Journal of Democracy*, 29(3), 9–23.

Walker, C., & Ludwig, J. (2017). From 'Soft Power' to 'Sharp Power': Rising Authoritarian Influence in the Democratic World. In J.P. Cardenal, J. Kucharczyk, G. Mesežniko & G. Pleschová (Eds.), *Sharp Power: Rising Authoritarian Influence* (8–25). Forum: International Forum for Democratic Studies. Retrieved from https://www.ned.org/sharp-power-rising-authoritarian-influence-forum-report/.

Wang, M. (2018, January 20). Finland welcomes China's panda pair. *China Daily.* Retrieved July 19, 2019, from http://www.chinadaily.com.cn/a/201801/20/WS5a62afc7a3106e7dcc1357a1.html.

Wigell, M. (2019). Hybrid interference as a wedge strategy: a theory of external interference in liberal democracy. 95 *International Affairs* 2: 255–275.

Xinhua Agency. (2017, July 17). *Xinhua.* Retrieved October 10, 2018, from http://www.xinhuanet.com/politics/2017-07/17/c_1121333722.htm.

Xu Klein, J. (2018, September 14). It's not just the US: around the world, doors are shutting on Chinese investment. *South China Morning Post.* Retrieved September 10, 2019, from https://www.scmp.com/business/banking-finance/article/2163974/its-not-just-us-around-world-doors-are-shutting-chinese.

Yang, M. (2017, November 30). Polar Tourism: A New Favorite in China. CGTN. Retrieved June 15, 2018, from https://news.cgtn.com/news/3267544d7a637a6333566d54/share_p.html.

Zellen, B. (2009). Arctic Doom, Arctic Boom: The Geopolitics of Climate Change in the Arctic. Praeger Security International.

Zhou, L. (2019, August 3). Canada's detention of Huawei executive Meng Wanzhou 'angered Chinese people'. South China Morning Post. Retrieved September 3, 2019, from https://www.scmp.com/news/china/diplomacy/article/3021306/canadas-detention-huawei-executive-meng-wanzhou-angered.

Interviews

Interviewee 1, June 13, 2018.

Interviewee 2, June 12, 2018.

CHAPTER 7

Chinese-Finnish Economic Relations within the Arctic Context: Hopes and Disappointments

Adam Stepien, Timo Koivurova, Juha Käpylä, Harri Mikkola and Matti Nojonen

7.1 Introduction

In its 2013 Arctic Strategy, the Finnish government stated that there is great value in bilateral Arctic partnerships with various actors (Prime Minister's Office, 2013: 15). In light of the increasing Chinese economic activities in the Arctic (see Chapter 6 in this volume), Chinese investors, companies and clients could be, in principle, interesting partners for Finland in that regard.

This chapter focuses on the economic relations between China and Finland in the Arctic context. This is done from two perspectives. First, we consider China's investments and presence in northern Finland and particularly in Finnish Lapland, the country's northernmost province, the majority of which is located north of the Arctic Circle. At present, the sectors with Chinese investment presence are bioeconomy and tourism. In terms of future prospects, mining, renewable energy, data centers, testing facilities, and participation in the Arctic railway project could become relevant. Second, we look at the instances of economic cooperation in areas of Finnish Arctic expertise. These include Finnish investments in China, Chinese in Finland, and joint ventures.

There is scant data available in terms of the monetary value of current Chinese investments in Arctic sectors and even less in terms of assessing future potential. The potential for Sino-Finnish economic cooperation is thus discussed here without quantifying the overall value of investments or contracts. In most of the identified areas for business collaboration, there have been few or no examples of implemented Arctic-specific actions. Therefore, rather than providing uncertain and indicative monetary calculations of Chinese investment potential, this chapter presents a broad overview of sectors in which activities have already been implemented or in which cooperation may occur in the future. Rare cases of implemented or announced investment and other activities or plans are described in greater detail. The potential for Sino-Finnish economic ties was considered by taking into account the following: the sectors

© KONINKLIJKE BRILL NV, LEIDEN, 2020 | DOI:10.1163/9789004408425_008

of Finnish Arctic expertise,[1] the developmental trajectories in northern Finland, China's main areas of interest in the Arctic,[2] and recent investments and current plans.

The work on this chapter was carried out as a desk study supported by personal communication with experts and stakeholders dealing with or engaged in instances of Sino-Finnish cooperation, persons promoting Finnish Arctic expertise, as well as relevant public and private actors in Finnish Lapland. The interviews had a semi-structured format and they were carried out in person, by phone or by email. All interviews are anonymized with the exception of interviewees who explicitly wished to be mentioned by name. For contemporary and ongoing developments, these interviews are often the main source of information included in this chapter in addition to recent media reports.

7.2 Overall Economic Relations between China and Finland

Finland has established a broad range of ties with China, ranging from diplomatic, trade and investment relations to scientific collaboration and tourism. Historically, Finland was one of the first Western countries (with Sweden and Denmark) to recognize (in 1950) the People's Republic of China and to establish diplomatic relations. The Finnish embassy was established in Beijing in 1952. In the following year, Finland and China signed an economic cooperation agreement – the first of its kind between a Western (capitalist) state and the newly established People's Republic. In practice, however, bilateral relations did not intensify before the late 1970s because of domestic turmoil caused by the Cultural Revolution in China. Moreover, Finland's foreign policy was heavily directed by the *Agreement of Friendship, Cooperation, and Mutual Assistance* (1948–1992) with the Soviet Union, which had ideological tensions with China since the Sino-Soviet split in the late 1950s. A crucial step in bilateral relations was taken in 1979, when China entered its opening and reform period, with Chinese Premier Geng Biao's official visit to Finland. In the same year, an Agreement on economic, industrial, scientific and technological cooperation was signed. Numerous state visits took place in the 1980s and the 1990s[3] (Embassy of Finland, Beijing, 2014).

---

1 Based on Finland's official Arctic documents: 2013 Strategy and 2017 Action plan (Prime Minister's Office, 2013, 2017).

2 Chinese interests in the Arctic; and thus, potential activities of Chinese public and private actors are those identified by the Chinese government in its Arctic Policy White Paper from January 2018 (PRC State Council, 2018).

3 For instance, Finnish Foreign Minister Paavo Väyrynen visited Beijing in 1984, Prime Minister Kalevi Sorsa in 1986, and President Mauno Koivisto in 1988. Chinese President Jiang Zemin

Today, there are about 400 Finnish companies engaged in various operations in China (Finnish Business Council Beijing, n.d.), in a broad variety of activities. For instance, to name a few illustrative examples, Finnish company Valmet supplied a waste-fired boiler to Shanying Huazhong Paper's paper mill in Jingzhou in Hubei province, Nokia will deploy a cloud-native core network in seven Chinese provinces, laying the foundation for future 5G connectivity (Business Finland, 2018, February 5), and Wärtsilä in 2017 won a contract for the construction of a gas-fueled power plant (30 MW combined heat and power plant) in Guangzhou.

For Finland, China is an important trade partner. Recently, Finnish-Chinese trade has been generally growing year-to-year, both in terms of imports and exports (however, service imports from China went down by 16 percent and exports to China fell by four percent from 2016). In 2017, the import of goods from China reached €4.560bln (€4.995bln when services are included), constituting 7.3% of all Finnish imports and representing a 12% year-to-year growth. The export of goods was at €3.392bln, representing 5.7% of all Finland's exports and a year-to-year growth at 27% (€4.242bln when services are included) (Statistics Finland – Finnish Customs, 2017). Within these international trade numbers, Finnish high technology imports from China reached €1.573bln (representing 22.1% of all high technology imports and the annual growth by 23%) and high technology exports to China stood at €517m (representing 12.9% of all exports and the annual growth by 25%) (Customs Finland, 2018). Finland's overall trade relations with China are therefore strong and China is clearly of high importance for the Finnish economy.

In 2009–2018, Chinese foreign direct investments in Finland stood at US16.28$bln, compared to US$11.96bln in Sweden and US$4.31bln in Norway (AEI, n.d.), although the high number for Finland is primarily a result of a couple of major company takeovers, such as Tancent's acquisition of the shares of Finnish game maker company Supercell. Due to the latter transaction, Finland statistically became one of the largest recipients of Chinese Foreign Direct Investment in the EU in 2016. Nonetheless, compared both to the total level of foreign investment in Finland and to overall Chinese overseas direct investment (ODI), only a small percentage of Chinese investments have been located in Finland and Chinese investments constitute only a small part of foreign investment activity in the country (10% in 2016–2017, mostly accounted for by the Supercell transaction, see OECD Data, n.d.). Overall, the majority of Chinese investments in Finland focus on high tech. These include the aforementioned Tecent Supercell purchase, as well as the acquisition of the Finnish

visited Finland in 1995, and after that, several official meetings have taken place between the two countries (Embassy of Finland, Beijing, 2014).

company Okmetic by China-based National Semiconductor Industry Group, and Rightware being bought by Thundersoft. Huawei operates two research and development (R&D) units in Finland. Among others, the predominance of technological investments may be a result of "structural upgrade to knowledge intensive industries" in China (Zhu Bin at Business Finland, 2017, April 11). Considering the structure of the Finnish economy, such a shift may be beneficial for Sino-Finnish economic relations. A stronger focus on innovation in China – both in terms of innovative products and 'innovative markets' – makes Finland an attractive partner for Chinese companies. Finland can also become a testbed for Chinese products and solutions due to developed business-research clusters, the Finnish startup landscape, the culture of innovation, and the stable and predictable business environment. Good transport connections between Helsinki and China may also play a role in encouraging Chinese investors to look at opportunities in Finland. A synergy of particular value could be the combination of Finnish innovation and Chinese scaling-up capabilities (Ibid.). At present, Finland remains among the European countries perceived in China as most open and welcoming to Chinese investments. In some countries, Chinese companies may receive special treatment. That is not necessarily an advantage if there is a possibility of such a special status being revoked for political or other reasons, adding to business risk level. In Finland, Chinese investors are generally treated on par with European and Finnish business actors, which, in principle, may attract those who value long-term certainty over higher profits in the short term (personal communication, Interviewee 10, August 20, 2018).

On the other hand, among aspects discouraging Chinese investors are: the small size of the Finnish market, high operation costs and high taxation, as well as a lack of familiarity with Finland among Chinese companies. In addition, slow and complex zoning and permitting procedures may be discouraging for Chinese firms. Of concern are also lengthy and (perceived by some as) "unfriendly" visa procedures, partly related to the limited capacities of Finnish consular services in China (personal communication, Interviewee 10, August 20, 2018).

The interest in and political support for Sino-Finnish economic relations was heightened following the visit of President Xi Jinping to Helsinki in April 2017. On the occasion of this state visit, a number of business and cooperation agreements were signed, including: the Memorandum of Understanding (MoU) between China's Ministry of Science and Technology and Tekes (at present Business Finland); a collaboration programme between Finpro (currently, following a merger with Tekes, operating as Business Finland) and China Development Bank; an agreement between Finpro and China Council for the Promotion of International Trade; as well as agreements related to two bioeconomy projects in Lapland, described later in this chapter. A committee for innovative business cooperation was also established. The Joint Declaration, signed upon Xi's visit, lists energy, information and communication technology (ICT), tourism and winter sports as among the sectors in which joint activities are to be encouraged. The commentators' expectations following Xi's visit were that it would raise interest in and awareness of Finland among Chinese companies and investors. Overall, there have been signs of Chinese encouragement for Nordic investment in the country. For example, in 2016, state-owned Beijing Capital Investment announced plans to start a €400mil fund aimed at finding Nordic companies with growth potential in China, with a focus on high-tech, cleantech, health care, renewables and production technology (YLE Uutiset, 2016, September 6).

Several companies from Finnish Lapland are present in China, making the Chinese market an important one in terms of the commercial success of Lappish entrepreneurs and the region's labor market. For instance, the Rovaniemi-based playground and outdoor sport equipment producer Lappset has gained a significant position as a foreign investor in the Chinese market in its area of business (including via the so-called "Happy Sport China Plan"). Rovaniemi LogHouses – producing log buildings for winter sports facilities, among other uses – is present in Chinese skiing resorts and golf courses (personal communication, Esko Lotvonen, Rovaniemi, June 20, 2018; Interviewee 11, September 03, 2018). Furthermore, the company operating the Santa Park theme park in Rovaniemi has been developing a project to establish a Santa Claus theme park in the northern Chinese province of Heilongjiang.

Business Finland and Team Finland, both of which support Finnish businesses in China, have offices in Beijing, Shanghai, Hong Kong and Guangzhou, although these support services conduct activities all across the country. Since 2005, the Finland-China Innovation Centre (FinChi) has been operating in Shanghai (FinChi, n.d.), offering support for Finnish high tech companies when entering the Chinese market and finding collaboration partners. Interviewees from Finnish companies based in Lapland and active in China described the support of these institutions as helpful.

7.3 Developments in Northern Finland: Potential for Chinese Involvement?

While Finland's 2013 Arctic Strategy (Prime Minister's Office, 2013) considers the whole territory of Finland as a part of the Arctic, Lapland and Northern

Finland were given particular attention. The strategy expresses a conviction that "Lapland has every chance of providing an attractive living environment in the future" based on infrastructure, expertise, existing networks and Arctic/ Barents economic developments (Ibid.: 20). In principle, Chinese companies and investors could support and influence the region's economic growth and job creation. The activity of Chinese companies in Arctic regions constitutes one dimension of China's Arctic policy. "To develop the Arctic" is one of the objectives of the 2018 White Paper (PRC State Council, 2018). This goal is to be achieved through contributing to the "economic and social development of the Arctic" and improving the "living conditions of the local people". The activities of Chinese companies in the Arctic can be expected to receive strategic and political support from the Chinese government, as they may be seen as beneficial for China's overall aims in Arctic regions.

At a declaratory level, "common development" and win-win approaches mean that China's presence in the Arctic should benefit the Arctic regions at the same time as it is profitable for Chinese actors. This is a language typically used, for example, with regard to the Belt and Road Initiative (BRI). The 2018 White Paper states that "all stakeholders in this area should pursue mutual benefit and common progress in all fields of activities" and "cooperation should ensure that the benefits are shared by both Arctic and non-Arctic States as well as by non-state entities, and should accommodate the interests of local residents including the indigenous peoples" (PRC State Council, 2018). Such statements are, however, declarations and it is not necessarily true that the Chinese government has full control over Chinese companies' activities at the operational level.

Chinese companies may be in a position to offer competitive prices for construction work and other services needed for the implementation of development projects in Northern Lapland. This may be, however, problematic for Finnish companies afraid of losing part of the domestic market and may affect the labor market in some sparsely-populated regions of Finland. Some experts in Lapland believe that the Chinese presence can be economically important for Lapland's economy, which is considered to be somewhat overlooked by domestic investors (Jaakko Ylinampa from Lapland ELY-Keskus at News Now Finland, 2017, November 6).

The three most prominent areas in which Chinese actors are already involved or where there is potential for future activities are bioeconomy in northern Finland, tourism in Lapland, and the plan to construct a new railway to the Arctic Ocean. These sectors are discussed below in greater detail, followed by other areas of regional economy such as mining and renewable energy.

7.3.1 *Biorefinery and Biofuels Projects*

The forestry sector remains one of the key industries in northern Finland, constituting between 8% and 17% of economic activity in Lapland.[4] Currently, a number of investment plans across Lapland, Northern Ostrobothnia and Kainuu are expected to add to the existing wood refining capacities. Among its many objectives, the Finnish Arctic Strategy (Prime Minister's Office, 2013: 54) sets the goal to increase the use of wood as a local renewable energy resource, as well as increase the diversity of business and entrepreneurship based on northern forests. Finland also adopted a 30% target for the share of biofuels in road traffic by 2029 (Business Finland, 2019, February 19).

The EU's revised Renewable Energy Directive (2018/2001/EU) integrates biofuels into EU targets, especially for transport transition, while setting new sustainability criteria for biofuels that can be accounted for. The new legislation is expected to support biofuel production in Finland, as it effectively promotes non-food-based biofuels and creates stable rules for business operations when national legislation implementing the directive is adopted.[5]

Bio-refining, bioenergy and biofuels constitute an important area for prospective Chinese investment. Many actors in Lapland believe that the region has significant potential in terms of underutilized annual forest growth and side-streams originating from the forestry industry (e.g. wood chips). Chinese companies have acquired a technological edge and expertise in bioenergy and biofuels. Currently, two bioeconomy projects in Lapland involve Chinese investors: the Kemi biofuel project (by the Chinese firm Kaidi) and the Kemijärvi Boreal Bioref Ltd. bio-refinery project.

The Kaidi biofuels project in Kemi (on the coast of the Bay of Bothnia) is a €900m investment plan for the construction of a refinery producing biodiesel (75%) and biopetrol (25%). Annual production is estimated at 225,000 tonnes of biofuel, utilising 2.8mil cubic meters of raw material originating from within a radius of up to 200km from Kemi (Kaidi, n.d.). The company – following the National Forest Inventory (VMI) assessment – claims that the planned annual wood use is within the sustainable harvesting limits in the region. Technology developed by the Chinese parent company, Kaidi Sunshine, would be utilized. Kaidi Finland estimates that 4000 work-years would be needed for the construction phase, and the operational phase would generate 150 jobs in Kemi. Annual tax output is projected at €200m.

4 Considering annual fluctuations in economic activity.

5 The text of the directive is, however, a compromise outcome and has been criticized for effectively supporting forestry (Searchinger et al., 2018).

Since early 2016, Kaidi Finland has been searching for investors. In April 2018, the project received a preliminary environmental and water management decision, but the investment decision has been postponed at least until 2021, following the adoption of the national law implementing the EU's Renewable Energy Directive (Kaihlanen, 2019, January 23). The project is likely to be seriously delayed or completely abandoned as the Kaidi parent company is facing challenges in China, and some experts have doubts about the efficiency of the proposed biorefining technology (personal communication, Interviewee 3, June 12, 2018; Interviewee 10, August 20, 2018).

Boreal Bioref Ltd. plans a single-line bio-refinery project in Kemijärvi in Eastern Lapland. If constructed, the refinery will produce bleached kraft softwood pulp, dissolving pulp and microcrystalline cellulose (MCC) – three kinds of cellulose utilized for different products and purposes in the industry. The refinery will utilise Lapland's timber production (2.8mil cubic meters including the local sawmill and glulam plant's leftover wood chips). In addition, biogas will be produced from waste products (Rautajoki & Lakkapää, 2018). In 2017, Chinese economic actors decided to invest in the Kemijärvi project. CAMC Engineering Ltd. (CAMCE) (*Zhonggong Guoji Gongcheng Gufen Youxiangongsi* 中工国际工程股份有限公司) has become a shareholder in Boreal Bioref Oy, and the engineering, procurement and construction contract was signed (also including CAMCE Swedish partner, Silvi Industries AB). The financing agreement for the construction of the bio-refinery was signed with the Chinese Development Bank (*Guojia Kaifa Yinhang* 国家开发银行). Shenyang Investment Management Ltd. and Shanying International Holding (*Shanying Guoji Konggu Gufen Gongsi* 山鹰国际控股股份公司) were originally to become the majority shareholders as well as product buyers and operational partners. Shanying is a Chinese paper and wood company with a presence in Japan, the U.S. and Europe, including Sweden. In contrast to Kaidi, the Kemijärvi project is to operate based on technology developed primarily in Finland (personal communication, Interviewee 8, June 28, 2018). In January 2020, the shareholding of Chinese partners in the project was decreased to below 50% due to concerns over Chinese companies holding majority control. China is Finland's largest single export market for pulp, so the interest of Chinese investors in Finnish bioenergy projects should not come as a surprise (Rautajoki & Lakkapää, 2018: 29–42). So far, no specific contracts have been signed for the purchase of the Boreal Bioref production, and while it is expected that the majority of production will be exported to China, the market for pulp – according to project developers – is diverse and broad enough at the moment to prevent dependence on a single buyer or exclusively on the Chinese demand (personal communication, Interviewee 8, June 28, 2018). The Boreal Bioref Oy project is fairly advanced, awaiting a formal environmental permit (at the time of finalizing this book). Multiple changes in the project structure and investments value, however, raise doubts about the chances of its implementation.

Globally, Chinese companies are currently particularly interested in biorefinery investments. This is due to the expectation among Chinese producers that shortages of raw materials may occur in connection to newly introduced limits on the imports of cardboard and paper waste into China. At the same time, the opportunities for biorefining in China are limited. In the Arctic context, Finland appears more attractive than, for instance, Russia, owing to its political stability and strong forestry and biorefining traditions, EU market access, as well as the availability of technological solutions provided by companies such as Valmet or Andritz (Ibid.).

It is possible that investments such as the Kemijärvi biorefinery would be followed up by other Chinese activities. For instance, as most of the produced pulp is planned to reach Chinese clients, the improvement of transport connectivity could be among interesting areas of future long-term engagement, including the railway project discussed further in this chapter. The current economic feasibility of the biorefineries under development is not, however, dependent on transport connections additional to the currently available ones (personal communication, Interviewee 3, Rovaniemi, June 12, 2018).

An emerging challenge related to biorefinery investments in northern Finland is the availability of raw material. National assessments indicate that economically-used forests in the region are underutilized. This situation may change if all projects currently in the pipeline are implemented. Recently, Metsä Group announced its own investment plans for the Kemi biorefinery, with estimated raw material needs reaching 6.7mil cubic meters. It could be the case in the future that wood for Finnish refineries would need to be imported from Russia, Sweden and the Baltic states (Kallio, 2018, September 25). However, project developers believe that the amount of wood in Lapland is sufficient to allow sustainable use by all biorefineries planned at present (personal communication, Interviewee 8, June 28, 2018). There are, however, environmental concerns related to biodiversity in the areas of increased wood production. Old-growth forests are biodiversity hotspots, forests provide other ecosystem services than wood, and forestry may also adversely affect the forest bedding and the multiple species dependent on it (see e.g. WWF, 2016).

7.3.2 *Tourism*

The Finnish Arctic tourist attractions include the Lappish natural environment, winter conditions, skiing resorts, cultural heritage, as well as Christmas-related sights and activities. The whole Arctic region has recently become an object of public interest owing to media attention related to climate change impacts, among other factors. Good transport connections make Finnish Lapland one of the easiest circumpolar locations to access. Due to the emergence of Helsinki as a hub for Europe-Asia flights, northern Finland is already easily accessible for Asian tourists. In 2016, the StopOver Finland offers were launched (potentially leading to increased numbers of Chinese tourists also in the North). There is a possibility for direct Beijing-Rovaniemi flights in the near future, making it an even more attractive destination. Among the goals of Finland's Arctic Strategy is to improve tourists' access to Finnish Lapland.

In general, "sustainable tourism" – a term largely undefined and abstract[6] – is one of the central themes of Finland's Arctic Strategy in regard to Lapland's regional development. Moreover, the connections between the Arctic bioeconomy and tourism are sought, for instance, via the focus on endemic food production in the North and integrating it into tourism offers (Prime Minister's Office, 2017: 5). Policymakers declare the aim towards the "sustainable concentration of tourist services" (Prime Minister's Office, 2013: 55).

The tourism industry in Lapland has been growing dynamically in recent years, with almost 3 million overnight stays in Lapland (not including AirBnB and private cabin rentals), 52% of which were foreign tourists (6% year-to-year growth). Chinese tourists are still a relatively small group – 67,674 within the 1,563,495 nights spent by foreign tourists in Lapland – although their numbers are growing every year (35,084 in 2016 and 63,668 in 2017) (Statistics Finland, 2019, April 9, see also Regional Council of Lapland, 2017; Yle Uutiset, 2019, February 11). Markedly, in 2017, Chinese tourists constituted 12% of foreign visitors in Rovaniemi alone (a higher percentage than for the whole of Lapland). The length of stay for Chinese tourists is quite short – 1.58 nights per stay as

6 The portal VisitFinland defines sustainable tourism as "committed to having a positive impact on nature, society and the economy, leaving a low ecological footprint and honouring local cultures. Keep nature clean by choosing environmentally-friendly options in modes of travel, and recycle, reuse and reduce your overall consumption and waste. Choose locally-produced and ethically-made food and products [...]" (Visit Finland, n.d.). Such a definition would, in fact, be a better fit to describe responsible tourism or even responsible nature tourism. It is unclear how encouraging the increased number of (often long-haul) flights for hundreds of thousands of new visitors is to be presented as sustainable, especially considering that China declares a commitment to promote "low-carbon tourism" (PRC State Council, 2018). A report for the Nordic Council of Ministers (Øian, 2018) provides a less ambitious definition: "[t]ourism is held to be sustainable to the extent tourism-specific planning and management systems take full account of current and future economic, social and environmental impacts. The interests of visitors, the industry, the environment and host communities should accordingly be balanced against each other".

compared to an average of 2.41 nights for all tourists in 2017. This may be related to Chinese visits in Lapland often being part of package tours around Finland or Nordic countries.

In the 2018 White Paper (PRC State Council, 2018), the Chinese government places a special focus on Arctic tourism, mainly due to China being an increasingly important source of visitors in the region. Chinese companies are encouraged "to cooperate with Arctic States in developing tourism in the region". China is to contribute to environmentally conscious, sustainable, and respectful Chinese tourism in the Arctic regions, and commitments are being made for the Chinese government to take some actions towards achieving that aim:

> China conducts training for and regulates Chinese tourism agencies and professionals involved in Arctic tourism, and endeavors to raise the environmental awareness of Chinese tourists. China advocates low-carbon tourism, ecotourism and responsible tourism, and hopes to contribute to the sustainable development of Arctic tourism.
>
> PRC State Council, 2018

The discourse on tourism presented in the White Paper resonates with the Finnish Arctic strategy objectives. Moreover, the aforementioned commitments are important, as the growing number of Chinese tourists in Lapland has already been followed by an increased interest in Lapland's tourism sector by Chinese investors. One hotel is being built at the Arctic Circle in Rovaniemi (so far, this is the only major Chinese investment in Lapland to have been implemented) and another hotel is planned for Saariselkä (Inari) with the involvement of Alitrip, a major Chinese player in the tourism industry. In the vicinity of Rovaniemi, several small cabin areas have also been recently developed by Chinese companies and there are initial plans for further investments (personal communication, Esko Lotvonen, Rovaniemi, June 20, 2018). A major, rather ambitious tourism development project north of Rovaniemi proposed by the Republic of Santa Claus Dream Work company is currently searching for investors, with Asian capital likely to be a part of the project portfolio (Nilsen, 2019, September 27; Republic of Santa Claus website). Furthermore, Chinese tourism operators organize tours across Northern Fennoscandia.

Importantly, investments in the tourism sector are often followed by real estate investments. While Chinese companies require approval from the government to invest their domestic resources in real estate abroad, which may slow down such processes, many Chinese business actors have assets abroad. Using such assets does not require Chinese governmental consent (personal communication, Interviewee 10, August 20, 2018).

A potential barrier for Chinese tourism in Lapland could be the lengthy visa procedures in China. While *VisitFinland* has had major success in promoting Finland in China, the service experience in the process of acquiring a visa appears to continue to be a roadblock (personal communication, Interviewee 10, August 20, 2018). However, 13 new visa application centers were opened in China in 2016. By the end of 2019, the Finnish Arctic tourism communication and marketing strategy is to be drafted, likely including some focus on Chinese or Asian visitors and their expectations.

Many tourists, especially from outside Europe, perceive Northern Fennoscandia as a single tourism destination. Therefore, increased integration/complementarity of tourism services and improved transport connections between tourism locations may be beneficial for encouraging Chinese tourism in the region in different seasons (e.g. Husebekk, Andersson & Penttilä, 2015; Stępień, 2016; personal communication, Interviewee 1, Rovaniemi, June 2016).

The Chinese 2018 White Paper also emphasizes the question of safety and security in tourism (to a great extent referring to cruise tourism), areas in which Finland claims to have special expertise. Finnish Lapland has a "safety cluster" (with a tourism focus, amongst others) as one of the key components of its Smart Specialization Strategy (see Arctic Smartness, n.d.). Finnish operators highlight their excellence in maritime safety issues, which is potentially relevant to Arctic cruise tourism (Prime Minister's Office, 2013).

The growth in numbers of Chinese tourists, while generally seen in the region as a positive development, comes with its own set of challenges. There is an ongoing debate in Lapland regarding the problems related to mass tourism, potentially lowering both the quality and the value generated for the regional economy per visitor. Rising numbers of Asian visitors contribute to the transformation of some of Lapland's tourism activities towards mass tourism. Moreover, while welcoming Chinese tourists and investors, the actors in Lappish tourism wish to avoid labeling Lapland or Rovaniemi as "Chinese tourism destinations", so that the perception of the region remains as a place of interest for different nationalities and the composition of foreign visitors continues to be diverse (personal communication, Mika Riipi, June 27, 2018).

There are also concerns regarding the possibility that Chinese tourists in Lapland are serviced primarily by Chinese tourism operators as well as Chinese accommodation or other businesses. For local companies in Lapland, this possibility could limit the benefits coming from the increased number of visitors from China. Major tourism investments, Chinese or not, may cause disturbances in the local tourism market. The recent growth in tourism implies that the market is big enough and expanding fast enough to accommodate any investment. However, there is a risk that one major investment, especially in small localities, will dominate the local tourism market and constrain the development of local tourism businesses, thereby preventing the emergence of diverse offer for tourists. A long-term strategic approach may be needed with consideration as to what sorts of tourism investments and in which locations are the most beneficial for the region (personal communication, Mika Riipi, Rovaniemi, June 27, 2018).

7.3.2.1 The Arctic Railway: A Connection to China but would there be Chinese Involvement?

Physical and digital infrastructure are considered by the Finnish government to constitute the basis for the investment attractiveness of Finland and Lapland (Prime Minister's Office, 2017: 6). The Arctic region has gained a more prominent role in national connectivity planning. The most ambitious Arctic project in Finland is the proposal for connecting Lapland (and thereby whole Finland) by railway to the Arctic Ocean and thus repositioning northern Finland from the European periphery to one of the central nodes of the envisaged new northern transport route linking Europe and Asia via the Northern Sea Route (NSR). In turn, China's 2018 White Paper highlights the importance of the northern transport route to Europe for China. The alignment of Chinese and Finnish objectives can lead to the potential for involvement of Chinese companies and investors in project implementation.

The project for a new "Arctic corridor" has been debated in Finland for many years. The questions include the overall economic feasibility, the costs of different routings and the possible impacts on Sámi livelihoods and on the environment. Notwithstanding the transit traffic via the NSR, the railway project has also been discussed in terms of Finland's own security of supply (there is no agreement as to whether the project will actually improve Finland's overall supply security) and the transportation of the outputs of industries in Lapland and wider Barents region to Central Europe via the Baltic or Barents seas. However, it is clear that the commercial viability of the railway would significantly increase if it were to become an element of global, inter-continental transport networks.

The discussion has gained pace significantly in the past two to three years. A number of studies analyzed the potential of the Arctic railway project (e.g., Kirkenes Nearingshage, 2018; Norconsult, 2018). In 2018, the Finnish and Norwegian ministries of transport chose the route between Rovaniemi and Kirkenes for further analysis (Finnish Transport Agency, 2018). The working group, established to investigate the feasibility of the investment, concluded that it is not economically justified at present (Ministry of Transport and Communications, 2019). Even if it had been evaluated as feasible, its implementation would require clear political will, focused planning efforts and financial commitments, none of which is present at the moment. Following the termination of public efforts for the time being, a proposal for a privately-funded railway was tabled by Peter Vesterbacka, the developer of the Angry Birds game and franchise and the leader of the private project to construct a tunnel between Helsinki and Tallinn. In May 2019, a memorandum of understanding with the development company of the Sør-Varanger municipality was signed (YLE Uutiset, 2019, May 9). The proponents of the project suggested that they might be capable of attracting private investment, primarily originating from Chinese funds. One way or the other, the project is likely to keep resurfacing in the coming years and decades.

The Arctic shipping routes have been promoted as a future component of the global logistical system with the Northern Sea Route (NSR) connecting Asia and Northern Europe. Arctic sea lanes were integrated into the BRI in 2018. However, currently, the growth is primarily registered for destinational shipping (export of Arctic resources, cruise tourism, Arctic construction projects), while transit shipping has not picked up so far. While the NSR offers shorter shipping distance between Northern Asian ports and Northern Europe, there are numerous challenges for maritime transport, including: high costs, limited volumes, short shipping season with year-to-year fluctuations in terms of season length, environmental and safety risks, and a mismatch with global shipping logistics (see Chapter 6 in this volume; Sander et al., 2016).

Studies dedicated to the Arctic railway concept (Finnish Transport Agency, 2018; Kirkenes Nearingshage, 2018; Norconsult, 2018; Ministry of Transport and Communications, 2019) and actors promoting such an investment (e.g. personal communication, Interviewee 6, June 20, 2018) often highlight the possible advantages of the new transport corridor and the construction of a port in Kirkenes at the Barents Sea coast. As there are high costs related to polar class vessels sailing directly to Central European ports through non-Arctic waters, Barents Sea ports offer the possibility of transshipment to regular vessels or to terrestrial transport. The railway could lower the costs for exports of Lapland's extractive industries and biorefineries outputs, especially to Asia. The investment could reposition Lapland and Finnmark from peripheries to transport hubs, resulting in regional development and employment opportunities. The railway, if constructed, is also believed to have the potential to decrease lorry transport in Northern Fennoscandia. A report by a Kirkenes-based consultancy (Kirkenes Nearingshage, 2018) claims that "even a share of 3–4% of the combined container imports from China, Taiwan, South Korea and Japan to Northern Europe [that is, the Nordic countries, the Baltic states, Germany and Poland, as well as the St. Petersburg region (clarification added)] would generate comprehensive activity at the Port of Kirkenes and on an Arctic railway to Rovaniemi". Such an assessment is based on the assumption that there will be a 70% increase in overall container cargo shipping between Asia and Europe by 2040. For China, the NSR would constitute a shipping route located mostly outside of the control and operations of the United States Navy (Gavrilov & Kripakova, 2017; as quoted in Lim, 2018).[7]

However, the same studies suggest a number of constraints. As far as the container shipping from Asian manufacturing centers is concerned, for example, empty containers would need to be transported back to China from Central Europe via the Port of Kirkenes. Moreover, the transshipment to non-polar vessels in one of the Barents Sea ports may be competitive to the train transport from these ports to Central Europe. So far, there is very limited regional cargo basis for the transport hub, as various mining and biofuel projects in Northern Finland are still in the planning stage. There are also concerns regarding the environmental, social and cultural impacts of the new rail route (Finnish Transport Agency, 2018; Kirkenes Nearingshage, 2018; Norconsult, 2018). The Finnish-Norwegian working group also highlighted alternative options for improving cargo and passenger transport connections in Northern Finland (Ministry of Transport and Communications, 2019).

The potential of the Arctic railway as a part of the Arctic transit corridor depends to a great extent on China (alongside other Asian actors), namely, choices made by Chinese shipping companies, Russian and Chinese political focus on the NSR, and trade volumes between China and Northern Europe. Equally, the feasibility of an Arctic railway for container shipping depends, according to studies (Kirkenes Nearingshage, 2018: 29), on appropriate connections to Germany, as Chinese imports to Germany would need to constitute a vast majority of container shipping transported by rail. Therefore, the completion of Rail Baltica, improvement of the capacity of Finland's main rail line between Helsinki, Tampere and Oulu and the highly challenging Helsinki-Tallinn tunnel (currently in the early conceptual stage, envisaged – ambitiously – to be built by 2035) might prove crucial for the Arctic railway to become economically feasible in terms of East Asia-Europe transit.

Moreover, the potential export of raw materials and products from northern Finland to China and other East-Asian countries could become an important

7 However, there is a remote possibility – and a rather unlikely one, considering the expected Russian reaction – that the U.S. could attempt to conduct Freedom of Navigation operations in the Russian Exclusive Economic Zone (Department of State, 2019). There is also disagreement regarding the status of several straits between the Russian mainland and Arctic archipelagos, which Russia considers its internal waters. Any action, if taken, is most certainly temporarily limited.

element of the rationale for developing the railway project. For instance, part of the outputs of the planned Sakatti mine[8] in Finnish Lapland would be likely exported to China. However, some actors in the mining industry emphasize that the new railway connection may not be competitive at the present levels of mineral production, and, even if the Arctic Railway is built, road transport may remain more feasible than the rail transport at least for some Finnish mines (Sorjanen, 2018, November 16).

Chinese investments in biorefineries in Lapland – where the majority of production is to be exported to Chinese clients – could, in principle, serve as an incentive for the biorefinery owners or other Chinese investors to engage in transport infrastructure projects that provide supply for the Chinese market (personal communication, Interviewee 3, Rovaniemi, June 12, 2018). The export of Kemijärvi biorefinery pulp products via Kirkenes (in the summer via the NSR and possibly in winter via the Suez Canal) might lower the costs compared to the currently planned transport via Kemi or Oulu ports with transshipment in major hubs in Central Europe, although the difference in transport costs appears to be of a secondary consideration in economic feasibility assessment for these projects (personal communication, Interviewee 6, June 20, 2018; Interviewee 8, June 28, 2018).

Chinese financial institutions could become key investors, especially if the 2019 private initiative makes progress. Greater Chinese involvement in the Arctic railway project could include Chinese companies entering into private-public partnerships (PPP), and thus the construction and long-term operation of the railway. Stakeholders supporting the railway project believe that investment loans or PPP, despite low return, could be attractive for international investment banks and companies, including Chinese actors. Presumably, this is because Nordic countries are considered safe locations to invest in, and such an investment would generate secure long term revenue (e.g. personal communication, Interviewee 6, June 20, 2018). As Chinese construction companies are in constant search for international contracts, if the Arctic Railway project enters into the implementation phase, some degree of interest by such Chinese firms can be expected (personal communication, Interviewee 10, August 20, 2018). There appears to be political interest from China to promote the above-mentioned forms of engagement in Arctic infrastructure projects. In the 2018 White Paper, the Chinese government "encourages [Chinese] enterprises to participate in the infrastructure construction for [Arctic] routes". Furthermore, the NSR is considered in China as a security alternative or a backup in the case that disturbances along the Indian Ocean shipping lanes occur. This

8 Currently, the copper-nickel-platinum deposit is still in the exploration phase.

security perspective could further fuel the interest of the Chinese state and also state-owned actors in the NSR-related infrastructure projects such as the Arctic Ocean railway.

The development of the infrastructure within the BRI is to be carried out through cooperation between China and other states. Chinese interest in the NSR as part of the BRI network could therefore extend to the European access points, including the Port of Kirkenes and the Arctic railway project. So far, there has been no open expression of interest from Chinese investment banks or companies. This is not surprising, as the project is at an early stage of planning. However, there has been interest from the Chinese media and informal initial expressions of interest from business actors (personal communication, Interviewee 6, June 20, 2018; Esko Lotvonen, Rovaniemi, June 20, 2018).

China's BRI initiative is to bring direct economic benefits to Chinese economic actors. BRI projects can translate into profits for Chinese financial institutions in many ways, from loans related to infrastructural developments, to contracts for Chinese construction companies and operators of infrastructure, as well as to benefits for Chinese shipping companies if the new BRI infrastructure results in lower shipping costs (Rana, 2017). Chinese involvement in projects such as the Arctic railway, even if being of strategic nature, will therefore depend not only on strategic calculations but also on the potential of this particular investment to bring returns and provide new contracts for Chinese companies.

If the Chinese involvement in infrastructure projects such as the Arctic railway become significant, concerns related to control over what can be considered a strategic transport corridor may arise. This could be the case, for instance, if a Chinese company acts as the main constructor and operator of the railway in the format of public-private partnership. There might be also questions about undesirable political influence or corruptive relationships. Recent controversy related to Greenland airports is a good example of such concerns. The Danish government stopped the procurement procedure for the upgrading of three Greenlandic airports – a procedure in which Chinese state-owned enterprise was likely to acquire the contract. The Danish concerns were related to the possibility of Chinese actors gaining partial control over important infrastructure (and even specific construction elements of that infrastructure) at a strategically important location[9] (Breum, 2018, June 30; Lim, 2018).

9 For instance, the United States (U.S.) military operates the Thule base in northern Greenland.

7.3.2.2 Other Sectors: Mining, Renewables, Cold-climate Testing, Data Centers, Fiber-optic Cables

There are a number of sectors that are already important or have some growth potential in northern Finland, including mining, renewable energy, cold-climate testing and fiber-based broadband infrastructure. While in principle there is some space for Chinese actors' presence in these sectors as clients, manufacturers or investors, so far no activity has been registered.

Finland's objective is to attract further foreign investments in its growing mining industry (Prime Minister's Office, 2013: 9). The Finnish regulatory environment is perceived as favorable to mining activities, including good availability of geophysical data. However, many actors in Lapland have concerns regarding extractive industries, considering their impacts on the environment, livelihoods and culture. Challenges for mining projects are numerous, including financing, fluctuating global resource markets, or high costs of mitigating and responding to environmental risks. While many mining developments have been canceled or postponed in recent years, several projects are in advanced planning stages, including the expansion of production in the mines in Kemi (chromite concentrate), Kittilä (gold) and Kevitsa (copper-nickel).

In the 2018 White Paper, the Chinese government "encourages [Chinese] enterprises to engage in international cooperation on the exploration for and utilization of Arctic resources by making the best use of their advantages in capital, technology and domestic market". This is in line with the overall policy promoting Chinese economic expansion abroad (see Chapter 6 in this volume). Chinese investors have been interested in Arctic raw materials (see Section 6.7.), but the Northern Fennoscandian mining sector has so far been overlooked by Chinese players. In principle, there might be potential for Chinese involvement in the Finnish mining sector, considering the global activities of Chinese investors and companies, including construction companies, and the fact that China will be among the main markets for most new mining projects. International players such as Anglo American, Agnico Eagle and Boliden are already active in Lapland. However, despite focus on Arctic minerals in China's Arctic strategy, the potential for Chinese involvement in the Finnish mining sector in the near future primarily depends on the situation in the resource markets and the profitability of particular projects rather than on any political considerations.

Finnish metals exports to China stood at US$193m (2016 statistics, WITS, n.d). Globally, Chinese demand is one of the key factors shaping raw materials prices. Some minerals for which there is high demand in China are either produced or have high discovery potential in Finland, including in Lapland. China imports 95 percent of chrome used in its production, 90 percent of its cobalt,

79 percent of its gold, 73 percent of its copper, as well as 73 percent of its iron ore (data for 2017, Zhang, 2018). In 2016, China was responsible for 26.4% of global copper imports, 25.6% of global nickel imports, and 9.1% of zinc imports (UN Department of Economic and Social Affairs, 2017). All these metals are produced (for iron ore there are advanced projects) or have further moderate-to-good discovery potential in Finland (Geological Survey of Finland, 2010; Kaiva.fi, n.d. website for the current situation).

Wind power has seen a period of significant expansion in northern Finland. In the mid-term perspective, an overall maximum investment potential is assessed at over €4b (Rautajoki and Lakkapää, 2018). China is a major global player in terms of wind and solar power. However, so far there has been no Chinese investment interest in projects in northern Finland.

A vibrant cold-climate testing industry has emerged in Finnish Lapland. A number of companies provide testing services in particular for cars and tires. In recent years, this has generated high turnover and employment. So far, there have been no Chinese manufacturers using Lapland's testing facilities and the likelihood of Chinese clients using Lappish testing facilities is currently low. However, the situation may change within the next two or three decades as Chinese manufacturers expand their activities and portfolios. For instance, Korean Hankook is already testing its winter tires in Lapland and the facilities could be used by Chinese manufacturers if they decide to gain a stronger presence in the global winter tires market (personal communication, Interviewee 3, Rovaniemi, June 11, 2018).

Northern regions are attractive as locations of data centers and cloud services due to the colder climate, which decreases the costs for cooling down servers. Of importance is also the availability of relatively cheap renewable energy, as many information technology (IT) companies aim at exclusively using renewable energy sources. Up to 80% of energy consumption when using online applications occurs in data centers (Nilsen, 2016; Warrenstein et al., 2016). The overall potential of Northern Fennoscandia also depends on the availability of low-latency broadband connectivity, which usually requires fiber cables considering the amount of data transferred (see the discussion further in this section). The forerunner in terms of attracting data center investments in Northern Fennoscandia has been the Luleå-Boden area in the Swedish Norrbotten region (Facebook, Bitcoin and other data centers). Several Chinese companies have already joined the boom of data centers in Sweden or are deliberating investments. For instance, Alibaba is considering central Sweden for its second European data center location (Invest in Dalarna, 2017, September 29). From 2017, Chinese blockchain company Canaan Creative is using data storage capacities in Boden (Smolaks, 2017, February 9). Swedish Vattenfall has been negotiating further deals with Chinese companies interested in Sweden-based data centers (Karagiannopoulos, 2018, May 9).

So far, there have been no major data or cloud center investments in Northern Finland, although this sector's investment potential in Oulu is assessed as at up to €400m (Rautajoki and Lakkapää, 2018).[10] If Finnish policymakers decide to more strongly pursue the opportunities related to data centers, Chinese companies could be among the possible investors and users of the data storage space. Security and regulatory considerations could also play a role in future developments, limiting the interest of Chinese clients. This would be the case, for instance, if China forces companies to store more Chinese data on servers located in China. From 1 June 2017, "critical information" has already had to be stored domestically in China.

A prospective avenue for Chinese investors or for involvement of Chinese companies could become a marine fiber-optic cable project linking Asia and Europe via the NSR, linked to European networks via Lapland and Finland. The project would decrease the latency (delay in data transfer) as compared to the Europe-Asia connections via the U.S. and Indian Ocean. Such latency decrease would benefit financial markets, data centers located in Northern Europe and major internet companies. Originally, in Russia, the development company PolarNet had been studying the potential of the connection since 2011, making plans for a UK-to-Tokyo connector. Finnish policy-makers also place much emphasis on this project (Prime Minister's Office, 2017: 7; Lipponen & Svento, 2016). There were informal expressions of initial interest by Chinese investors in the project (personal communication, Interviewee 2, May 04, 2018). Moreover, China's 2018 Arctic policy White Paper clearly states that among "[c]oncrete cooperation steps" in the Arctic is "enhancing Arctic digital connectivity" (PRC State Council, 2018).

At present, the Finnish company Cinia is bringing together investors towards realizing the fiber broadband project. In 2019, it secured an agreement with Russian company MegaFon to establish a joint development company to prepare and implement the project, a major milestone towards project success (Cinia, 2019, June 6). Chinese companies are likely to be involved in the fiber optic cable projects as key clients rather than investors. Chinese investment banks could be potential sources of funding. However, at the moment, financial institutions across the globe are eager to invest in prospective infrastructure projects. Therefore, Cinia does not expect acquiring funding to be a

10 Southern Finland has attracted some major data center investments, including the Google facility in Hamina, with recent new investment evaluated at €2 billion (Yle Uutiset, 2019, September 20).

challenge as long as agreements with potential clients are in place. While the Chinese financing is thus not crucial for the project, the agreements with Chinese companies may be of key importance for finding investors and the project's ultimate success. China Telecom (*Zhongguo Dianxin* 中国电信) has already declared its interest (Bannerman, 2019, August 30). Baidu or Alibaba may be other potential clients. At present, Cinia has a network of cables stretching from Frankfurt via the Baltic Sea to Lapland (3,000km of the 13,000km needed between Frankfurt and Tokyo). The NSR cable project is expected to be implemented within three years from the commencement of seabed surveying (personal communication, Interviewee 7, June 26, 2018). While the project had been expected to encounter challenges related to Russia's security concerns (personal communication, Interviewee 2, May 04, 2018), the involvement of a major player such as MegaFon significantly raises the chances of success.

7.4 Finnish Arctic Expertise: Finnish Solutions for Chinese Arctic Activities

Among China's goals in the Arctic is to "improve the capacity and capability in using applied Arctic technology, strengthen technological innovation, environmental protection, resource utilization, and development of shipping routes in the Arctic" (PRC State Council, 2018). The development of technical Arctic equipment is seen as particularly important:

> ...upgrade of equipment in the fields of deep sea exploration, ice zone prospecting, and atmosphere and biology observation, and [...] technology innovation in Arctic oil and gas drilling and exploitation, renewable energy development, navigation and monitoring in ice zones, and construction of new-type icebreakers.
>
> PRC State Council, 2018

Finnish political and economic actors believe that Finland has much to offer in regard to practical Arctic technological solutions, Arctic shipping safety and services, and environmental technology. In principle, acquiring technologies developed in Finland and cooperating with Finnish partners towards further innovative solutions should be seen as contributing to China's goals in the Arctic.

The Finnish government and businesses have long highlighted Finland's "Arctic expertise", meaning the set of products and skills developed in the country due to its geographical location (in the North and by the seasonally ice-covered Baltic Sea). Such know-how originates from the need for all actors to adjust their products, design, materials and services to cold temperature, challenging weather conditions, sparse population, and remoteness. The long list of areas identified as constituting Finland's Arctic expertise includes:

- Icebreaking
- Polar shipping technology
- Shipping safety (Search and Rescue, communication and construction technologies, weather and information services)
- Mechanical oil recovery in ice conditions
- Energy resources expertise (structural and materials engineering in Arctic conditions, risk assessment and risk prevention, icebreaking assistance, contingency planning, prevention of oil spills and oil cleanup)
- Arctic cleantech (water processing technologies, efficiency of production facilities and a low level of emissions)
- Renewable energy and energy efficiency solutions (including district heating systems/solutions)
- Digital infrastructure and e-services in peripheral areas
- Arctic construction (including wood construction)
- Cold-climate civil engineering
- Arctic circular economy
- Blue bioeconomy
- Climate resilience
- Arctic-relevant space technologies
- Wellbeing technologies
- Environmental technologies
- "Green mining" and "Arctic mining" technologies
- Arctic research (both natural and social sciences)
- Environmental monitoring
- Cold-climate expertise of security forces
- Arctic design

According to Finland's 2013 Arctic Strategy (Prime Minister's Office, 2013: 28), the competitive edge of Finnish companies "lies in environment-friendly solutions and the ability to carry out business operations with due regard to the limitations imposed by the natural environment". In order to commercially utilize their expertise, "Finnish companies need to be able to form alliances and offer a broad range of solution-type products and services". Experts (Paavola et al., 2017) advised that long-term development of commercializable Arctic expertise in Finland requires regional and sector-specific clusters to emerge, suggesting that ecosystem funding and performance-based funding instruments are needed. Activities of Team Finland and Business Finland are seen as an important component in the effort to promote Finnish Arctic expertise.

A recent report (Paavola et al., 2017) highlights challenges for commercializing Finnish Arctic expertise. Only a few everyday cold-climate competences are labeled by companies as "Arctic expertise" and often businesses see little value in branding their services and products as "Arctic". Partly this is due to the limited size of the markets that are considered specifically "Arctic". Therefore, the "Arctic" label may be not only a "new name for old things" (a common criticism of the "Arctic expertise" concept), but one having limited actual commercial utility. This notwithstanding, the branding of products, solutions and services as "Arctic", while not necessarily attractive for operators already present in the Arctic, may prove important in gaining the attention of actors taking their first steps in the northern regions of the globe, such as Chinese companies looking for partners in their new Arctic endeavors. In China, Finland's brand is strongly associated with expertise in cold conditions. The experience of some Lappish companies shows that being located in Northern Finland and being able to present their products in Arctic conditions is of advantage in relations with Chinese customers (e.g., personal communication, Interviewee 11, September 03, 2018). However, a general "Arctic" or northern labeling of technologies and products coming from Finland may also be a barrier for Finnish companies that offer products not related to cold conditions, as clients may assume that such products are not suitable for warmer climates and an urban environment (personal communication, Interviewee 4, June 13, 2018). That is a concern that Finnish industry promotion agencies need to seriously take into consideration.

7.4.1 *Areas of Finnish Arctic Expertise with Potential for Sino-Finnish Cooperation*

Finnish Arctic expertise can be an object of Sino-Finnish cooperation in various ways, including sales of Finnish technologies or designs, employment of Finnish experts or collaboration between institutions. From the perspective of Chinese Arctic activities, there may be interest in sectors such as mining, cleantech, winter sports, occupational health and safety, renewables and cold-climate construction, and in particular icebreaking services, shipbuilding and polar maritime design. The latter are here of central importance and they are discussed separately in the following section.

Currently, few Chinese companies are present in the Arctic and therefore the demand is limited and only some areas may be of direct interest for Chinese operators that are considering engaging in Arctic projects or activities.

The 2013 Arctic Strategy underlines that the further development of Finnish Arctic expertise is dependent on "international networks, contacts and mobility", among other factors (Prime Minister's Office, 2013: 13). In the future, Chinese institutions and companies may become important partners in research and training collaborations. In turn, the 2018 White Paper states that China "has spared no efforts to contribute its wisdom to the development of the Arctic region" (PRC State Council, 2018). In principle, Chinese companies and institutions should have a strong political incentive to be involved in activities, the aim of which is to provide technological solutions for Arctic developments. However, any such collaborations need to be economically feasible.

Finland promotes mobility of labor in the Arctic region (Prime Minister's Office, 2013: 23), not only to fill labor market demands within Finland's Arctic but also to facilitate contracts and employment possibilities across the region for Finnish companies and Finnish Arctic experts. Chinese Arctic activities can potentially contribute to the expansion of such a market for Finnish expertise-holders.

As discussed above, while there has been little interest among Chinese investors in northern Finland's mining projects, Finnish companies claim that they can offer not only investment opportunities but also technological solutions for carrying out operations in northern conditions (e.g. in Greenland or Canada) in a responsible manner. The delivery of technologies and services for Chinese projects in Russia – which could be the most attractive opportunity – may be challenging.[11] The situation can, however, change in the future.

Similarly to mining technologies, Finnish cleantech (including mechanical oil recovery in ice conditions) could be offered to Chinese businesses operating in the Arctic. A report by Azure International and Cleantech Scandinavia (supported by Tekes – nowadays Business Finland) suggests that Nordic cleantech could be of particular interest for Chinese investors, due to increased focus on clean energy, renewables, and a general shift in China's outbound investment towards technology (Azure International and Cleantech Scandinavia, n.d.).

Finnish Arctic policy statements also highlight the experience and Finnish technological solutions in the field of renewable energy and low-carbon development, both in terms of business cooperation and the sharing of best practices. China's 2018 White Paper clearly emphasizes the value of such expertise for China and Chinese operators:

11 Among others, due to the ongoing EU sanctions targeting Russian Arctic hydrocarbon projects or due to Russian political/security considerations.

> The Arctic region boasts an abundance of geothermal, wind, and other clean energy resources. China will work with the Arctic States to strengthen clean energy cooperation, increase exchanges in respect of technology, personnel and experience in this field, explore the supply of clean energy and energy substitution, and pursue low-carbon development.
>
> PRC State Council, 2018

Furthermore, Sino-Finnish collaboration with regard to winter sports has recently commenced. This has been connected to the preparations for the Beijing 2022 Winter Olympic Games and the increasing interest in winter sports in China. Finland has high levels of expertise in winter sports training, technologies and facilities. In 2015, the Chinese vice-premier visited Rovaniemi with sport cooperation being among the focal points. An agreement between the Rovaniemi Santa Sport sports institute and the Sport University of Beijing, in effect since 2017, is one of the elements of this collaboration. A major cooperation program has been carried out by the Vuokatti-Ruka Sport Academy. For instance, 150 Chinese young sportsmen and sportswomen visited the school in the Summer of 2018. In 2019, China and Finland organized a joint thematic winter sports year. The collaboration in the field of sports could also facilitate further exports of Finnish products for the construction of Chinese skiing resorts, e.g., by Rovaniemi-based companies Lappset and Hirsitalot (personal communication, Esko Lotvonen, Rovaniemi, June 20, 2018).

Finland's 2013 Arctic Strategy also highlights Finnish expertise and research in occupational health in Arctic conditions and in creating a safe working environment. This may be of particular interest for new operators entering the Arctic region.

Cooperation between institutions from northern Finland and their Chinese partners in the area of education is yet another dimension of Sino-Finnish relations. For instance, Rovaniemi is engaged in a number of school exchanges and experience-sharing programmes with Chinese schools. This is partly related to the reputation of the Finnish education system (personal communication, Esko Lotvonen, Rovaniemi, June 20, 2018). Markedly, sub-university education was among Finland's Arctic Council 2017–2019 chairmanship program priorities (Ministry of Foreign Affairs, 2017).

An area of particular interest for cooperation with Chinese institutions is Finnish Arctic shipping technology (construction and design, services) and Finnish icebreaking services, discussed in greater detail below.

7.4.1.1 Finnish Arctic Maritime Technology and Services

Finland's Arctic Strategy (2013) identifies shipping and maritime technology as one of Finland's most important commercializable Arctic export sectors.

Finnish strengths include: national Arctic shipbuilding, offshore and winter navigation operations, shipping safety solutions, as well as the overall low-temperature, winter, ice and weather research and expertise. Among the products that Finnish actors hope to commercialize are vessel traffic, reporting, monitoring, identification and communications systems (including satellite services), including weather and ice information services (Prime Minister's Office, 2013: 30, 53; Prime Minister's Office, 2017). One of the strategy's objectives is maintaining "Finland's position as a leading expert in the Arctic maritime industry", which to a great extent arises from the tradition of operating in the Baltic Sea. The Strategy stresses that "the best practices developed in the Baltic Sea region offer highly suitable export products for the Arctic market".

China is identified as one of the main markets for the export of Finnish Arctic shipping technology (Prime Minister's Office, 2013: 9, 29). This is, in fact, the only context in which cooperation with China is mentioned specifically in Finland's 2013 strategic Arctic statement. It is believed that countries such as China will "need new equipment and fleets capable of operating offshore oil and gas fields as well as mining under Arctic conditions" (Prime Minister's Office, 2013: 29). Moreover, Chinese operators new to Arctic areas may find Finnish experience with international rescue operations and the management of maritime accidents a useful theme for collaboration. In turn, China's 2018 White Paper clearly states that China will strive "for the upgrade of equipment in the fields of deep sea exploration, ice zone prospecting, and atmosphere and biology observation, and promotes technology innovation in Arctic oil and gas drilling and exploitation, renewable energy development, navigation and monitoring in ice zones, and construction of new-type icebreakers". Currently, in addition to operating two research icebreakers (Xue Long I and II, the second entering service in 2019), China is in the process of planning for a nuclear-powered icebreaker. China General Nuclear Power Group leads the project (Sun, 2018; Nilsen, 2019, March 21). Moreover, the 2018 White Paper states that "[i]n order to effectively protect the marine environment of the Arctic, China works with other States to enhance control of the sources of marine pollution such as ship discharge, offshore dumping, and air pollution" (PRC State Council, 2018). Such statements can be seen as the political encouragement for Chinese operators to utilize foreign Arctic shipping technology and shipping services, and thus, an opening for the commercialization of Finnish expertise in the sector.

In terms of providing icebreaking services for Chinese Arctic operations, there has been no concrete cooperation thus far. However, some discussions on future joint projects have taken place, in particular regarding the support for Chinese research operations in the Arctic Ocean. For Arctia, a Finnish state-owned ice-breaking company, the latter area appears the most prospective at the moment (personal communication, Interviewee 9, August 01, 2018). It appears unlikely that enhanced Chinese icebreaking capacities – e.g. the potential nuclear icebreaker – would create competition for Finnish service providers in the near future (personal communication, Interviewee 9, August 01, 2018). However, acquiring increased icebreaking capacities may limit the future Chinese demand for icebreaking services.

There seems to be little interest among Finnish shipbuilding and shipping companies in acquiring Chinese investors. Finnish companies at the moment see East Asia as a prospective market for their products and technologies rather than a source of investment capital. There is a more general concern related to foreign investment in this sector in Finland (personal communication, Interviewee 10, Zhu Bin, August 20, 2018). Some space for joint ventures between Finnish and Chinese companies regarding particular Arctic shipbuilding projects likely exists. However, the general approach is to keep technological development in Finland itself and under fully Finnish ownership (personal communication, Interviewee 13, November 13, 2018).

At this stage, the companies Aker Arctic and Wärtsilä have had the most visible presence of all Finnish shipping and shipbuilding actors in the Chinese market.

In 2012, Aker Arctic was contracted by the Polar Research Institute of China (PRIC) to provide the concept and basic design for a Polar research vessel. The construction work was carried out in the Jiangnan Shipyard (*Jiangnan Zaochuan (Jituan) Youxian Zeren Gongsi* 江南造船 (集团) 有限责任公司) in Shanghai and the 122m-long Polar Class 3 icebreaker was completed in 2019. Aker Arctic advertizes the icebreaker it designed as "the world's most advanced polar research vessel" (Aker Arctic, n.d.). In 2014, Aker Arctic produced the concept and basic design for two Arctic module carriers, *Audax* and *Pugnax* (Polar Class 3, length of 206.3m with an icebreaking capability of 3 knots in 1.5m level ice), which were built at Guangzhou Shipyard (*Guangchuan Guoji Youxiangongsi* 广船国际有限公司) in 2016. In 2016, Aker Arctic delivered the concept and basic design for an Arctic condensate tanker to the same Guangzhou Shipyard. This Arc7 ice class vessel – *Boris Sokolov* – built for Novatek with a deadweight of 43,400 tons with an icebreaking capability of 2 knots in 1.8m level ice was delivered in 2018. Wärtsilä produced, within its Chinese joint ventures, four engines for *Boris Sokolov*. *Boris Sokolov's* construction is based on Aker's Double Acting Ship (DAS™) principle that allows tankers and cargo ships to operate independently without icebreaker assistance in challenging ice conditions (Aker Arctic, 2018, December 4).

Aker Arctic management evaluates the engagement with Chinese partners as a positive experience (personal communication, Interviewee 13, November 13, 2018). Arctic maritime design is a highly specialized area of the shipping industry, with technological edge and purpose-built vessels dominating the landscape. Compared to general shipbuilding, where cost-cutting and serial production models dominate, polar ship design and shipbuilding constitutes a market niche in which Finnish and European actors have a competitive advantage. Nevertheless, China is a major player in global shipbuilding, and thus, it will likely be able to develop its own polar shipping design capabilities in the future (Ibid.).[12]

The current Aker Arctic portfolio is very broad, including the design of port icebreakers operating in Siberia and the LNG icebreaker *Polaris* delivered to Arctia (in Finland). Future Chinese contracts depend on the demand of Chinese shipyards and companies for polar class vessels, which is difficult to evaluate due to ever-changing predictions for Arctic shipping development. However, considering China Ocean Shipping Company's (COSCO, *Zhongyuan Haiyun Jizhuangxiang Yunshu Youxiangongsi* 中远海运集装箱运输有限公司) emphasis on engaging in Arctic shipping and the overall Chinese interest in utilizing the NSR, at least a modest level of future demand can be expected.

In addition to design, Finnish manufacturers have broad experience with Arctic maritime construction. Wärtsilä, a Finnish company specialized in power generation technology and other equipment in the marine and energy markets, formed a joint venture with China State Shipbuilding Corporation (CSSC *Zhongguo Chuanbo Gongye Jituan Youxiangongsi* 中国船舶工业集团有限公司) called CSSC Wärtsilä Engine Co Ltd (CWEC). The CWEC built a production facility in Lingang, Shanghai. The company, which produces medium-sized and large engines, had over 70 orders for various types of engines at the time of the opening of the production facility in January 2017. Wärtsilä has another production facility in China – Wärtsilä Qiyao Diesel Company (WQDC) – for small engines. Engines manufactured in both factories are fully suitable for

12 Recently, Finnish companies have developed increasing interest in high-tech advances in Arctic shipping and shipping in general, including autonomous vessels (Prime Minister's Office, 2017: 4). Such developments take place at the Meyer Turku shipyard, where autonomous ship technology using artificial intelligence is being developed (Business Finland, 2017, December 6). Technological advancement could generally allow Finnish actors to maintain a competitive edge. However, all companies in the sector attempt to strike an economic balance between the use of the most advanced technologies and the minimum needed by operators to conduct their activities in polar waters. Not every technological application necessarily translates to a market advantage if expensive advancements go beyond the needs of clients.

polar waters and some are used in these environments. The company also promotes its products as suitable for operations in polar waters (personal communication, Interviewee 12, October 22, 2018). Wärtsilä itself has a significant portfolio of engine design and construction for polar class vessels, especially for Russian clients. These include icebreakers (e.g. engines as well as integrated power and automation systems) and platform supply vessels. The company provided power generating sets for power plants operating in the Russian Arctic. Wärtsilä also builds engines for port icebreakers used at the Sabetta LNG terminal.

7.5 Hopes and Concerns

While the attitude towards Chinese investments in Finland and in Lapland has been generally positive, there are various noticeable concerns. These range from the apprehension that China and Chinese actors may gain too great an influence on national and local economy and politics to doubts about the environmental and social performance of Chinese companies. Many such questions could refer to any foreign investments. However, the concerns are exacerbated by reports of problems related to Chinese activities in other parts of the world and the fact that China is a new actor in the North. Nonetheless, the debate in Finland is characterized by divergent voices, where on the one hand there is a degree of anxiety and a perception of major presence, and on the other hand a notion of disappointment that Chinese investments are, in fact, very limited.

There are anxieties that Chinese investors and operators – and therefore the Chinese government – might gain an excessive long-term influence on the regional economy in Lapland and the national economy in Finland. Major land purchases or partial control over strategic infrastructure such as the Arctic Ocean railroad would be met with anxiety among many actors in Finland. There are doubts regarding the environmental and social performance of Chinese businesses operating in the North and the reliability and feasibility of many investments plans. Concerns related to Chinese projects in Finland and in the Arctic stem, to some extent, from experiences with some Chinese investors and operators in other parts of the world. Articles published by notable English-language media outlets exacerbate these fears (see, e.g., Mourdoukoutas, 2018; Cannon, 2019, February 8; see also Marsh, 2015). Direct investments in Finnish companies have sparked speculations over the protection of intellectual property rights, industrial espionage and, in the long-term future, Finnish companies losing their competitive advantage in certain Arctic-related industries such as ice management and ship design. In addition, Chinese companies' corporate social responsibility practices have been a source of unease in Finnish public debate. Some analysts underline, however, that Chinese operators are capable of adjusting to local conditions and regulatory frameworks, and that the performance of Chinese investors has overall significantly improved over the last decade (Rosen and Thuringen, 2017). Being aware of and critically assessing these concerns is key for long-term Sino-Finnish collaboration in Arctic affairs.

Current Chinese investments in Finland can be seen as paving the way for other Chinese investments in the Nordic states, in the European Union and across the circumpolar Arctic. For this reason, it may be expected that Chinese companies – striving to strengthen their international reputation – are willing to apply high standards and benefit Finnish northern regions. Some Finnish private actors believe that Chinese investors are driven by long-term goals and long investment perspectives. That, in principle, makes Chinese companies attractive business partners (personal communication, Interviewee 8, June 27, 2018).

Some types of Chinese economic presence may adversely affect the current, generally positive attitude towards Chinese investors in Northern Finland. These include: major land purchases, especially in areas of high environmental, biodiversity or landscape value; bringing in Chinese workforce in significant numbers; and the involvement of Chinese construction companies on terms that would be perceived by local actors as unfair competition (personal communication, Mika Riipi, June 27, 2018). Furthermore, if small Arctic economies become heavily dependent on Chinese capital, they may become highly vulnerable to economic fluctuations in China. This is a concern, as the country's economy undergoes ongoing structural changes.

Regarding the currently planned investments in Lapland, such as the construction of biorefineries and hotels, no significant inflow of Chinese workers is planned with the exception of engineering and managerial staff. In principle, incoming highly skilled staff can contribute to mitigating skills mismatch in sparsely populated areas. One hotel that has been constructed by Chinese investors employs both Finnish and international staff, similarly to any other accommodation venue in Lapland (personal communication, Jaakko Ylinampa, Lapin ELY-keskus, Rovaniemi, June 12, 2018).

Any major land acquisition could trigger a high level of anxiety as has been the case in Iceland, Greenland, North Norway or Svalbard (Higgins, 2014, September 27; Staalesen, 2014, October 21). However, thus far no such proposal has been made, and considering the aforementioned past experiences in other Nordic countries, it appears not very likely that a major Chinese investment project of that sort would be proposed for northern Finland. Local officials in Lapland believe that such projects would actually be harmful to the overall long-term Chinese investment potential in Lapland (personal communication, Mika Riipi, Rovaniemi, June 27, 2018; Esko Lotvonen, Rovaniemi, June 20, 2018).

Finns may also need to consider the views of their Western partners – the EU and U.S. – in making decisions on Arctic economic cooperation with China. The engagement with China at different levels (e.g. member states or regions like the Nordic region or Central and Eastern Europe) may raise concerns in EU institutions or other EU member states, because China is currently considered the EU's "systemic rival" (BDI 2019). In an extreme situation, this could adversely affect the position of Finland within the EU. Relations with the U.S. could also be at stake as intensifying global competition with China is considered a major international challenge in Washington. There appears to be a bipartisan agreement in that regard, making this a long term concern. The strong utterances about China in the speech by the U.S. Secretary of State Pompeo before the Arctic Council Ministerial Meeting in Rovaniemi in May 2019 may be interpreted as a warning signal to other Arctic states about China's growing presence in the region, including Chinese investments (Department of State, 2019, May 6). Finnish decision-makers must therefore apply particular scrutiny in the case of investments that would give Chinese companies influence over the construction and use of critical infrastructure such as railways, airports and perhaps also digital infrastructure. The cautious approach to foreign investments appears to be prevalent in regards to shipbuilding and ship design companies.

Another set of challenges related to working with Chinese companies or the presence in China are questions related to intellectual property rights (IPRs). Both Finnish companies operating in China and those collaborating with Chinese partners and investors in Finland should be aware of such risks. However, the IPRs regime has undergone a significant improvement since the beginning of the reform era, when practically no regulatory mechanism protected intellectual property rights in China. At the moment, the country conforms to the most important international conventions on IPRs. Furthermore, it has developed a national legal framework that entails laws on trademark and copyright protection and patents. What is more, the issue has been handled on the level of the highest political leadership, as illustrated by President Xi Jinping's speech in 2017 (Xinhua Agency, 2017, July 17). However, despite these advances, IPRs violations continue to constitute an unsolved problem for Sino-foreign business interactions both in China and abroad (see Global Innovation Policy Centre, 2018). Tackling this challenge is a slow process, as the "culture of copying" is a deep-rooted tradition in both the Chinese education system and the corporate world. For this reason, IPRs violations cannot be ruled out as a potential risk factor in Sino-Finnish Arctic business collaboration. In the case of Arctic ship design, for instance, in which the level of sensitivity to IPRs issues is high, so far there have not been any known cases of IPRs violations (personal communication, Interviewee 13, November 16, 2018).

Just as other investors, Lappish companies face problems related to differences between Finnish and Chinese business culture or the aforementioned IPRs issues. For instance, Lapland-based companies exporting wooden constructions to China are aware of the risk of their designs being copied (personal communication, Interviewee 4, June 12, 2018). Lappish companies underline the importance of strong personal relationships in order to develop their activities in China. Moreover, political support not only at the intergovernmental level but also at the level of region-to-region cooperation and city-to-city contacts can be sometimes needed for smooth investment processes. A good example is the Regional Council of Lapland. The Council approaches the collaboration with Chinese provinces strategically, cooperating with Heilongjiang, Hubei and Sichuan provinces where Lappish businesses have investment or market presence and where Lappish towns have ties with Chinese cities (Rovaniemi with Harbin and Chengdu, and Kemi with Wuhan, where the biofuels company Kaidi has its headquarters) (personal communication, Mika Riipi, Rovaniemi, June 27, 2018).

For Lappish companies active in China, the so-called "social credit system" (*shehui xinyong tixi* 社会信用体系) could also become an issue of relevance. The constantly expanded and developed system evaluates the behavior of individuals and companies against standards defined by the Chinese government (National Enterprise Credit Information Publicity System). Sanctions or blocking the possibility to operate further in the country may result in a low social credit score. The system (potentially) makes it more necessary for any private actors operating in China to comply with Chinese rules and triggers concerns that it may further influence the behavior of companies not only inside but also outside of China (Creemers, 2018; Hoffman, 2018, June 28; Munro, 2018, June 27).

The risks discussed above are highlighted by those who have misgivings about the Chinese economic presence in Finland. However, many actors, especially in Lapland, look at Chinese investments with a hope for economic development and job creation. For them, the main concern is that planned investments and partnerships will not actually materialize. And indeed, in Lapland, high expectations related to Chinese investments are mixed with the perception that little concrete developments actually take place (personal communication, Interviewee 2, May 04, 2018).

There is a perception that Chinese companies too often initially announce very ambitious plans but quit when more detailed business assessment is carried out. Also in the Arctic context, Lim (2018) asks whether "China's risk-taking approach in investing in mega Arctic projects that were previously deemed unrealistic raises questions about the sustainability and vulnerability of its investments". This is also a part of the Finnish experience. In 2017, Chinese investors pulled out from two biofuel projects in southern Finland, a decision supposedly related to the status of bioenergy within the EU regulatory framework. The current standstill in biorefinery projects in Lapland (Kemi and Kemijärvi) would appear to confirm such concerns. These and similar events increase the level of local uncertainty related to the current and future project proposals and plans. Chinese investors and companies do not appear to stand out in that respect, but as they are new actors in northern regions, they seem to be subject to relatively greater public scrutiny.

7.6 Conclusion

In general, Sino-Finnish economic cooperation is growing and it received a political boost with the visit of President Xi Jinping in 2017. This chapter shows that there is also modest activity regarding Arctic questions, and there is notable potential for enhancing Sino-Finnish collaboration in Arctic sectors. Finnish companies are operating in China, and Chinese investments are also starting to come to Finland, including the northern regions of the country. There are possibilities for Finnish Arctic expertise to bring commercial benefits for Finland by supporting China's expanding Arctic activities. However, at present, there are only a few instances of realized investments and implemented contracts, one outstanding example being tourism accommodation projects in Lapland. Most activities remain at the stage of planning or initial ideas, with high levels of uncertainty. The unclear future of the biorefinery investments in Kemijärvi and Kemi is a case in point. Also the project to extend the Finnish rail network to the Arctic Ocean faces many question marks regarding its feasibility and there are also challenges related to financing, with the new private initiative hoping for strong involvement from Chinese investors. Other potential investments in Finnish Lapland are yet to be realized. In Lapland and northern Finland, there remains potential for further winter tourism and sports investments, cold-climate testing, or data centers. The marine fiber-optic cable connecting Asia (including China) to Finland (Europe) has taken a step closer to the implementation stage in 2019. The role of Chinese partners may be limited to being clients, although there is space for Chinese investment.

There is, in principle, also some potential in commercializing Finnish Arctic expertise in China. However, currently the most prospective area of business is the design and construction of polar class vessels and components. It is in this field that examples of implemented projects can be found, including the role of Aker Arctic in designing China's second polar icebreaker (*Xuelong* II) or the construction of engines capable of operation in polar conditions by Wärtsilä and its joint ventures located in China. Interviewed experts note some potential in Finnish clean technology or the delivery of future icebreaking services. However, no concrete activities and plans have been put forth so far. Furthermore, while in some areas the "Arctic" labeling of Finnish products and expertise is of marketing advantage, that is not necessarily the case for all sectors.

Chinese activities in Finland and in its northernmost regions are characterized by dissonant voices. On the one hand, there is a perception and concern among commentators that China has too great an influence in the North. On the other hand, there is a sense of disappointment among many actors who hoped that Chinese investments would provide a needed economic boost for sparsely-populated and remote regions. The Chinese investment boom has not, so far, materialized. Many investments discussed in this chapter are indeed only in the planning phase, and the likelihood of their implementation is low. The Arctic Ocean railway may never materialize, and biorefinery projects are at a standstill. Many sectors have potential for Chinese investment, Chinese clients and the involvement of Chinese companies, but very little actual presence and activity is currently registered. Finland both believes in Sino-Finnish cooperation opportunities and is concerned about the risks of these opportunities materializing.

Literature and Sources

AEI (American Enterprise Institute). (n.d.). Global Investment Tracker – China. Retrieved October 8, 2019, from https://www.aei.org/china-global-investment-tracker/.

Aker Arctic. (n.d.). Website. Retrieved July 20, 2018, from https://akerarctic.fi/en/news/aker-arctic-designed-new-chinese-polar-research-vessel.

Aker Arctic. (2019, December 4). The naming ceremony for the Arctic condensate tanker. Aker Arctic website. Retrieved October 11, 2019, from https://akerarctic.fi/en/news/naming-ceremony-for-the-arctic-condensate-tanker/.

AMSA. (Arctic Marine Shipping Assessment). (2009). Arctic marine shipping assessment 2009 report. Arctic Council: Protection of Arctic Marine Environment.

Arctic Smartness. (n.d.). Arctic Safety. Retrieved September 25, 2019 from Arctic Smartness website at https://arcticsmartness.eu/arctic-safety/.

Azure International and Cleantech Scandinavia. (n.d.). China outbound investment strategies in the cleantech sector – Nordic opportunities. Retrieved July 5, 2018, from https://www.innovasjonnorge.no/globalassets/old/pagefiles/4014/china-outbound-investment-strategy_ver2.pdf.

Bannerman, N. (2019, August 30). Cinia moves full speed ahead with Arctic Connect. *Capacity.* Retrieved September 26, 2019, from https://www.capacitymedia.com/articles/3824070/cinia-moves-full-speed-ahead-with-arctic-connect.

Breum, M. (2018, June 30). How a dispute over China and Greenland's airports worked its way toward a solution. *Arctic Today.* Retrieved July 15, 2018, from https://www.arctictoday.com/dispute-china-greenlands-airports-worked-way-toward-solution/.

Business Finland. (2019, February 19). Finland sets new law to increase biofuel use in road traffic. *News. Business Finland website.* Retrieved September 25, 2019, from https://www.businessfinland.fi/en/whats-new/news/2019/finland-sets-new-law-to-increase-biofuel-use-in-road-traffic/.

Business Finland. (2018, February 5). Finnish heavyweights offer expertise worldwide. *Good News From Finland. Business Finland promotional website.* Retrieved June 15, 2018, from http://www.goodnewsfinland.com/finnish-heavyweights-offer-expertise-worldwide/.

Business Finland. (2017, April 11). Why does Finland attract Chinese investment (information in the format of an interview with Zhu Bin). *Business Finland.* Retrieved May 25, 2018, from https://www.investinfinland.fi/-/why-does-finland-attract-chinese-investment- (accessed 25 May, 2018).

Business Finland. (2017, December 6). Turku pushes boat out for maritime innovation. *Good News from Finland.* [Business Finland promotional website]. Retrieved June 15, 2018, from http://www.goodnewsfinland.com/feature/turku-pushes-boat-maritime-innovation/.

Cinia. (2019, June 6). Arctic Telecom Cable Initiative Takes Major Step Forward. Retrieved September 26, 2019, from Cinia website at https://www.cinia.fi/en/archive/arctic-telecom-cable-initiative-takes-major-step-forward.html.

Customs Finland. (2018). Korkean teknologian ulkomaankauppa vuonna 2017. *Customs Finland.* Retrieved June 10, 2018, from http://tulli.fi/documents/2912305/3492107/Korkean+teknologian+ulkomaankauppa+vuonna+2017.

Department of Defense (US). (2019). Department of Defense Arctic Strategy. Report to Congress. June 2016. Retrieved September 25, 2019, from https://media.defense.gov/2019/Jun/06/2002141657/-1/-1/1/2019-DOD-ARCTIC-STRATEGY.PDF.

Department of State (US). (2019, May 6). Looking North: Sharpening America's Arctic Focus. Speech by the US Secretary of State Mike Pompeo in Rovaniemi, Finland on 8 May 2019. Retrieved September 26, 2019, from the Department of State website at https://www.state.gov/looking-north-sharpening-americas-arctic-focus/.

Embassy of Finland, Beijing. (2014). Maatiedosto Kiina. Kahdenväliset suhteet. Retrieved September 30, 2018, from http://www.finland.cn/public/default.aspx?nodeid=44131&contentlan=1&culture=fi-FI.

Erokhin, V., Tianming, G., & Xinhua, Z. (2018). Arctic Blue Economic Corridor: China's Role in the Development of a New Connectivity Paradigm in the North. In L. Heininen & H. Exner-Pirot (Eds.), *Arctic Yearbook 2018*. Akureyri, Iceland: Northern Research Forum.

EU's Renewable Energy Directive. (2016). Proposal for a DIRECTIVE OF THE EUROPEAN PARLIAMENT AND OF THE COUNCIL on the promotion of the use of energy from renewable sources (recast). *European Commission*. Retrieved August 14, 2019, from https://eur-lex.europa.eu/legal-content/EN/ALL/?uri=COM%3A2016%3A767%3AFIN.

FinChi. (Finland-China Innovation Centre). (n.d.). [Website]. Retrieved June 15, 2018, from http://www.finchi.cn/.

Finnish Business Council Beijing. (n.d.). Website. Retrieved June 15, 2018, from http://www.fbcbj.org/.

Finnish Transport Agency. (2018). Arctic ocean railway report. *Finnish Transport Agency*. Retrieved October 2, 2018, from https://julkaisut.liikennevirasto.fi/pdf8/lr_2018_arctic_ocean_railway_report_web.pdf.

Gavrilov, V., & Kripakova, A. (2017). Arctic policy of the North East Asian countries. *Jindal Global Law Review, 8*(1), 69–86. DOI: 10.1007/s41020-017-0039-x.

Geological Survey of Finland. (2010). Finland's minerals strategy. *Geological Survey of Finland*. Retrieved December 12, 2018, from http://projects.gtk.fi/export/sites/projects/minerals_strategy/documents/FinlandsMineralsStrategy_2.pdf.

Husebekk, A., Andersson, M., & Penttilä, R.E.J. (2015). Growth from the North. How can Norway, Sweden and Finland achieve sustainable growth in the Scandinavian Arctic? *Prime Minister's Office*. [Report of an independent expert group]. Retrieved June 10, 2018, from http://valtioneuvosto.fi/documents/10616/1095776/J0415_Growth+from+the+North_net.pdf/2613b2d6-96f8-4ca1-813a-658eaad7f858.

Invest in Dalarna Agency. (2017, September 29). Alibaba eyes London and Sweden for second European cloud data centre. *Invest in Dalarna Agency*. Retrieved June 20, 2018, from http://www.investindalarna.se/2017/09/alibaba-eyes-london-and-sweden-for-second-european-cloud-data-centre/.

Jakobsen, S. (2018, August 24). Maersk sends first container ship through Arctic route. *Reuters*. Retrieved October 21, 2018, from https://www.reuters.com/article/us-arctic-shipping-maersk/maersk-sends-first-container-ship-through-arctic-route-idUSKCN1L91BR.

Kaidi. (n.d.). Website. Retrieved July 5, 2018, from www.kaidi.fi.

Kaihlanen, J. (2019, January 23). Yle: Kaidi Finlandin toimitusjohtajan usko Kemin biojalostamohankkeeseen ei horju – investointipäätös aikaisintaan 2021. *Maaseudun*

Tulevaisuus. Retrieved January 25, from https://www.maaseuduntulevaisuus.fi/metsa/artikkeli-1.366804.

Kaiva.fi (n.d.) Website. Retrieved July, 16, 2019, from www.kaiva.fi.

Kallio, H. (2018, June 25). Kemin biotuotetehtaasta tulisi koko pohjoisen pallonpuoliskon suurin puuta jalostava laitos. *Lapin Kansa*. Retrieved July 5, 2018, from https://www.lapinkansa.fi/lappi/kemin-biotuotetehdas-panisi-koko-maan-puuvirrat-uusiksi-201022044/.

Karagiannopoulos, L. (2018, May 9). After Facebook, Sweden set for more data center deals: Vattenfall. *Reuters*. Retrieved June 20, 2018, from https://www.reuters.com/article/us-sweden-vattenfall-datacentres/after-facebook-sweden-set-for-more-data-center-deals-vattenfall-idUSKBN1IA207.

Kirkenes Nearingshage. (2018, January). *An Arctic railway vision*. [Report for Finnmark Fylkeskommune and Sor-Varanger Utvikling].

Lim, K.S. (2018). China's Arctic policy & the Polar Silk Road vision. *Arctic Yearbook 2018*. Akureyri, Iceland: Northern Research Forum.

Lipponen, P., & Svento, R. (2016, November 25). Report on the Northeast Passage telecommunications cable project: Summary. *Ministry of Transport and Communications*. Report 3/2016.

Ministry of Foreign Affairs (Finland). (2017). Exploring Common Solutions – Finland's Chairmanship Programme for the Arctic Council. Retrieved September 26, 2019, from https://oaarchive.arctic-council.org/handle/11374/2027.

Ministry of Transport and Communications. (2019). Final Report of the Joint Working Group Between Finland and Norway on the Arctic Railway. Publications of the Ministry of Transport and Communications 2019:4. Retrieved September 25, 2019, from https://julkaisut.valtioneuvosto.fi/bitstream/handle/10024/161367/LVM_4_2019_Arctic%20Railway.pdf?sequence=1&isAllowed=y.

News Now Finland. (2017, November 6). The Ice Dragon cometh: China's Arctic ambitions. *News Now Finland*. Retrieved June 15, 2018, from http://newsnowfinland.fi/news-now-original/the-ice-dragon-cometh-chinas-arctic-ambitions.

Nilsen, T. (2016). Facebook and green energy key to economic boom. *The Barents Observer*. Retrieved June 10, 2018, from http://thebarentsObserver.com/industry/2016/01/facebook-and-green-energy-key-economic-boom.

Nilsen, T. (2019, March 21). Details of China's nuclear-powered icebreaker revealed. *Barents Observer*. Retrieved September 26, 2019, from https://thebarentsobserver.com/en/arctic/2019/03/details-chinas-nuclear-powered-icebreaker-revealed.

Nilsen, T. (2019, September 27). Giant Christmas theme park aiming at 10 million visitors annually. *Barents Observer*. Retrieved October 2, 2019, from https://thebarentsobserver.com/en/node/5902.

Norconsult. (2018, February). *Arctic railway*. [Report for Jernbanedirektoratet]. Retrieved September 26, 2019, from https://julkaisut.vayla.fi/pdf8/norconsult_arcticrailway_web.pdf.

OECD Data (n.d.). Inward FDI Stocks by Partner Country. Organization for Economic Cooperation and Development. Data Portal. Retrieved October 11, 2019, from https://data.oecd.org/fdi/inward-fdi-stocks-by-partner-country.htm.

Øian, H. Fredman, P., Sandell, K., Sæþórsdóttir, A.D., Tyrväinen, L. & Søndergaard Jensen, F. (2018). Tourism, nature and sustainability: A review of policy instruments in the Nordic countries. TemaNord 2018:534. Nordic Council of Ministers. Retrieved September 25, 2019, from https://norden.diva-portal.org/smash/get/diva2:1209894/FULLTEXT01.pdf.

Paavola, H., Kaihovaara, A., Blomqvist, K., & Hellenberg, T. (2017). Suomen arktisen osaamisen kaupallistamisen, tuotteistamisen ja viennin esteet, instrumentit ja mahdollisuudet. [The commercialisation, productisation and exportation of Finland's Arctic competencies: obstacles, instruments and opportunities]. *Publications of the Govenrment's analysis, assessment and research activities* 26/2017. Retrieved September 26, 2019, from https://tietokayttoon.fi/julkaisu?pubid=18001.

Prime Minister's Office. (2013). Finland's strategy for the Arctic region 2013.

Prime Minister's Office. (2017). Action plan for the update of the Arctic strategy. Retrieved October 8, 2018, from https://vnk.fi/documents/10616/3474615/EN_Arktisen+strategian+toimenpidesuunnitelma/0a755d6e-4b36-4533-a93b-9a430d08a29e/EN_Arktisen+strategian+toimenpidesuunnitelma.pdf.

PRC State Council. (2018, January 26). Full text: China's Arctic policy. *The State Council, The People's Republic of China.* Retrieved March 12, 2018, from http://english.gov.cn/archive/white_paper/2018/01/26/content_281476026660336.htm.

Rana, K.S. (2017). China's Belt and Road Initiative (BRI): Implications, prospects & consequences: Impact on India & its China diplomacy. Delhi: Institute of Chinese Studies. Occasional Paper, No. 16. Retrieved June 10, 2018, from http://www.icsin.org/uploads/2017/09/08/78c17f4569e5115c36b542e55ed1262d.pdf.

Rautajoki, T., & Lakkapää, V. (2018, April). *Arctic business forum yearbook 2018.* Lapland Chamber of Commerce. Rovaniemi: Painatuskeskus Finland.

Regional Council of Lapland. (2017, February 22). Matkailutilasto 2016. *Regional Council of Lapland.* Retrieved July 5, 2018, from http://www.lappi.fi/lapinliitto/c/document_library/get_file?folderId=3013126&name=DLFE-31215.pdf.

Republic of Santa Claus website at https://www.republicofsantaclaus.com. Retrieved October 2, 2019.

Rosen, M.E., & Thuringen, C.B. (2017, November). Unconstrained foreign direct investment: An emerging challenge to Arctic security. CNA Analysis and Solution.

Russian Federation. (2012). Federal Law 132-FZ on tourism. *Russian Federation.* Retrieved August 14, 2019, from http://www.fao.org/faolex/results/details/en/c/LEX-FAOC083016.

SADA. (Strategic Assessment of Development of the Arctic.) (2014). Stepien, A., Koivurova, T., & Kankaanpää, P. Retrieved June 20, 2018, from www.arctcinfo.eu/sada.

Sander, G., Gille, J., Stępień, A., Koivurova, T., Thomas, J., Gascard, J-C., & Justus, D. (2016). Changes in Arctic maritime transport. In A. Stępień, T. Koivurova & P. Kankaanpää (Eds.), The Changing Arctic and the European Union. Leiden, Netherlands; Boston, MA: Brill & Nijhoff.

Searchinger, T.D., Beringer, T., Holtsmark, B., Kammen, D.M., Lambin, E.F., Lucht, W., Raven, P. & van Ypersele, J.-P. (2018). Europe's renewable energy directive poised to harm global forests. *Nature Communications* 9: article 3741 (2018).

Smolaks, M. (2017, February 9). Canaan Creative is opening a 10MW bitcoin mine at the Node Pole. *Data Centre Dynamics*. Retrieved July 20, 2018, from http://www.datacenterdynamics.com/content-tracks/power-cooling/canaan-creative-is-opening-a-10mw-bitcoin-mine-at-the-node-pole/97793.fullarticle.

Sorjanen, T. (2018, November 16). Pohjoisin Lappi ei kiinnosta kaivosteollisuutta, kävi Jäämeren radan kanssa miten tahansa – "Tärkein kriteeri on, että on malmia". *Lapin Kansa*. Retrieved November 16, 2018, from https://www.lapinkansa.fi/lappi/pohjoisin-lappi-ei-kiinnosta-kaivosteollisuutta-kavi-jaameren-radan-kanssa-miten-tahansa-tarkein-kriteeri-on-etta-on-malmia-2817139/.

Statistic Finland (2019, April 9). Demand for accommodation services grew by 1.5% in 2018. Retrieved September 25, 2019, from http://www.stat.fi/til/matk/2018/matk_2018_2019-04-09_tie_001_en.html.

Statistics Finland – Finnish Customs. (2017). International trade in goods and services. *Statistics Finland*. Retrieved June 19, 2018, from https://www.stat.fi/til/tpulk/2017/04/tpulk_2017_04_2018-03-15_en.pdf.

Stępień, A. (2016, August). "Other futures for Arctic economies? Searching for alternatives to resource extraction", *ArCticles: Arctic Centre Papers* 5, Arctic Centre of the University of Lapland. Retrieved September 25, 2019, from https://lauda.ulapland.fi/handle/10024/62539.

Sun, H.H. (2018, June 28). China looks to build its first nuclear icebreaker. *Arctic Today*. Retrieved July 6, 2018, from https://www.arctictoday.com/china-looks-build-first-nuclear-icebreaker/.

UN Department of Economic and Social Affairs. (2017). 2016 International trade statistics yearbook. Vol. II: Trade by Product. New York: United Nations Publication. Retrieved December 12, 2018, from https://comtrade.un.org/pb/downloads/2016/VolII2016.pdf.

VisitFinland. (n.d.). Sustainable Finland. *Visit Finland website*. Retrieved September 25, 2019, from https://www.visitfinland.com/sustainable-finland/.

Warrenstein, A., Lind, F., Sundstrom, O., & Deutscher, S.A. (2016). Capturing the data centre opportunity: How Sweden can become a global front-runner in digital infrastructure. *The Boston Consulting Group. Business Sweden*. Retrieved November 25, 2018, from http://www.business-sweden.se/contentassets/cd7d2c2584d64e8694e92ec1f6408069/bcg-capturing-the-data-center-opportunity-june-2016.pdf.

WITS. (World Bank's World Integrated Trade Solution). (n.d.). Website. Retrieved December 9, 2018, from https://wits.worldbank.org.

WWF. (Worldwide Fund for Nature, Finland). (2016, August 30). Hallitus murentaa biotalouden kestävyydeltä pohjaa. *WWF.* Retrieved December 12, 2018, from https://wwf.fi/wwf-suomi/viestinta/uutiset-ja-tiedotteet/Hallitus-murentaa-biotalouden-kestavyydelta-pohjaa-2881.a.

YLE Uutiset. (2016, September 6). China's largest private equity investor eyes Finnish tech companies. *YLE Uutiset.* Retrieved June 15, 2018, from https://yle.fi/uutiset/osasto/news/chinas_largest_private_equity_investor_eyes_finnish_tech_companies/9147079.

YLE Uutiset. (2019, February 11). Record 3, overnight stays in Lapland last year. YLE. Retrieved September 25, 2019, from https://yle.fi/uutiset/osasto/news/record_3m_overnight_stays_in_laplandlast_year/10641452.

YLE Uutiset. (2019, May 9). Ex-Angry Birds marketing chief's involvement in Arctic Railway ruffles feathers in Lapland. YLE. Retrieved September 25, 2019, from https://yle.fi/uutiset/osasto/news/ex-angry_birds_marketing_chiefs_involvement_in_arctic_railway_ruffles_feathers_in_lapland/10776133.

YLE Uutiset. (2019, September 20). Google investment in Hamina data centre rises to €2bn. YLE. Retrieved October 10, 2019, from https://yle.fi/uutiset/osasto/news/google_investment_in_hamina_data_centre_rises_to_2bn/10981081.

Zhang, H. (2018, July 12). China relies more heavily on mineral imports. *Global Times.* Retrieved December 12, 2018, from http://www.globaltimes.cn/content/1110397.shtml.

Interviews

Interviewee 1, June 2016.
Interviewee 2, 4 May 2018.
Interviewee 3, 12 June 2018.
Interviewee 4, 12 June 2018.
Interviewee 5, 13 June 2018.
Interviewee 6, 20 June 2018.
Esko Lotvonen, Mayor of the City of Rovaniemi, Rovaniemi, 20 June 2018.
Interviewee 7, 26 June 2018.
Mika Riipi, Governor of Lapland, Rovaniemi, 27 June 2018.
Interviewee 8, 28 June 2018

Interviewee 9, 1 August 2018.
Interviewee 10, 20 August 2018.
Interviewee 11, 3 September 2018.
Interviewee 12, 22 October 2018.
Interviewee 13, 13 November 2018.

CHAPTER 8

Conclusion: China's Policy and Presence in the Arctic

Timo Koivurova, Sanna Kopra, Marc Lanteigne and Adam Stepien

8.1 Introduction

As the People's Republic of China has risen to great power status and the world's second-largest economy, its foreign policy no longer focuses only on regional affairs in East Asia and the Asia-Pacific, as Beijing now has interests at the global level as well. During the last decade, the Arctic has also become incorporated into China's increasingly confident global diplomacy. However, there are some noteworthy distinctive characteristics of China's Arctic engagement that differentiate it from the country's foreign policies in other parts of the world, especially given the Arctic region's distinct geography, demographics and economy. This volume has sought to identify these differences and offer an overview of China's policy and presence in the Arctic. Clearly, we confirm that China's manifold activities in the Arctic region have grown significantly in the past ten years. In this last chapter of the book, we summarize the key findings of the preceding chapters.

8.2 China as an Arctic Actor

Clearly, China is not an Arctic state because it has no sovereign territories or waters above the Arctic Circle, and it is therefore not likely to make any territorial claims in the Arctic in the future. Notwithstanding, it has sought to become a legitimate actor in the Arctic and has adjusted its cross-regional policies accordingly. China's Arctic policy is therefore a noteworthy exercise in identity-building that seeks to find tools to build an Arctic identity that would be acceptable, or at least not resisted, by the eight Arctic states. As Chapter 3 of this volume indicates, China's first ever official Arctic strategic White Paper (*Zhongguo de Beiji Zhengce Baipishu* 《中国的北极政策》白皮书) published in January 2018 can be seen as the party-state's final step in establishing itself very clearly as an Arctic actor.

In comparison with other non-Arctic states that have also been developing Arctic policies and strategies, including the United Kingdom, France, Germany,

© KONINKLIJKE BRILL NV, LEIDEN, 2020 | DOI:10.1163/9789004408425_009

Japan and South Korea, China's Arctic policies and activities have been subject to much greater global scrutiny, especially out of concern that Beijing may be seeking to develop a 'hard security' agenda in the region. This level of international attention strongly inhibits any sort of revisionist behavior on China's part. Because China's general lack of on-the-ground knowledge in the region makes any overt Chinese revisionist policies unacceptably risky, Beijing has been notably cautious about being seen as challenging the strategic status quo in the High North. Conversely, China's Arctic activities are highly dependent on economic and political cooperation with Arctic states and companies, given the state's status as an external actor to the region. Beijing does not want to antagonize the 'Arctic Eight' states, especially Russia. Rather, it is of utmost importance to China to be seen as a benevolent partner amongst the regional stakeholders. Furthermore, in light of very high international scrutiny that the media, experts and state officials place on any actions of China in the Arctic, it is highly improbable that China could significantly extend its reach and increase its power in the Arctic via covert means. Thus, at present the cost/benefit equation has strongly directed China to take a conservative and multilateral approach to the region, as well as one that respects international law and regional governance and existing regimes.

In its pursuit of expanding China's role in Arctic governance, Beijing continues to abide by public international law in its Arctic policy, including in the cases of the Arctic Council, the United Nations Convention on the Law of the Sea (UNCLOS), the Polar Code and the new fishing agreement in the Central Arctic Ocean. Regarding its Arctic activities, China's commitment to abide by international law and the legal frameworks of Arctic states was restated in the Chinese government's 2018 White Paper. In the policy statement, China's role in the region was directly connected to existing legal and political frameworks. However, the South China Sea case shows that Chinese and Western interpretations of international law, including UNCLOS, may differ. International law is interpreted, in some occasions, by states in a way that best supports their interests and objectives. It cannot be excluded that there will be future disagreements between China and Arctic states on particular international law rules in the Arctic or of those provisions' applicability to the Arctic.

8.3 China's Role in the Arctic

In addition to Arctic governance, Beijing seeks to expand other dimensions of its presence in the region. Chapter 4 of this volume makes it clear that China has significantly increased its scientific facilities, thereby enhancing its scientific potential in the North, over the course of a relatively short time. At present, among others, China has a research station in Svalbard Archipelago, is an active member of the International Arctic Science Committee (IASC), conducts regular icebreaker science expeditions in the Arctic, and is becoming increasingly involved in international science cooperation projects. The scale and expansion of Chinese investments in research and development over the last twenty years remains largely unparalleled. The country has become increasingly interested in climate change in the Arctic, not only in terms of impacts occurring in the region itself but also in the effects of these changes in China. Yet, China's scientific activities have recently raised concerns amongst some Arctic states and stakeholders. The United States, in particular, has warned about the potential dual use of Chinese research facilities. Growing geopolitical tensions may increase these suspicions, making the Sino-Arctic research cooperation more difficult in the coming years.

Although climate change is an important driver of China's Arctic engagement, Chapter 5 of this volume points out that the state's Arctic strategy does not specify additional efforts to mitigate climate change. Beijing, regrettably, does not currently participate in the Arctic Council Expert Group's work on black carbon and methane, which could present an important contribution to addressing the impacts of climate change in the North. Some of the black carbon that is deposited in the Arctic originates from China. Beijing faces the same challenge in terms of other pollutants. The country participates in global cooperation on persistent organic pollutants (POPs) and mercury as well as on plastic waste, but it also produces a lot of these substances that then end up in the Arctic ecosystems and food chains. After the United States announced its decision to withdraw from the 2015 Paris Agreement, the international community has hoped for China to take a leadership role in international climate politics. To some extent, China appears to be willing to assume this role. Yet, its climate policies are not ambitious enough to prevent dangerous climate change from happening. Moreover, the Belt and Road Initiative (BRI) continues to invest in coal and other fossil fuels, and Chinese demand for resources constitutes the key contributor to the market incentives for the expansion of resource extraction in the Arctic.

In addition to environmental issues, Indigenous Peoples' issues are an important element of Arctic governance. As Chapter 3 of this volume notes, Beijing's approach to these questions is complex. China does not consider any of the ethnic or minority groups inhabiting its territory to have the status of an Indigenous People, and in a broader ethnopolitical context, China has been sensitive to the potential for ethnic unrest, especially in the cases of Tibet and Xinjiang in the country's far west. China, however, is a fairly consistent supporter of Indigenous rights at the United Nations. This is politically easy for

China, as Beijing believes indigenous status arises exclusively from the history of colonization and is not applicable to China itself. Chinese international stance does, however, potentially matter in the Arctic context. As an Observer to the Arctic Council, China has accepted the organization's Nuuk Observer criteria, which calls upon Observers to "respect the values, interests, culture and traditions of Arctic indigenous peoples and other Arctic inhabitants" as well as have "demonstrated a political willingness as well as financial ability to contribute to the work of the Permanent Participants and other Arctic indigenous peoples" (see Arctic Council, 2019). Thus far, however, Beijing has not spoken of Indigenous issues in terms of Indigenous rights, nor has Beijing organized any practical cooperation with the Arctic Council Permanent Participants organizations, in contrast to, for instance, Singapore or the European Union.

Furthermore, China's global economic role has grown rapidly, and this expansion can be expected to continue in the future. Chapter 6 of this volume indicates that the country is preparing to utilize the emerging navigational opportunities and to invest in the Arctic's energy resources in particular. At present, Chinese actors focus mainly on Russia in terms of oil and gas investments, Greenland with respect to mining, and biorefining in Finland. In Iceland and Finland there are investments and cooperation in the tourism sector. However, Chinese economic activities in the region remain limited. Some planned activities have been delayed and in some cases Chinese investors pull out. There were cases of infrastructural investments in Arctic states, where security concerns made Arctic states to reject Chinese investment plans. This is visible in the case of Finland, which is considered separately in Chapter 7 of this volume. At present, there are only a few instances of realized investments (such as tourist accommodation in Lapland), and only a handful implemented contracts. Most projects associated with Chinese actors remain at the stage of planning or initial ideas, and the specific place of Finland within the BRI is yet to be clarified. However, economic cooperation between Finland and China is growing, and there is a notable potential for enhancing collaboration in Arctic questions.

8.4 Risks and Future Prospects

It is apparent that China's great power status will only consolidate with time, which means that Beijing's Arctic presence in various policy areas will also likely grow. It is not likely that China's military presence will grow in the Arctic in the near future. While scientific diplomacy will probably continue to be the vanguard of Chinese Arctic interests, economic interests are also starting to be important, given China's ongoing need for energy and raw materials as well as new shipping lanes. As for Arctic governance, China does not presently challenge the existing general Arctic security and governance frameworks; however Beijing is starting to make changes in the realm of regional norms by affecting the informal understandings that govern the behavior of actors in international society, including states and governments.

Thus, China is no longer content to be merely a 'norm-taker' in the Arctic. Instead, it is becoming more comfortable with acting as a norm-maker, that is, an actor proposing its own ideas and norms and not only observing and participating in existing frameworks. This is evident from the 2017 extension of the BRI into the Arctic Ocean, a multidimensional and global development endeavor seeking to establish and fortify China as an economic pole in the international system and launched by Chinese President Xi Jinping in 2013. Conservative estimates place the overall cost of the BRI, which extends to many parts of the world, including Africa, Central Asia, Europe, the Middle East and Russia in addition to the Arctic, at US$1 trillion. The BRI has coalesced into the primary foreign policy of President Xi Jinping. However, that also means that the BRI has become an overarching frame for Chinese overseas investment and cooperation, which results in many projects being labeled as BRI actions in order to gain political support and easier access to Chinese financing.

In addition to the economic benefits of collaboration between China and Arctic, there are various concerns and risks related to cooperation with Chinese partners. Many perceived risks are based on the negative assessment of past Chinese activities in regions such as Africa and South Asia. The situation in developed Arctic states and relatively well-governed Arctic regions may not be easily compared to other parts of the world. However, the adverse experiences and resulting negative image do affect the perception of Chinese actors in the Arctic. We can identify some types of Chinese activities that are particularly likely to cause anxiety within Arctic states: major land purchases, especially in areas of high environmental, biodiversity or landscape value; investments in critical infrastructure; and bringing in Chinese workforce in significant numbers. On the other hand, studies have underlined that Chinese operators are capable of adjusting to local conditions and regulatory frameworks, and that the performance of Chinese investors overseas has, overall, significantly improved over the last decade. The hope is that the Arctic would be a place where Chinese investments follow best practice.

According to Chapters 6 and 7 of this volume, three dimensions of risks related to the growing Chinese economic presence in the Arctic can be distinguished. First, there are anxieties related to the perception of Chinese investment and economic, scientific and other forms of cooperation as constituting instruments of increasing Chinese influence. Chinese investors and operators (and similarly any single major foreign investor) may gain excessive long-term influence on the regional economy. At the same time, there is a belief that China – as an authoritarian state with significant control over its economic actors – may gain too great an influence on the Arctic states' national economies, also leading to political influence. Such fears are exacerbated by the fact that China has a history of using economic pressure to retaliate against what it perceives as actions directed against Chinese national interests. The collapse of Sino-Norwegian relations following the Nobel Peace Prize controversy in 2010 constitutes a clear case in point. The authors of Chapter 6 highlight the possibility that sharp power mechanisms could be utilized by China also in the Arctic.

Second, there are concerns related to the environmental and social performance of Chinese actors as investors or business partners. The impacts of Chinese investments on the local business landscape and labor market need to be assessed for each project, as there is no single pattern of Chinese investors and companies' behavior. Moreover, issues related to intellectual property rights remain problematic for Arctic businesses cooperating with Chinese partners. Lastly, local actors, who are often strongly in favor of Chinese investments, have misgivings that plans announced by Chinese investors often remain unimplemented or ephemeral.

Clearly, the ways in which these potential risks can be addressed and mitigated are case-specific. Decision-makers are advised to apply particular scrutiny in cases of investments that would give Chinese companies influence over the construction and use of critical infrastructure such as railways or airports. Some of the risks may be avoided by increased cultural understanding. In general, thus, it is highly recommended for Arctic states to dedicate resources towards better understanding Chinese foreign influence, the modes of operation of Chinese business actors and a generally improved understanding of the Chinese society and culture, including facilitating Mandarin language skills. At the same time, China should also devote resources to increasing their knowledge of the special characteristics of the Arctic region: the culture, traditions, history, norms and values of the Arctic populations. Without understanding one another's backgrounds and needs, collaboration is unlikely to thrive and the current level of mistrust will not be successfully addressed.

Literature

Arctic Council. (2019). Observers. Retrieved October 22, 2019, from https://arctic-council.org/index.php/en/about-us/arctic-council/observers.

Index

www.ingramcontent.com/pod-product-compliance
Lightning Source LLC
Chambersburg PA
CBHW071225230926
51849CB00001B/33
9789004408418